THE COLDER WAR

THE COLDER WAR

How the Global Energy Trade Slipped from America's Grasp

Marin Katusa

WILEY

 CASEY RESEARCH

Cover design: Jan Linke
Cover Images: Obama/Putin: © Evan Vucci/Associated Press; clouds/oil field © Mick Roessler/Corbis

Published by John Wiley & Sons, Inc., Hoboken, New Jersey, and Casey Research, LLC, Stowe, Vermont.
Published simultaneously in Canada.

For general information on our other products and services or for technical support, please contact our Customer Care Department within the United States at (800) 762-2974, outside the United States at (317) 572-3993 or fax (317) 572-4002.

Wiley publishes in a variety of print and electronic formats and by print-on-demand. Some material included with standard print versions of this book may not be included in e-books or in print-on-demand. If this book refers to media such as a CD or DVD that is not included in the version you purchased, you may download this material at http://booksupport.wiley.com. For more information about Wiley products, visit www.wiley.com.

ISBN 9781118799949 (Hardcover)
ISBN 9781118800058 (ePDF)
ISBN 9781118800072 (ePub)

Printed in the United States of America.

10 9 8 7 6 5 4 3 2 1

To my wife, Marina.
Your support and undying love carry me in all I do.

Contents

Foreword

Let me be candid. I really like this book because it's original, it's well reasoned, and its conclusions are correct. It's important that you read it.

Let me take a couple of pages to explain why the subject of energy is even more important than most people imagine, and why Marin is not only the right man to explain it but a winning player in the rough-and-tumble energy arena.

Marin wasn't planning to write a book until I twisted his arm. Although he's a competent writer, as you'll see, he's first and foremost a deal maker. But what has brought him so much success in that career is being a preternaturally shrewd analyst and an independent big-picture thinker. His take on many things—not least the Putinization of energy and the incipient Colder War—is likely to give you a new view on what is going on in the world. He won't be echoing the conventional wisdom you're likely to hear on network TV or read in the *New York Times*.

Energy

It's a commonplace that "the world runs on energy," but few appreciate the mercilessness of that truth for an industrialized world. Putting it quite simply, energy is the sine qua non of civilization itself. Without large quantities of it, most of us would literally starve and would do so while freezing in the dark.

Your food requires large quantities of fossil fuel to be grown, packaged, transported, refrigerated, and later cooked. That dependence may not be ideal, but it's reality for at least another generation of mankind. For your car to run, for planes to fly, and for trucks and trains to deliver goods, it's going to take a lot of fossil fuel for many years to come. Fossil fuels are the raw material for many of the things we use, from plastics to clothing. Without a river of energy, you can forget about communications, TV, computers, and the Internet. Without oil, natural gas, coal, and nuclear power, modern civilization would wither in a matter of days.

But that's only a description of how things are now. Despite greenism and the widespread enthusiasm for the idea of conservation, energy isn't going to become less important; it's going to become vastly more important. The Second Law of Thermodynamics states, in essence, that without continual inputs of energy, all systems wind down. Entropy, like gravity, conquers all. Only inputs of energy can hold the process at bay.

The world's population will likely grow to 10 billion people by the end of the century, and their energy requirements will grow much, much faster. Today two-thirds of all people are still poor and consume little energy. As they approach a Western standard of living, they're going to want more—say, about 10 times more—than they have now of the things you and I take for granted. And all those things are made with energy inputs and run on more energy inputs.

Now, it's true that technology is making rapid improvements in the efficiency of renewable or sustainable energy, mainly solar and wind. They will likely become economical, at some point, for many applications. But in the foreseeable future, there is no remotely practical substitute for the high-density energy of fossil fuels.

There eventually will be such a substitute, I'm sure, if only because there are more scientists and engineers alive today than have lived in all of previous history. Vastly improved, much smaller, much cheaper, much safer uranium-fueled power plants are on the way. So are thorium reactors. Fusion may eventually obviate all energy problems. And in the meantime, we're always improving the efficiency of using fossil fuels. The Boeing 787, for instance, is more than three times more fuel efficient than a Boeing 707; a 2014 Corvette can cruise at 30 miles per gallon, whereas its 1960 predecessor would be pressed to make 12.

Solutions will be found and innovations will appear. In the meantime, the use of fossil fuels will continue to rise, albeit at higher costs per unit of energy. The commercialization of fracking, horizontal drilling, coal bed methane recovery, deep-sea drilling, and tar sands recovery are just a few new sources of oil and gas.

Mankind's sources of energy will continue to evolve. But for the next few decades, fossil fuel will be critical just for maintaining civilization as it is today, and the expected escape from poverty by billions of people will require even more of it. The Second Law is always there, grinding away. And over the coming generation, the companies and countries that control fossil fuels are going to have more influence on the rest of the world than they ever had before. It's going to be, at the nicest, the Colder War that Marin posits.

... and the Man

Marin is that rare person who is both academically smart and street smart. He was a university math professor and has a bent for science. And it didn't take him long to put theory into practice, analyzing the fundamentals of mining companies and oil companies—geology, mineralogy, engineering, permitting, management, and a score of other disciplines.

There are thousands of such companies, and they're represented by the most volatile class of stocks you can find. Over the course of a commodity cycle, many of the small ones are capable of moving 100 to 1 in price, or more. Most of them turn out to be just black holes for capital, however. Speculators in this area seldom appreciate how great the potential can be and the severity of the risk. Paradoxically, however, companies with the lowest risk can have the highest potential—if the speculator knows what to look for.

And this is an area where Marin really shines. He not only has a strong academic background in oil, gas, unconventional energy, uranium, and mining, he also has a proven hands-on, boots-on-the-ground record of building and running successful companies. In particular, he's largely responsible for putting Canada's third-largest copper mine into production—all the way from property acquisition to financing, construction, and profitable operation. That's a rare accomplishment and extraordinary for a 30-year-old (his age at the time).

He was one of the largest investors in the company early on. He's even now one of the most successful financiers in the resource exploration business and runs four hedge funds, where he and I are the largest investors. (He puts his money where his mouth is.) The funds have outperformed the TSX-V index by 600 percent over the past five years, despite holding large cash balances. In both relative and absolute terms, it's one of the most exceptional performances I've ever seen.

But it's not just knowledge and technical expertise that put Marin at the top. It's also his people skills. The son of Croatian immigrants, Marin had (what turned out to be) the good fortune to be born on the wrong side of the tracks. So he's not just book smart, but street smart. Whether it's with the president of a company or the president of a country, he knows how to relate to them over a bottle of something potent. Watching him ask questions and get answers as few people can, I'm forced to remark that he could have been the type of police detective they do TV shows about. And he's a world-class poker player.

With that background, he's now concentrating on finance. I've been in the resource finance business for about 40 years and have gotten to know most of the movers and shakers. Many of them—like Robert Friedland, Lukas Lundin, Frank Giustra, and Ross Beaty—are multibillionaires. Marin will join their ranks, quite possibly in this cycle—since, as I write, resource stocks are at a historic bottom. I saw him cut the deal that founded the largest shale gas company in Europe. And we were recently in Albania together to assess what may become Europe's largest onshore oil producer.

I've been to more than 135 countries, but Marin is starting to close in on me. We've traveled through the Balkans, across Iraq, through Asia and South America, as well as all over North America together. Travel becomes an aggravation once you've done enough of it, but it's essential in this business. One reason is that you want to meet a company's management in their element and see how things are going with your own eyes. Another is to understand the local political situation, a theme that's central to this book. In today's world—much more so than in even the recent past—the world's 200+ governments are the biggest factor in resources. Their leaders and bureaucracies determine whether a resource can even be exploited, what workers are paid, and how much will be left over after the government extracts its royalties and taxes.

Hence, a good part of this book explains how international politics relate to energy and how the worldwide energy picture is likely to evolve over the next decade—especially with regard to Russia, and more particularly with regard to Vladimir Putin, who, at age 62 as I write, is likely to be on the scene for years to come. He's both a lot smarter and a lot tougher than any of his counterparts in the West, and he will be a big part of what will make the next decade among the most "interesting" (to use that word as the Chinese do) in world history.

You're going to be glad you read this book.

Doug Casey
Author of *The International Man, Strategic Investing, Crisis Investing, Totally Incorrect,* and *Right on the Money,*
Chairman, Casey Research

Acknowledgments

As I sit at my office desk, in midsummer 2014, going through the last chapter of the manuscript and responding to all of Terry Coxon's comments and edits, I wonder how many wrong turns I might have left uncorrected but for the attention Terry and other members of the Casey Research team have given the project.

When Doug Casey, the founder of Casey Research, broached the idea of writing about my theories of the Colder War, I was reluctant. I'm much more of an investment analyst than a writer, and I've never felt a yearning to see my work sitting on a bookshelf. But Doug persisted, and when I took up his idea of writing the book, he responded with advice that helped make it what its first reviewer termed "such a good read."

The support and guidance I received from Doug's partner, Olivier Garret, the CEO of Casey Research, were critical to making *The Colder War* happen, and to making it happen well. Olivier believed in the concepts and ideas I've been sharing with Casey Research subscribers for most of the past 10 years, and he saw the value in assembling the core of those ideas into a book for a wider audience. Without Olivier, the group of funds I manage would never have happened, and together we have been able to deliver to our shareholders some of the best returns in the sector over the past five years, beating our comparable index by over 600 percent.

Doug Hornig and Terry Coxon both were prime movers in the evolution of *The Colder War*, and they deserve much credit for any success it enjoys. Doug Hornig worked tirelessly to organize my early jumble of notes and jottings, to identify and hunt down needed details, and, most important, to impose some literary discipline on the technical topics—material that for me is music, but for most readers just isn't. Terry Coxon, as you may notice as you read the book, is an exceptional editor; he did much to streamline the story and ease its flow from the first page to the last.

I've been fortunate to find a career I love and that has invited me to travel the world many times over—and doubly fortunate for the friends and colleagues who've greeted me along the way. Jim O'Rourke, a member of the Canadian Mining Hall of Fame, and Rick Rule of Sprott Global have been generous mentors who for many years have shared their knowledge and experience. David Galland, of Casey Research, gave me a platform to excel at what I most enjoy, which is finding the best resource investments around the world.

My parents came to Canada with nothing but a dream of a better life for their kids than they had experienced growing up under the communist regime of Yugoslavia. I can never thank you enough. My appetite for work came from watching the two of you work to live out that dream. And to my brothers, Jad and Karlo, who nurtured my competitive, never-give-up attitude in the uncompromising way only big brothers can, thank you.

It is my brilliant and beautiful wife, Marina, whom I must thank the most. Her support and undying love carry me in all I do.

Marin Katusa
Vancouver, British Columbia, 2014

THE COLDER WAR

Chapter 1

The End of the Lost Decade

I am going to tell you a story you'll wish weren't true.

Sometime soon, likely in the next five years or so, there is going to be an emergency meeting in the White House Situation Room. It probably will start in the wee hours of the morning, when the early risers among Europe's oil traders and currency speculators have already begun to scramble out of the way of what's coming. None of the worried participants in that meeting will have a good solution to propose, because there will be no way for the United States to turn without embracing calamity of one kind or another.

The president will listen as his closest advisers lay out the dilemma. After a long silence, he will say, "You're telling me that everything—*everything*—is coming unglued."

He'll be right. At that point, there will be no good options, only less awful ones.

Don't count on the wise and worldly who occupy the highest echelons of government power to know what they are doing when they sit

1

in that meeting. Solving the puzzle of what to do will fall to the same kind of people who today are standing by and letting disaster build.

Some of them just don't know any better. They see all of mankind's turmoil as cartoonlike conflicts between white hats and black hats. Others know that reality is more complex, but it's so easy, and often politically convenient, to let everything boil down to good guys battling bad guys.

For years, political power players in the United States have joined their media allies in portraying Vladimir Putin as a coarse bully, a leftover from the KGB, a ruthless homophobic thug, a preening would-be Napoleon who worships men of action—especially himself. Even Hillary Clinton, who should know better, likened him to Hitler.

The ruthless part is quite real, but there is so much more to the truth. I've been studying Putin's moves for as long as I've immersed myself in analyzing world energy markets—which at this point is a long time. He's a complicated man whom Americans have been viewing through the simplifying lens their leaders like to hold up. He is less of an ogre but far more dangerous than politicians and the media would lead you to believe.

It has been a terrible mistake for Washington's political circles to dismiss him for so many years as just a hustler temporarily running a country, to cast him as a shooting star destined to flame out in the unforgiving world of Russian politics. It has been to his advantage that short people tend not to be taken seriously, even if, like Putin, they are martial arts champions and have a chiseled physique to display at age 62. And his less than dignified moments posing as He-Man have played into our readiness to treat him more as a clown than as a dangerous competitor.

But Washington should never have thought of him as a Cold War relic, any more than it should have thought of Russia as a once-lionlike country that had devolved into a goat. It should have seen that Putin has a long-range plan for Mother Russia—a map covering decades, not the four-year election cycles that dominate the attention of U.S. politicians—and both the vision and the resources to make the plan work. For 15 years, Putin has been formulating, bankrolling, and directing Cold War: The Sequel. Or, as I like to term it, the Colder War. He's in it to win it.

And the way he plans to win it isn't through the sword, but through control of the world's energy supplies.

There's no undoing the U.S. government's failures to date. What I can do now is tell you the true story of the Colder War. I can trace the connections of world events you've read about and that only seemed unrelated. I can explain why Putin does what he does, so that you can anticipate what he's likely to do next. I can show you the world-changing power shift that is little recognized even though it is unfolding in plain sight, right before our eyes.

It's all about energy—oil, gas, coal, uranium, hydroelectric power. Today, when you're talking about energy, you're talking about Putin. And vice versa.

Energy is what makes the world go round. For most of the past 60 years, the United States has prospered, largely because it has dominated the energy market but also because it issues the currency in which energy and other resources are traded—a nice monopoly to have. The United States has been top dog for so long, it's a shock to imagine how things might be different.

Slowly but surely, however, U.S. strength has been ebbing as Putin positions himself for the final push. While the United States dithers over green energy, Russia has a Putin in its tank.

The Lost Decade

To understand where Vladimir Vladimirovich Putin is taking Russia, you need to go back to the country's lost decade, the years after the collapse of the Soviet Union in 1989. If you were an average Josef Vodka caught up in the chaos that followed the demise of communism, it was a time of hardship, dislocation, and frightening uncertainty. If you were a Westerner, it was a time of prosperity and of self-congratulation for having won the Cold War. If you were Vladimir Putin, it was a time of anger and hardening—and preparing. (See Figure 1.1.)

Given the country's stunning rise since the 1990s, it's easy to forget how bad things were. (See Figure 1.2.)

It was 10 dismal years of lawlessness presided over by politicians who had been left bewildered by the task of bringing their country into

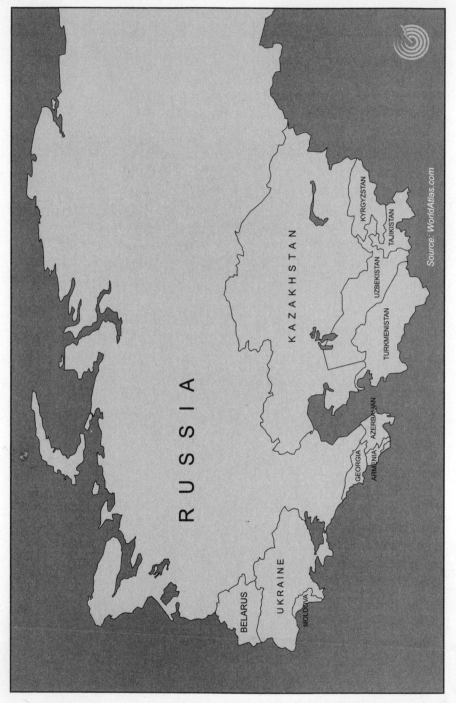

Figure 1.1 Commonwealth of Independent States (CIS)
SOURCE: World Atlas.

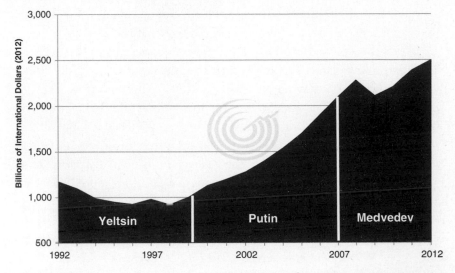

Figure 1.2 Russian Gross Domestic Product (Producer Price Parity) since the
Fall of the Soviet Union

SOURCE: International Monetary Fund. © Casey Research 2014.

the modern world. The sad decade was marked by the ascent of wildly profitable criminal syndicates and a coterie of oligarchs who fed on the government's naive plans for turning state enterprises into private ones. Operating as barely legal businessmen, they became billionaires almost overnight.

While the few celebrated, morale among ordinary Russians sank. They had just suffered through a long war in Afghanistan and its humiliating end. Then came the implosion of the Soviet Union, the grand empire they'd been told had been built for the ages. National pride had become a painful memory.

When the communist economy ground to a halt, no one in the government of the newborn Russian Federation knew what to do. Free markets were just beginning to emerge. Sizable and mature private businesses didn't exist. There were no banks competent to judge credit risks. Almost no one understood stocks, bonds, commodities, or any kind of market other than the black one that had long flourished—and continued to do so. Property rights were a slogan with uncertain application. The ruble was worthless outside the country while internally inflation ran wild. Jobs disappeared, leaving millions unemployed. Infrastructure was crumbling. Millions of Russians fell into destitution.

It was the very definition of hard times. People's prospects were so bleak that many clamored for a return to communism, a regime under which they at least knew where they stood ("We pretend to work; they pretend to pay us," as the Soviet-era joke went). And the problems weren't just with the economy.

There was, in particular, Chechnya. A secessionist movement of Islamic Chechens were reading the disorganization in Moscow as an invitation to press their bid for independence. They accepted the invitation, and in late 1994 the First Chechen War began.

Putin's predecessor, Boris Yeltsin, was still in office at the time. Despite Moscow's superior manpower, weaponry, and air support, by December 1995 Chechen guerrillas had fought Yeltsin's mighty Russian army to a bloody, embarrassing stalemate.

The Chechens' military success was largely a dividend from their long-running success at crime. Even during the Soviet era, Chechen *mafiyas* had controlled much of the Russian criminal underworld, so the lawlessness of the 1990s played to the insurgents' advantage. Need sophisticated weapons to fight the Russian army? No problem. The rebels knew which Russian army officers were willing and able to deliver the weapons in exchange for a bag of dollars or a deposit to an account in Zurich. The cash was readily available to the rebels from the Chechen crime syndicates operating throughout Russia.

By the end of 1995, Russian forces were utterly demoralized. That, along with a Russian public still smarting from the Afghanistan disaster and deeply opposed to the conflict, led Yeltsin's government to declare a ceasefire at the end of the following year.

It had been a vicious conflict, with atrocities committed by both sides. The official figure for Russian military deaths was 5,500; the truth may be twice that. For Chechen fighters, the death toll neared 15,000. Civilian casualties, which are more difficult to tally, numbered 30,000 to 100,000 killed and multiples of that injured. More than 500,000 people were displaced, and cities and villages across Chechnya were in ruins. But for Moscow, the suffering and loss weren't the price of victory; they were an advertisement of failure.

Putin was watching the debacle from afar, and it ground away at him.

During most of the conflict, he was just another minor political figure in St. Petersburg, serving as an adviser to the mayor on international affairs and far removed from Kremlin politics. But he was filled with ambition and had already set his sights on higher office. To that end, he had begun gathering a circle of confidants. These "St. Petersburg boys," intensely loyal to Putin, were the only people he trusted.

This inner circle would benefit enormously. Dmitry Medvedev, for example, would eventually inherit the presidency from Putin when the latter was barred by law from a third consecutive term. Medvedev would keep Putin close by appointing him prime minister. Then, after serving a single term, Medvedev would step down, allow Putin to be reelected, and accept his own appointment as prime minister in return—a revolving door that could be kept turning for decades.

Other loyalists, like Igor Sechin, Putin's right-hand man in St. Petersburg, were rewarded with control of vast stretches of the economy, particularly in the energy industry.

Move to Moscow

In June 1996, bringing the St. Petersburg boys with him, Putin moved to Moscow, where another former colleague had invited him to join the Yeltsin administration. Surrounding himself with loyal supporters was a shrewd strategy, or it might have been simply a matter of caution, given the hazards of Russian politics. Either way, it insulated him from potential enemies and would give him an unassailable base when he later moved to consolidate power.

At the time Putin entered the capital, Yeltsin's economic policies were failing on a grand scale, and his army had just been fought to that embarrassing standstill in Chechnya. Putin knew he could do better, and began his ascent to the pinnacle of power. First order of business: crush those rebellious Muslims once and for all—and do it right.

The years following the end of the First Chechen War had been troubled. The Chechen government's grip on its little would-be republic was weak, especially outside Grozny, a capital that lay in rubble. Areas

controlled by splinter groups operating beyond the capital were expanding. The ravages of war and lack of economic opportunity left thousands
of brutal, heavily armed former separatist fighters idle but still ready for
violence.

Warlords outside Grozny scorned the authority of the capital and
busied themselves raiding other parts of the Northern Caucasus. Kidnapping emerged as the country's principal source of income, bringing
in over $200 million during the fledgling state's three-year existence.
Between 1996 and 1999, more than 1,300 people were abducted in
Chechnya, and in 1998 four Western hostages were executed.

Tensions rose among all segments of the public. Political violence
and religious conflicts with Islamist Wahhabi forces[1] were widespread.
Confrontations between the Chechen National Guard and the Islamist
militias grew in intensity and frequency. In 1998, the authorities in
Grozny declared a state of emergency.

Enter Vladimir Putin, a once-obscure KGB agent but now an ascen-
dant political star to whom Yeltsin had taken a liking. First, in July 1998,
Yeltsin had installed him as head of the Federal Security Service (FSB,
successor to the KGB). Then, barely a year later, he appointed Putin to
the office of prime minister.

In retrospect, it seems a meteoric rise. At the time, though, no one
thought much of Putin. After all, he was Yeltsin's sixth prime minister
in eight years; it was a dead-end job. The new guy wasn't expected to
last longer than any of his predecessors.

Not for the last time, he was badly underestimated.

Becoming prime minister immediately drew Putin into the Chechen
fray. But rather than see it as a hopeless mess, he saw an opportunity
to prove how different he was from the indecisive Yeltsin, whom he
already felt confident he could replace. But that was for later. For now,
as Russian prime minister, he could engineer an ending very different
from the first Chechen conflict.

The presumed trigger of the Second Chechen War was an invasion
of the neighboring Republic of Dagestan in August and September 1999
by two freelance armies of about 2,000 Chechen, Dagestani, and Arab

---

[1] Wahhabism is a reactionary Islamist sect originating in Saudi Arabia.

mujahideen and Wahhabist fighters. Their invasion failed, and by mid-September they had been pushed back into Chechnya.

With that, the adventure might have ended with a return to the status quo ante, but for the bombs about to explode.

The Bombings

The first of four closely spaced terrorist attacks came on September 4, 1999, in Buynaksk, Dagestan. Late that night, an enormous truck bomb leveled a barracks that housed Russian soldiers and their families. Left within the pile of burning rubble and pancaked floors were the bodies of 64 Russian men, women, and children. An Islamic Chechen claimed responsibility for the deed. Though he later changed his story, he had set the pattern of blaming for the incidents that would follow.

Five days later, bombers struck Moscow. The target was an eight-story apartment building on Guryanova Street, in a working-class neighborhood in the city's southeast. Rather than being delivered by truck, the device had been stashed on the building's ground floor, but the result was similar. The explosion brought down all eight floors and killed 94 residents as they slept.

For the Russian public, trouble in Dagestan was unremarkable. But Guryanova Street was in the heart of the homeland. It was there that the alarm first sounded. Within hours, Russian government officials all but certified that Chechen terrorists were responsible. Cities everywhere went into a state of high alert. As thousands of police fanned out to question—and in several hundred cases, arrest—anyone resembling a Chechen, residents of apartment buildings organized themselves into neighborhood watch patrols. Calls for retaliation rose from all political quarters.

Notably, instead of treating the site as an active crime scene and sifting through the ruins, Russian authorities razed 19 Guryanova Street just days after the blast and hauled the rubble away to a municipal dump. If any evidence had been gathered—and it wasn't clear that any had been—it was locked away in an FSB storehouse. Nothing was left for examination by third parties.

Four days later, on September 13, 1999, amid the near hysteria that gripped Moscow, authorities were called early in the morning to check on suspicious activity at the apartment building at 6/3 Kashirskoye Highway, on Moscow's outskirts. Finding nothing untoward, security personnel left at about 2 A.M. Somehow, inexplicably, they had failed to notice the massive bomb in the building's basement. At 5:03 A.M., the bomb detonated, and the nine-story building collapsed; 121 died.

Then came another oddity. That same morning, Gennady Seleznyov, Speaker of the Duma (Russia's lower parliamentary house), relayed to parliament a report he had just received that an apartment building in Volgodonsk, a city 700 miles south of Moscow, had been blown up the previous night.

A building had in fact been destroyed by a bomb the previous night (6/3 Kashirskoye Highway), but Seleznyov was citing an entirely different location. It seemed no more than an inconsequential blunder until three days later, when an apartment building in Volgodonsk was indeed blown up.

"How did it happen," one Duma member asked, "that you told us on Monday about a blast that didn't occur until Thursday?"

In lieu of an answer, the questioner had his microphone cut off.

To many observers, this was an early hint of conspiracy. It suggested that the bombings had been scheduled with the knowledge of the FSB and that someone in the organization had confused the order in which the disasters were to be announced to parliament.

The Volgodonsk bombing did actually happen, but not until three days later, on September 16. It, too, was a truck bomb, and it left another 17 apartment dwellers dead.

By that time, in the minds of most Russians, Chechens had been fingered as the perpetrators in all four attacks. It was an easy idea to sell. Russian antipathy toward Chechens runs deep, and it had grown stronger during the secessionist war. During that conflict, Chechen rebels had shown no reluctance about taking their fight to Russia proper and targeting civilians.

Still, a few felt uneasy with the official explanation. What, some asked, was the Chechens' motive? The war had ended in 1997 with Boris Yeltsin agreeing to Chechen autonomy. Why would the Chechens want to risk provoking the Russian government when they already had what they had fought for?

And then something very strange happened in the sleepy provincial city of Ryazan, some 120 miles southeast of Moscow.

Hypervigilance was still the order of the day, so it was no surprise that residents of 14/16 Novosyolov Street in Ryazan looked with suspicion on a white Zhiguli sedan that pulled up to park beside their apartment building on the evening of September 22. They became downright panicky when they saw two men removing several large sacks from the car's trunk and carrying them into the basement before speeding away.

The residents called the police, who discovered three 110-pound sacks wired to a detonator and timer in the basement. As they quickly evacuated the apartment building, a local FSB explosives expert was called in to disarm the device. He determined that the sacks contained RDX, an explosive powerful enough to bring down the entire building. In the meantime, all roads out of Ryazan were blocked, and a massive manhunt for the Zhiguli and its occupants began.

By the following afternoon, word of the incident in Ryazan had spread across Russia. Acting Prime Minister Putin flexed his rhetorical muscles and congratulated the residents for their vigilance. The Russian interior minister chimed in, lauding recent improvements in the readiness of security forces that had foiled the bombing.

And that might have been that, except the night of the failed bombing, two of the Ryazan suspects were apprehended. To the local authorities' astonishment, both produced FSB identification cards, and soon a call came down from FSB headquarters in Moscow that the two were to be released.

The following morning, FSB director Nikolai Patrushev appeared on television to report a wholly new version of events in Ryazan. Rather than an aborted terrorist attack, he explained, the incident at 14/16 Novosyolov Street had actually been an FSB "training exercise" to test the public's alertness. Further, he said, the sacks in the basement had contained no explosives, just sugar.

The sacks of sugar did not help the medicine go down. How was one to reconcile FSB headquarters' sacks-of-sugar claim with the local FSB's chemical analysis finding RDX? If the incident truly had been a training exercise, how was it that the local FSB branch wasn't informed ahead of time? How was it that Director Patrushev himself hadn't seen fit to mention the training exercise for a day and a half after the terrorist alert was raised? For that matter, why did the apartment building bombing spree cease after the Ryazan confusion? Surely, if the attacks had been the handiwork of Chechen terrorists, they wouldn't have stopped after one setback.

We'll probably never learn the truth, although several investigators have died trying, as we will see.

Second Chechen War

Whatever the case, Putin saw and seized the day. This was his opportunity to capitalize on the Russian public's endemic fear of Islam and its lingering sense of humiliation over failure in the First Chechen War.

On the night of September 23, 1999, even as newly installed Prime Minister Putin was praising the residents of Ryazan for their watchfulness, Russian warplanes were striking Grozny. A week later, the Russian armored battalions that had been amassed on the border for months crossed into Chechnya. The Second Chechen War was on.

This time around, following a scorched-earth strategy, Russian forces turned their weapons on civilian targets. To avoid repeating the heavy Russian casualties of the First Chechen War, they advanced slowly and in force, using artillery and air power to soften Chechen defenses. Nearly 300,000 of Chechnya's 800,000 civilians fled from the Russian advance and sought refuge in neighboring Russian republics.

The Russian army took no chances with the Chechen populace. They set up so-called filtration camps in northern Chechnya for detaining suspected members of *bandformirovaniya* militant groups (literally: bandit formations). Once again they flattened the capital of Grozny, which was under the control of anti-Russian rebels.

Observers likened the scene to Dresden or Hiroshima. But few details leaked to the outside world, as human-rights groups and journalists were barred from the war zone. Not for the last time, Putin kept blinders on the media.

Success with Chechnya positioned Putin perfectly for the stunner that came next: On December 31, Boris Yeltsin—whose approval rating had fallen to single digits—abruptly resigned. As provided in the Russian constitution, Prime Minister Putin succeeded Yeltsin and became acting president.

Putin had jumped from an appointment as head of the FSB in July 1998 to an appointment as prime minister barely a year later, and then to acting president less than five months after that. It was an astonishing rise, unprecedented in Russian politics.

Had Putin expected to move so far so fast? Was it all planned? Of course we can't know. But whether it happened mostly by design or mostly by chance, we do know that he played *carpe diem* masterfully.

He knew the kind of leader Russians had been pining for, so he gave priority to advancing his persona as the fearless tough guy. Rather than sit in the president's office, he flew into the war zone to express his support of, and solidarity with, the troops. That was something his predecessor never would have done. The Russian people notice shows of strength.

After a winter siege beginning at the end of 1999, the Russian military took control of Grozny on February 2 of the following year. This time, the war had been brief.

Though Putin was able to claim victory, the end of the full-scale offensive didn't mean peace. Chechen militants throughout the North Caucasus went on killing Russians in large numbers. Their challenge to Russian political control of Chechnya continued for several more years.

Between 2002 and 2004, Chechens and Chechen-led militants carried out a campaign of terror against civilians in Russia. About 200 Russians were killed in bombings. Two large-scale hostage takings added to the headlines. The 2002 Moscow theater hostage crisis (916 hostages) and the 2004 Beslan school siege (1,120 hostages) ended in the deaths of hundreds of civilians. In the Moscow standoff, FSB Spetsnaz forces stormed the buildings on the third day with lethal chemical agents.

Nevertheless, Putin acted as if the revolt were over. He established direct rule of Chechnya in May 2000 and the following month appointed Akhmad Kadyrov president of the Chechen Republic. On March 23, 2003, a constitution—keeping the republic tethered to Moscow while allowing it a significant degree of autonomy—was adopted by referendum in Chechnya.

The referendum had been promoted by the Russian government, rejected by separatists, and boycotted by many citizens. Akhmad Kadyrov was assassinated by bomb the following year. His son Ramzan Kadyrov, leader of the pro-Moscow militia known as *kadyrovtsy*, became Chechnya's de facto ruler. In February 2007, with support from Putin, the younger Kadyrov was installed as president, where he remains despite several attempts on his life.

Questions about the alleged Chechen terrorist bombings of September 1999 linger. Although the Chechens certainly had motive, means, and opportunity, some Putin skeptics continue to ask: Did the FSB conspire to elevate one of their own, Putin, to the presidency? Were the bombings a false-flag operation?

No, say the Russian courts. A criminal investigation into the bombings was completed in 2002. That investigation and the court that reviewed it concluded that the bombings were the work of Islamic militants retaliating for Russia's counteroffensive against their incursion into Dagestan. Six suspects were convicted.

Putin Installed

Whatever the truth of the bombings' origins, the offensive in Chechnya—begun by Yeltsin but largely managed by Putin—served to move a very dark horse to the front of the Russian political pack, where President Putin used the bombings to leverage his prominence.

In an August 1999 poll, Putin had garnered less than 2 percent support as a presidential candidate despite (or perhaps because of) Yeltsin's backing. By the time Election Day arrived, his situation had changed entirely.

Putin faced a lot of opposition. But the candidates had been preparing for the regularly scheduled presidential election, which would have occurred in June 2000 had Yeltsin not resigned. Instead, Yeltsin's resignation pulled the balloting up to March. At that point, Putin's total-war policy in Chechnya was still fresh in people's minds, and he was riding a wave of popularity. His opponents were sandbagged by events. Putin took 53 percent of the vote and became president.

The reign of Vladimir Putin had begun. Like Peter the Great, the historical figure he most admired, he vowed to restore his country as a power of consequence. He knew that it wasn't going to happen easily. But he believed he had been endowed with all the right qualities to bring it off: physical stamina, a keen intellect, a deep understanding of the ways of politics in the real world (and the role that energy plays), and an unwavering boldness of vision.

It was time to tighten his hold on power by dealing with his enemies. Next in Putin's sights: the oligarchs.

Chapter 2

Humbling the Oligarchs

For a national leader wishing to cement a hold on power—especially a would-be autocrat—nothing beats war. Turning the children of the common folk into soldiers and sending them to do battle with a feared or hated enemy tends to unite those folk in support of whoever is in charge, no matter what the actual reason for the fighting. It works in any country.

So it was with Putin and Chechnya. Although the breakaway republic wasn't exactly a foreign country, to most Russians it might as well have been. So they fell right in line behind their aggressive new president and his Chechnya campaign.

Putin is always ready for the next move, the zag after the zig. He recognized that as quickly as war wins the population over to your side, the advantage can just as quickly be lost. The longer a war goes on, the more likely people are to turn against it. Lose a war, and everyone decides they were against it all along. So to gain from a bloody conflict, a leader needs a swift, decisive victory.

The First Chechen War had left Russians with a sour taste in their mouths. It went on for two years and ended with their well-equipped, modern army failing against a posse of back-country guerrillas—a replay of Afghanistan in Russia's own backyard. No one was in the mood for more of the same.

The people rallied behind Putin because they detected his willingness to do whatever it took to get the job done. What else would you expect from an ex-KGB officer?

Predictably, Putin went at the Chechens with maximum firepower and subdued them with minimum loss of Russian lives. After that, Russia's lingering troubles with the republic hardly mattered. The war had ended quickly, and it had ended in victory, a demonstration of Putin's strength for all to see. No more wishy-washy leaders in the Kremlin. A real man was back at the helm. The people cheered.

Disposing of an outside threat was important as a first step toward Putin's goal of reestablishing Russian might, with himself as the revered leader. It was the relatively simple part, however.

Next, he had to deal with his political enemies. Some were easy to identify. The drifting policies of the Yeltsin years had fostered a small class of crafty and often violent billionaires, a wild bunch known as the oligarchs.

In the words of a former deputy chairman of Russia's central bank: "All Russian oligarchs are fiendishly ingenious, fiendishly strong, malicious, and greedy—tough customers to deal with."

Land of Opportunity

During the 1990s, the country was struggling to adopt the ways of a free-market society. After 70 years of enforced collectivism, suffocation by central planning, and the quashing of individual initiative, Russia's freedom makeover wasn't going smoothly.

The transition from centralized command and control to free markets was hindered by a massive flight of domestic capital, foreign investors deserting the country, a sharp rise in unemployment, widespread failure to meet payrolls for those who actually held jobs, and a precipitous drop in the foreign-exchange value of the ruble (which hit its all-time low in late 1993). Before the early 1990s, there wasn't even a stock market.

Three generations of Russians had toiled under the threat of communism's gulags and been trained to look to Moscow for decisions in all matters. And that was after three and a half centuries of submission to czarist rule. Suddenly, people were thrown into a situation they weren't prepared for and had no experience with. That they were overwhelmed by their first whiff of freedom was hardly a surprise.

Most were utterly lost, but not all. As state control of enterprises withered, a few crafty individuals saw they could exploit what was happening. Some were already wealthy, whereas others simply seized the opportunity to start a fortune. What they all had in common was an aptitude for business that was in such short supply in Russia.

The best that can be said of the oligarchs is that they were ready for economic freedom when almost no one else was. They certainly helped with the transition to a market economy. But in a society where cronyism, bribery, extortion, and murder for hire are normal, it would be a stretch to argue that these newly minted billionaires came by their fortunes in an honest way.

They were utterly ruthless. But they would soon learn that someone else was even more so: Vladimir Putin.

Nailing Khodorkovsky

Putin realized early on that the key to Russia's rebirth was its vast wealth of natural resources. Oil, gas, uranium—the country had them all in abundance. All figured into his master plan. And because of their importance, energy companies could not be allowed to fall under the control of foreign investors, no matter what. Even domestic private owners would have to answer to the state or, more to the point, to Putin.

The oligarchs mattered to Putin not merely because of their wealth but because energy was precisely the industry in which they were most prominent. Mikhail Khodorkovsky was the richest and most powerful of them, with a fortune of $18 billion. In his struggle with the oligarchs, Putin's contest with Khodorkovsky was the decisive battle.

When it ended—with Khodorkovsky and others stripped of their wealth and imprisoned, exiled, or dead—there was no doubt that Putin would be the overlord of Russia's energy sector. And he would be thanked for what he did. As with Chechnya, attacking the oligarchs was a hit with the public, who resented both their great wealth and how they had gotten it. Seeing them humbled amped up Putin's popularity yet again.

The Khodorkovsky match was not the only front in Putin's war with the oligarchs. But it was the splashiest, and it best illustrates his methods.

Like Putin, Khodorkovsky had spent his childhood in a shabby communal apartment and, also like Putin, he had ambition to spare. After working as a leader in Komsomol, a communist youth organization, he opened the Youth Center for Scientific and Technological Development. Later he founded an import/export firm.

As he transitioned from communist to capitalist, Khodorkovsky came to believe that the new Russian economy should be centered on high-tech industries rather than on natural resources. That put him in conflict with Putin's notion that resources are the natural engine for Russia's economic progress.

Khodorkovsky became a prominent advocate for a free market. In 1993, he published the Russian capitalist manifesto, *The Man with the Ruble*. In it he wrote: "It is time to stop living according to Lenin! Our guiding light is Profit, acquired in a strictly legal way. Our Lord is His Majesty, Money, for it is only He who can lead us to wealth as the norm in life."

Khodorkovsky's compliance with the law was noticeably far from strict. But that was the norm at the time. Several of his early millionaire colleagues had gotten so closely involved with criminals that they eventually had to flee the country to save their lives and the lives of their families. Shootings in public view were common, as were kidnappings of women and children. It was all part of the cost of doing business. That Khodorkovsky's import/export company was known to violate dozens of laws surprised no one, and by comparison with many others he was a goody-goody.

It was entering the financial arena that put Khodorkovsky on track to join the billionaires' club. And it was through Bank Menatep that he positioned himself to become the richest man in the new Russia.

Vouchers

Bank Menatep, which Khodorkovsky established in 1989, made significant profits, reportedly enhanced by diverted state funds. The bank also operated a lucrative market for trading state privatization vouchers, which turned out to be more than just another profit center.

Though it seems crazy now, the voucher program must have made sense to Boris Yeltsin at the time. He initiated it in 1992 on a day when, perhaps, he was heavily into the vodka.

Yeltsin proposed that every man, woman, and child in Russia be issued a voucher that could be exchanged for shares in one of the state enterprises undergoing privatization. That way, Yeltsin was convinced, every citizen would gain a stake in the emerging capitalist economy. However, consistent with capitalist principles, everyone would be free to trade or sell his or her voucher if one chose to.

The voucher idea had been imported to Russia by consulting economists from the United States. It made good sense in a textbook kind of way. But it made no sense at all if the vouchers were going to be issued to people who didn't understand what the pieces of paper represented.

Over 140 million Russians participated in the grand voucher program, the great majority of them cash poor and lacking even a rudimentary comprehension of capital markets. Most chose to capture a little cash immediately by selling their vouchers.

That played right into the hands of anyone with a bit of investment sense—especially the oligarchs. They were ready and able to accommodate the millions of Russians who knew nothing about the vouchers except that they could be turned into instant cash. Buying on the very cheap, they gained control of formerly state-run companies, which concentrated an astronomical amount of wealth and power in the hands of a very few.

Khodorkovsky topped the list of those who made the people's ignorance his gain. Through Bank Menatep and a separate holding company, he took control of a string of companies for mere kopecks on the ruble. It wasn't quite theft, but it was a process in which informed consent played no role whatsoever.

In 1995, Group Menatep moved on Yukos, a major petroleum con-glomerate. Yukos had been assembled by the Russian government in 1993 to roll up dozens of state-owned production, refining, and distri-bution assets, including one of the most productive oil fields in west-ern Siberia. Like most other Russian companies struggling to adapt to a market economy, its performance had been dismal. Oil production rates were declining, employees were months behind in getting paid, and financial controls were haphazard.

Khodorkovsky set out to grab Yukos and fix it.

He captured Yukos in two bold moves and in so doing demonstrated that he was a wily businessman, someone to be reckoned with. Vladimir Putin—at the time still working for the mayor of St. Petersburg, but with his eye on higher office—took notice. Perhaps, given his dispassion in separating ends from means, he even admired how Khodorkovsky operated.

It happened this way: First, knowing that the Yeltsin administra-tion was strapped for cash, Bank Menatep participated in the ill-fated "Loans for Shares" program. Under the arrangement, Yeltsin's govern-ment pledged shares in several of Russia's most profitable companies as collateral for loans from oligarch-controlled banks. The value of the collateral was several times more than the value of the loans secured. If the state defaulted—and its debilitated condition made that likely—the lending bank was supposed to auction off the shares. But the auctions that actually took place were rigged. Everything was carefully planned to exclude anyone who might outbid the lending bank.

In this instance, Bank Menatep lent the Kremlin $159 million under conditions that virtually ensured default. For collateral, the Kremlin pledged 45 percent of Yukos, which at that point was worth over $3 billion, or some 20 times the size of the loan. Then, when the gov-ernment indeed defaulted, Khodorkovsky effectively swapped the IOU Bank Menatep was holding for nearly half of Yukos.

Days later, to gain full control, Menatep purchased another 33 per-cent of Yukos from Yeltsin's desperate government for just $150 million, or about 15 cents on the dollar.

Over the next several years, Khodorkovsky brought the company back to health. In 2002 Yukos became the first Russian oil company to pay dividends to its shareholders, and by 2003 it was accounting for

20 percent of all Russian oil production and 2 percent of the world's. It had become the country's second-largest taxpayer, covering 4 percent of the Russian federal budget.

This was quite a high standing for a company about to be smashed. Whether Putin could have succeeded in moving on Khodorkovsky in a different political and economic climate is difficult to judge. But he clearly made savvy use of the man's past.

During the postrevolutionary fallout of the 1990s, every large Russian business, including Bank Menatep, engaged in shady practices. Tax evasion, loose accounting, and bribery of government officials were flat-out necessities. In a transition to private enterprise rife with distortions and wrong turns, the roughest of the freshly minted capitalists modeled their enterprises after the powerful crime syndicates.

The Yukos Way

Nevertheless, as the revolutionary dust settled and the backbone of capitalism began to take shape, Yukos was an exemplar of clean and transparent business practices, at least by the standards of the day. Yukos was the first large Russian company to adopt international accounting standards and the first Russian oil company to issue financial statements in accordance with generally accepted accounting principles (GAAP). The company added accountants who had been trained in the West to its staff, and retained PricewaterhouseCoopers to audit its annual reports.

Bank Menatep also set up an international advisory board to help it integrate into the global business community. The bank was rapidly moving away from the Wild West practices of the 1990s. Wanting to be taken seriously as a legitimate global business, it decided to act like one.

Khodorkovsky also began imitating the philanthropic practices of his Western counterparts. Both personally and through Yukos, he donated hundreds of millions of dollars to charities. The company gave college scholarships to the high-achieving children of its employees, as well as to students focusing on oil-related industries. Khodorkovsky personally bankrolled numerous organizations such as the Eurasia Foundation, an American nonprofit that supports the development of small businesses.

Nonprofits are powerful political players in this part of the world, and Khodorkovsky's involvement with them would prove to be a major contributor to his downfall.

The Yukos education programs reflected and promoted Khodorkovsky's personal vision for Russia. In one such project, New Civilization, high school students designed an imaginary country, chose its political system and currency, and elected a government. It was Khodorkovsky's effort to instill democratic and free-market principles in Russia's youth. That put Khodorkovsky at odds with Putin and his belief that Russia's greatness required a very strong—autocratic, if necessary—hand on the helm.

In addition to supporting organizations hostile to Putin's government, Khodorkovsky personally spoke out against the man, loudly and often. He lambasted the Kremlin for infringing on civil rights, accused state officials of corruption, and criticized the government's control of oil transportation through its pipeline company, Transneft.

Openly critical of what he referred to as "managed democracy," he claimed that the military and security services exercised far too much authority. In a 2003 interview with the *Times* of London, he said:

> It is the Singapore model ... in Russia these days. It means that theoretically you have a free press, but in practice there is self-censorship. Theoretically you have courts; in practice the courts adopt decisions dictated from above. Theoretically there are civil rights enshrined in the constitution; in practice you are not able to exercise some of these rights.

His observations may have been spot on, but without doubt he was baiting the bear, perhaps under the foolish belief that his great wealth would protect him.

His largesse reached deep into the political arena. He gave freely to opponents of Putin's own party, United Russia. As the 2003 elections approached for the Duma (Russia's lower parliamentary house), Khodorkovsky increased his financial support of the Union of Rightist Forces, the Russian United Democratic Party, and even the Communist Party. By supporting the opposition, Khodorkovsky hoped to keep United Russia and other pro-Putin politicians from achieving a two-thirds majority in the Duma. He pointedly refused to contribute to Putin's United Russia, despite the party's repeated requests.

Putin's Best Offer

Khodorkovsky was ignoring the rules Putin had issued in earlier meetings with the oligarchs. To obtain at least an uneasy peace, Putin offered a policy of "live and let live." He was willing to turn a blind eye to the origins of the oligarchs' wealth, and he would allow them to accumulate more. But he knew he had to protect himself from the influence their wealth could buy. So, in return for his forbearance, Putin insisted that the oligarchs deny financial support to his political opponents.

It was a classic Putin maneuver: Dangle the carrot, but keep the stick at hand. Those who went along stayed rich; those who declined the offer . . .

Still moving to expand his business empire, Khodorkovsky announced that Yukos would merge with Sibneft—another oil company that, on its own, was already larger than Rosneft, which was Putin's pet. Fellow oligarchs Roman Abramovich and Boris Berezovsky had acquired Sibneft during Yeltsin's Loans for Shares auctions, each paying $100 million for a half interest, which they rapidly turned into billions. Abramovich later bought out Berezovsky, and at the time of the planned merger, he owned most of Sibneft.

The new entity, which was to be known as YukosSibneft Oil Company, would have produced 30 percent of Russia's oil, and it would have held the third-largest privately owned oil reserves in the world, right behind Exxon Mobil Corporation and Royal Dutch Shell. In addition to the merger, Khodorkovsky was also in talks to sell the company to Exxon Mobil or Chevron. At one point, he was secretly shuttling between rooms at two hotels as he tried to drum up a bidding war between the two. He planned to become the largest shareholder in one or the other of the American petro-giants and to become rich and powerful on a Rockefeller scale.

The oligarch knew he wasn't going to get Putin's support for his dalliance with a foreign company, but he felt strong enough—and was greedy enough—to try to make an end run around the president. If

Putin found out, he would be furious. That the deal involved the sale of energy rights would make it doubly offensive.

In the emerging system, widely known as Kremlin Incorporated, striking a deal with foreign partners was simply not the prerogative of a private businessman. Proper procedure would have been for Khodorkovsky to seek Putin's blessing before advancing such an initiative. As with any big deal, it wouldn't become official until a TV broadcast featured the president signing off on it.

Putin did find out. The Exxon representative—then-CEO Lee Raymond—became suspicious of the game Khodorkovsky was playing and phoned the president to ask whether the deal had his backing. Absolutely not, Putin said. He wasn't aware of the negotiations at all.

That was enough for Raymond, who recognized that Putin's magic wand was never going to be waved over Khodorkovsky's proposal and that the deal was dangerous. So Exxon backed off. Shortly thereafter, negotiations with Chevron also collapsed.

Nevertheless, the slight wasn't forgotten. Khodorkovsky had gone too far. He had shown major disrespect to Russia's leader.

That the Yukos/Sibneft merger threatened Putin's plan to steer Russia's oil industry was by itself enough of an insult. But in addition to Khodorkovsky's growing domination of oil, other factors—his great wealth, his outspoken scorn for Putin's policies, his eagerness to throw his financial might behind Putin's competitors, his readiness to flout protocol, and his overt disdain for the natural resources industry that had given him his power—made him an adversary too dangerous and irritating for Putin to ignore.

The conflict reached a crescendo in February 2003. At a public, media-attended meeting at the Kremlin between Putin and the oligarchs, Khodorkovsky sparred recklessly with Putin, challenging him on questions of government misconduct and implying that state officials were pocketing millions in bribes. He all but accused Putin of involvement in the theft of state assets.

It was a left hook to the jaw: Khodorkovsky versus Putin, broadcast live for all of Russia to see.

The president did not dispute the accusations, which was widely taken to mean that Khodorkovsky was correct.

But Putin clearly understood how damaging the allegations would be if left unanswered, so he quickly mounted a counteroffensive. He turned the tables on Khodorkovsky by pointing out the enormity of Yukos's oil reserves and asked how the company obtained them. He also referred to Yukos's history of tax issues and the question of whether those issues had been disposed of through bribery.

Right uppercut from Putin.

Everyone—from the media to government to business to ordinary Russian viewers—understood Putin's veiled threat. He was stronger than the richest of the rich. Any disfavored oligarch would be prosecuted and held accountable for his anything-goes behavior in the 1990s. As of that pivotal day, all of Russia's wealthy were on notice that they would always be subject to Putin.

He stood as the man of steel, a man cut out for the times, just the sort Russians were looking for in their leadership.

Unfortunately for Khodorkovsky, he did not have the charisma for an effective media personality. He was no match for Putin as a propagandist, and his high-pitched voice was a poor instrument for delivering any message. Like most of the oligarchs, he was a Jew, which for many Russians made him a ready scapegoat for the country's problems. The public never saw him as one of them, as opposed to Putin, who seemed a latter-day Slavic warrior straight from the pages of their history books—despite his diminutive stature and even though almost nothing was known of Putin's ancestry before his grandparents.

Despite Khodorkovsky's offensive, Putin came out victorious in his first big media battle.

Later, privately, Putin would tell Lord John Browne, the former head of British Petroleum, "I have eaten more dirt than I need to from that man."

Indeed. No one could be allowed to challenge the authority of the state in so many ways. And now, unforgivably, Khodorkovsky had offended the president in front of the whole nation. Putin had no choice but to take him out.

Dropping the Hammer

But gone were the days when Soviet dictators merely shipped their enemies to a hellhole in Siberia. Putin was determined to maintain his public image as a democratic leader by acting within the letter of the law.

He bided his time. He went quiet after the TV spat and Khodor-kovsky's announcement of the Yukos/Sibneft merger, leaving many to believe that Putin had lost control, especially when he also with-drew the government's opposition to private oil pipeline projects that would further enrich Russia's tycoons. Many analysts were duped into thinking that the president was yielding to his adversaries and that the country's oil sector would belong to the oligarchs and be dominated by Yukos.

Putin was far craftier than that, though. His retreat, in fact, was strategic. He knew that a rich opportunity had presented itself, one that in a single stroke could eliminate the Yukos threat, further domination by Rosneft, his own favored company, and warn off anyone who might stand in his way. But everything had to be done carefully.

As noted earlier, if you wanted to find something damaging to a veteran of Russia's 1990s business world, you didn't have to look too closely at his books before it smacked you in the face.

The Putin forces did their homework and then made their first move in July 2003. Moscow police arrested Platon Lebedev, a principal share-holder and director of Bank Menatep and member of the executive committee of Yukos. Armed with a warrant from the Russian prose-cutor general, they dragged Lebedev from a Moscow hospital bed and charged him with embezzling state assets. Additional charges followed: tax evasion, abuse of trust, and so on.

Three months later, masked FSB agents stormed Khodorkovsky's airplane and arrested him. He was charged with tax evasion, embezzle-ment, fraud, and forgery.

The Russian government also froze the assets of the two men, including a large block of shares in Yukos, which made it impossible to sell the company to Chevron or any other buyer. Without its two largest shareholders and lacking a financial white knight with the courage to enter the battle, Yukos was helpless.

Ironically, as Russia inched its way toward greater respect for law and transparency, Putin was attacking the company that had taken the longest strides in that direction. Had he merely been looking to make an example of a tax evader, he had plenty of better targets. But he wasn't. Putin was looking for an opening to prevent the Yukos/Sibneft merger, to shake down Khodorkovsky, and to reverse the privatization of the energy sector—and to do so without having to renationalize any company outright.

Despite having approved Yukos's tax standing in July 2003, the Russian Tax Ministry began a series of audits of the company's tax accounts in December of the same year, about two months after Khodorkovsky was arrested. The Tax Ministry adopted novel legal theories invented solely for attacking Yukos, and twisted Russian tax law to retroactively assign subsidiaries' profits to Yukos.

Ultimately, Yukos was handed a $30 billion bill for back taxes for the years 2000 to 2004. The company was given exactly two days to pay the tab for 2000; but its assets were frozen, so the two-day meter ran out.

Although tax claims in Russia are supposed to be settled by first selling off the taxpayer's nonessential assets, the Russian government went straight for the heart. In June 2004, it seized Yuganskneftegaz (YNG)—Yukos's largest enterprise, which was responsible for 60 percent of its oil production—for an auction later that year. At the time, YNG was valued at $15 billion to $22 billion. However, prior to the December auction, the Russian Ministry of Justice announced that YNG was worth a mere $10.4 billion. To drive the price down even further, the government assessed new taxes against the company.

Yukos tried to block the sale through the Russian courts. It also sought relief in the European Court of Human Rights and even filed for Chapter 11 bankruptcy in the United States. Although Yukos was unable to prevent the sale of YNG, the Russian bankruptcy court did issue a temporary restraining order preventing third parties—including Gazprom and banks under the court's jurisdiction—from participating in the auction.

With Gazprom excluded, the only bidder left was Baikal Finance Group. Baikal acquired YNG at the bargain basement price of $9.35 billion, which it paid out of a loan from state-controlled (i.e., Putin-controlled) Rosneft. This was quite a leap for a shell company with net capital of just $300 (yes, three hundred dollars). Three days later, Rosneft swallowed up Baikal.

That tripled Rosneft's production overnight, from barely 5 percent of Russia's output to 15 percent. Its reserves grew almost fivefold. Rosneft had become the third-largest oil producer in Russia.

In the meantime, the Yukos/Sibneft merger was unwound in the wake of Khodorkovsky's arrest, restoring Sibneft to essentially the condition it had been in prior to the deal. The prospects of survival for what remained of Yukos, however, looked dim.

Rosneft purchased Yukos's remaining debts in 2007, making the Russian government indirectly the company's main creditor. After the company's proposed restructuring plan was rejected, a Russian court declared the company insolvent. A bankruptcy sale followed, at which Rosneft purchased most of Yukos's remaining assets for about one-third of their value.

Khodorkovsky and Lebedev were put through a show trial. The court allowed gross procedural violations and accepted all of the prosecution's claims at face value. It questioned witnesses on the prosecution's behalf, whereas the two defendants weren't allowed to introduce evidence of their innocence. The court routinely denied defense motions and requests, and restricted Khodorkovsky's and Lebedev's contact with their attorneys.

The trial ended in May 2005, with Khodorkovsky and Lebedev each being sentenced to prison for nine years. On appeal to the Moscow City Court, the sentences were reduced to eight years. Yet eight years later, neither prisoner would be free.

After serving half of their respective sentences, both men became eligible for parole. In order to secure Putin an extended vacation from his nemeses and to prevent Khodorkovsky's return to Russia's economic and political landscape, the two were charged with additional crimes: embezzlement and money laundering.

In 2009, the two political prisoners were tried and once again convicted. Each of their sentences was extended to 2016. Later, Natalia Vasilyeva, the assistant to the presiding judge throughout the trial, stated that the judge's verdict was foisted on him by higher authority. No one had to ask who that authority might be.

Khodorkovsky left prison in December 2013, and Lebedev followed in January 2014.

What Putin accomplished with the Khodorkovsky affair is remarkable. In one move, he crippled a troublesome political critic and asserted state (and, by extension, personal) control over a huge element of Russia's natural resources industry.

In Putin's view, that control benefited the nation. But it may also have resulted in a financial windfall for Putin himself because of the large increase in the value of the shares he is believed to own in the companies involved. His actual net worth is a secret, because if he does own those shares (he denies it), it would be through nominees and shell companies. Unsubstantiated estimates that he might be worth upwards of $70 billion, which would make him the richest man on the planet, could be just so much hot air. Or not.

Putin accomplished it all within the formalities of the law and without alienating the public. In the latter, he was supported by the public's perception of the oligarchs as thieves who deserved whatever they got. Widespread dislike of Jews was also a help.

Putin would likely do anything to keep the respect of his people, but he cares little about outsiders' opinions of him. He ignored foreign criticism of the show trials of Khodorkovsky and Lebedev. It has been of no consequence to him that international nongovernmental organizations (NGOs) such as Human Rights Watch and Amnesty International criticized the trials as political, with the latter organization labeling the two men prisoners of conscience.

The Parliamentary Assembly of the Council of Europe Committee on Legal Affairs and Human Rights found the first trial riddled with violations of due process. In 2007, the European Court of Human Rights found that Lebedev had been illegally detained and that the Russian courts had conducted hearings without Lebedev or his attorneys present. None of those findings mattered.

A Trail of Bodies

While the überwealthy Khodorkovsky may have been Putin's highest-profile target, he was by no means atypical. Vasily Aleksanyan, at one time Yukos's general counsel and executive vice president, was arrested in 2006 on the by then familiar charges of tax evasion and money laundering.

As Putin was working to dismember Yukos, Aleksanyan had stepped up during the bankruptcy proceedings to try to preserve what was left of the company. He was repeatedly threatened and harassed and then arrested. During his incarceration, although known to be HIV-positive, he was denied medical treatment.

Or rather, treatment for his condition was offered as a bribe for giving false testimony against Khodorkovsky and Lebedev. He refused. Eventually, in January 2009, he was released on bond. By then it was too late. In 2011, he died of lymphatic cancer brought on by AIDS.

And what became of Boris Berezovsky, the former mathematician who helped Abramovich buy Sibneft? The prominent billionaire was yet another of Putin's victims. In a stunning progression, Berezovsky had turned from one of Putin's biggest boosters to his critic, and then to a high-class political refugee.

Berezovsky was a media magnate, with an empire anchored by ORT-TV. He also had interests in Aeroflot, the largest Russian airline. He'd been a member of President Yeltsin's inner circle and was elected to the Duma as part of Putin's slate. When Yeltsin tapped Putin to be prime minister, Berezovsky used his Russian television empire to turn the relative unknown into a household name in a matter of months.

But Berezovsky soured on the new president early in Putin's first term and began using ORT-TV as a platform for criticizing the Kremlin.

Opposing Putin through his television network wasn't Berezovsky's only offense. As a member of the Duma, he attacked the constitutional changes Putin was planning and announced that he would lead a fight against them. Berezovsky had become a major headache for Putin, a man who might block his plans for himself and the motherland. He had to be disposed of.

One transgression Putin could capitalize on was that Berezovsky, also Jewish, had accepted an Israeli passport, even though it was illegal for a Russian official to have a second citizenship. Another avenue of attack was to revive an old investigation of Aeroflot. When the prosecutor general demanded that Berezovsky appear for questioning, he could read the writing on the wall. The prospect of martyrdom did not appeal to him.

So, since he was abroad at the time, Berezovsky simply exiled himself to London.

The Russian government seized his media assets, tried him in absentia, and convicted him of embezzlement and fraud. Although Putin sought his extradition, the courts in the United Kingdom refused and granted Berezovsky permanent political asylum.

Despite narrowly escaping a fate similar to Khodorkovsky's, Berezovsky still met a bad end. He was found dead in his Berkshire home in March 2013, at the customer service end of a hangman's rope. Although his death appears to have been a suicide and police found no signs of violent struggle, assassination theories persist.

Daring to Notice

Berezovsky's death should have come as no surprise, since enemies of Vladimir Putin who don't wind up either in prison or in exile tend to wind up dead.

Journalists, for instance. Some 20 of them have been murdered since Putin ascended to the presidency. Yet only two of those cases have been solved, according to the Committee to Protect Journalists. Three of the most notorious were Yuri Shchekochikhin, Paul Klebnikov, and Anna Politkovskaya.

Shchekochikhin died in July 2003 from an undisclosed illness, just a few days before his scheduled departure to the United States to meet with FBI investigators. His medical documents ended up "classified" by the Russian authorities. His symptoms, however, fit the pattern of poisoning by radioactive materials used as an assassination technique by the KGB and its successor, the FSB.

In April 2004, Klebnikov, the American editor of *Forbes—Russia*, was shot to death in Moscow. Prosecutors accused a Chechen of being the shooter. You've probably noticed that Chechens, all but universally despised among Russians, make for very convenient fall guys, as do old foes: Also prominently mentioned as one of the masterminds behind the operation was none other than Boris Berezovsky. Where the truth lies we will never know. But the Chechen was acquitted in a jury trial closed to press and public. He fled the country.

Then there is Anna Politkovskaya, a writer for *Novaya Gazeta*. In October 2006, she was found shot dead in the elevator of her apartment block in central Moscow. Politkovskaya was known for her opposition to Putin in general and to his Chechen campaign in particular. She made her reputation reporting from Chechnya and had raised questions about who was really behind the apartment building bombings that supposedly provoked Putin's attack on Chechnya in 1999.

Politkovskaya had already survived a poisoning attempt in 2004. Shortly before her death, she was warned by Alexander Litvinenko—a former FSB security officer turned critic in exile—that her life was in imminent danger and that she should leave Russia immediately. He stated that the contract had been placed by Putin himself, who was reported to have said he would take her head, "literally, not figuratively," if she didn't shut her mouth about the bombings.

The identity(ies) of the murderer(s) remained a mystery for nearly eight years. The suspects weren't limited to Putin and his henchmen. Politkovskaya had made enemies not only in Moscow but also in Chechnya, where she had gathered evidence that President Kadyrov's subordinates were involved in kidnapping and murder. The FSB was also on the suspect list, and, yes, Berezovsky's name surfaced yet again. In 2009, three accused conspirators were tried and acquitted.

In June 2014, a Russian court convicted two Chechen professional hit men and their three Chechen accomplices of the murder. The identity of the person who sent them remains unknown.

And Litvinenko, who had tried to warn the soon-to-be-murdered journalist? Just three weeks after Politkovskaya's death, he met with two Russians in a London hotel, where he drank tea dosed with polonium-210.

The substance is colorless and odorless and doesn't set off ordinary radiation sensors; it is extremely difficult to detect in the body. Scientists identified it in Litvinenko only hours before his death three weeks later. Litvinenko was a fitness enthusiast. Doctors say it was only because he was in such good shape that he lingered so long. Had he died sooner, the actual cause wouldn't have been discovered.

Other Putin opponents have suffered similar fates.

Vladimir Gusinsky, a media tycoon and a skeptic about the Chechen bombings, used his television station, NTV, to back a candidate against Putin's Unity Party in the 1999 Duma elections. He also aired a program highly critical of Putin just days before the 2000 presidential election. After being arrested and threatened with prosecution for fraud, Gusinsky jumped bail and took exile in Spain.

Arkady Patarkatsishvili, an oligarch and business associate of Berezovsky, was another Putin supporter who changed sides. He went into
exile after Putin's election. In December 2007, he told the London Sun-
day *Times* he was the target of an assassination plot. He died little more
than a month later at his Surrey mansion of what is listed as a "heart
attack."

Finally, there was Alexander Perepilichny, a wealthy businessman
who sought refuge in Britain after supplying evidence against an alleged
Russian crime syndicate. He collapsed while jogging outside his home
in Weybridge, England, right after returning from a trip to Paris. Toxi-
cology tests on the 44-year-old's body failed to reveal a cause of death,
although poisoning is suspected.

Survive and Thrive

But there's another side to the coin, and to understand Putin, it needs
to be noticed. Though so many of Russia's 1990s-era oligarchs came to
a bad end, others managed not only to survive but to thrive in the new
Russia.

Alisher Usmanov could serve as a model for an acceptable player in
the country Putin wants: amass wealth from natural resources and deploy
that wealth for the build-out of a modern Russia. Despite not being
a native (he's from Uzbekistan), despite being a Muslim in a country
hostile to Muslims, and despite having done jail time in his homeland
(for charges later dismissed), Usmanov has become the country's richest
oligarch, with a fortune exceeding $18 billion. He made the money
in metals and now has interests in telecommunications and media. He
owns a stake in British soccer team FC Arsenal, was an early backer of
Facebook, and profited nicely from a $100 million position in Apple.

Mikhail Friedman is another oligarch with whom Putin has no problems. This in spite of Friedman being a Jew who is active in Jewish
organizations in Russia and Europe.

More important to Putin than ethnicity is that Friedman honors
Russia through membership in numerous public-service bodies, includ-
ing the board of directors of the Russian Union of Industrialists and
Entrepreneurs and the National Council on Corporate Governance. He

also helps promote the national literary award, "Big Book," and is a member of the board of the Center for Support of Native Literature, which encourages cultural programs, promotes the ideals of humanism and respect for the values of Russian culture, and supports creative writing in Russia. *Forbes* assesses Friedman's fortune at $17.6 billion, making him the country's second-richest man (or third, if tales of Putin's own net worth are true).

Roman Abramovich, the exiled Berezovsky's associate at Sibneft, is another example of how to succeed. He has become a two-digit billionaire and remains in Putin's good graces, probably because he doesn't have his former partner's penchant for political criticism, contributes generously to the president's party, and invests in important infrastructure projects in the country. It likely didn't hurt that, as court documents show, he handed out billions of dollars in bribes for political favors and protection fees in the course of obtaining a big share of Russia's oil and aluminum assets.

Be wary of U.S. media's portrayal of Putin as a one-dimensional ogre. True, he can be as ruthless as he needs to be. But he's no Stalin, who saw an enemy's face at every window. Putin is practical. He knows he needs the cooperation of other powerful and able people to realize his vision. He doesn't care who you are if you can help him and agree to play by his rules. There's no evidence he's personally misogynistic, homophobic, or anti-Semitic (though he exploits Russian homophobia when it suits his purpose). His motto could be written this way: "Align with me and I will hold nothing against you; oppose me and you will surely lose."

Putin has a singular vision for Russia, and it includes only one man at the top: Putin. For him to securely hold that spot, many of the oligarchs had to go—along with hostile journalists and political opponents, of course. But the oligarchs were the easy part. They were widely resented. Much of their wealth derived from seemingly underhanded deals, even though they generally operated within the legal and economic mores of the time. Some were simply thugs. Ordinary citizens could rationalize that they got what was coming to them.

While the wealth of the surviving oligarchs may have been ill gotten, Putin has no interest in pushing them to right their past wrongs. He's not in the justice business. His vendettas against Khodorkovsky and others took Russia away from respect for property rights and closer to being a country where, if a powerful man wants something, he just has to reach out and take it. And that suits Putin.

The oligarchs want to be rich. Putin is distinguishable from them only in that he has a grand vision for Russia. In every other way, he is one of them and can comfortably coexist with them—as long as everyone understands who runs the club.

Vision and Principle

Putin's treatment of the oligarchs arose from his grand vision for Russia. In the chapters that follow, we'll see how that vision guides his actions in all matters. Here are the man's 10 principles.

1. Russia must be secure against attack and intimidation.
2. The country with the greatest material ability for intimidating or attacking Russia is the United States.
3. For the sake of security, countries bordering Russia must serve as buffers against the West; that is, they cannot be aligned with the United States.
4. Russia should be prosperous—for the sake of prosperity itself, as a necessary element in achieving security, and for Putin's personal political survival.
5. Development of natural resources, especially energy, is Russia's clearest path to prosperity.
6. In addition to paying the bills for security (chiefly military expenditures), energy exports support Russia's security by drawing customer countries into quasi-dependence, disposing them to defer to Russia in international matters. Quasi-dependence is especially desirable in countries that border Russia or are near it.
7. Russian dominance in energy-related industries—refining, processing, shipping—reinforces quasi-dependence, at least for some countries. It gives Russia the power to withhold a needed service from a target country or from the target country's other suppliers of oil, gas, or uranium.

8. Speedy development of energy resources requires outside capital and technology, so foreign partners are welcome. But because energy production is part of a strategy for security, energy industries must be under the control of the Russian government.

9. Russia's position as an energy exporter implies that disruption of energy production anywhere outside of Russia works to Russia's advantage. In particular, turmoil in the Middle East is always to Russia's advantage or can be turned to it.

10. Because the United States is the country with the greatest ability to intimidate or attack Russia, anything that weakens the United States leaves Russia more secure. On that principle, Russia should subvert the dollar's position as the world's reserve currency, and for that purpose should subvert the petrodollar system.

It's a plan that has already produced results. Putin is a man of remarkable intelligence, determination, and ruthlessness. In the eyes of many Russians, that last quality is not a fault but a virtue. While our media paint him as a cold-blooded dictator, Russians see him as a man's man who restored their country's pride, economy, and position after a humiliating period they'd rather forget. If getting it done required trampling the rights of a few citizens and knocking heads among the country's new capitalist class, well, nothing's free.

We'll see where else these principles lead.

Chapter 3

The Great Game and the End of the Cold War

It has been known as the "Great Game" since Rudyard Kipling introduced the term in 1901, in his novel *Kim*.

For some, the "Great Game" refers simply to the British and Russian empires' nearly century-long joust for supremacy in Central Asia. Both considered the region critical for their goals elsewhere.

For others, though (and I count myself among them), the Great Game in Central Asia never ended. The build-out of the Soviet Union was another round in the contest, which continued into the Cold War. Today it is central to the Colder War, which is only now coming to be recognized for what it is.

A player has been replaced, with the United States taking over Britain's role. But what hasn't changed in two centuries is that Russia remains a pivotal figure in geopolitical maneuvering in a grand arc from Europe through the Middle East to Central Asia.

Back in the old days, while the United States was busy expanding from sea to shining sea, the British were wrestling to maintain their position as the dominant global power—and, more important, to preserve the pound sterling as the world's reserve currency.

Control of international commerce wields enormous power. So does control of the world's reserve currency. It can dictate terms of trade; it can move the price of commodities in distant markets; it can extract a fee when money passes from one hand to another. For a long time, the country holding that control was Britain, which prospered enormously. Then, after the devastation of World War II, the baton passed to the United States, where it has resided ever since.

The British Empire was always a shaky proposition. Its very implausibility added to the celebration of every victory. That such a small country should hold sway over such a large part of the planet seems all but inexplicable today. The British did manage it, of course, but building an empire is one thing; holding on to it is another project entirely. To succeed, you have to deal with the discontent of the people you rule while continually facing down countries that covet what you have.

India was called "the jewel in Britain's crown," and British policy in Asia during the nineteenth century was concerned chiefly with expanding and strengthening Britain's hold on the subcontinent. The chief threat to that goal, from the British point of view, was Russia.

Russia had been expanding for centuries, even before Czar Peter the Great—the historical figure with whom Vladimir Putin most closely identifies—proclaimed Russia an empire in 1721. The expansion proceeded southward and eastward during the seventeenth and eighteenth centuries, and by the nineteenth century Russia had swallowed up most of present-day Kazakhstan, Kyrgyzstan, Tajikistan, Turkmenistan, and Uzbekistan.

Britain feared that Russia was knocking at India's door and would try to grab the territory and its wealth. The British invaded Tibet and fought two tribal wars in Afghanistan solely to establish buffer zones against the advancing Russian bear.

The Great Game was afoot. Though usually thought of in terms of territory, it also was about money and the ways in which it could be manipulated. The twentieth century added what proved to be the most important of those ways by far: access to and control of the energy sources upon which the world now depends.

Those sources include natural gas and uranium. But the one that matters most is oil. Oil has become the primary expression of wealth in the world. It finances economies and funds political regimes. It props up the standard of living wherever it is plentiful.

Once used primarily as a cheap substitute for whale oil in street lamps, it now is the fuel for most transportation and much electricity generation, and is the feedstock for plastics and most other organic chemicals. There is little in modern life that does not depend on oil for either its production or its delivery. Crayons, heart valves, heart medicine, pesticides, toy airplanes, and real airplanes all come to you from an oil well.

And it's not just tangible goods. Oil is the underpinning of the global financial structure. It separates the rich from the poor. That—not just its use in cars and jet engines—is why it is the planet's most sought-after commodity.

Control oil and you control money. That's how you become a dominant player in the new Great Game—the one that Putin has been playing so masterfully in his effort to engineer the demise of the dollar.

The First Drop

Let's go back to the very beginning.

Petroleum is not a modern discovery. In ancient times, people gathered oil that seeped naturally from the ground. According to Herodotus, asphalt was used more than 4,000 years ago in the construction of the walls and towers of Babylon. And depending on who's reading the clay tablets, the upper strata of ancient Persia employed oil in medicine and for lighting.

The Chinese have been drilling for oil and gas, which they found occurring with brine (their primary target), for centuries. The date of their first use of petroleum is unknown, but there was drilling in Szechuan as early as 400 BC. Bamboo pipelines were built to carry the accompanying gas over short distances. By the first century BC, Chinese engineers were drilling to depths beyond 800 feet.

By the late sixteenth century, wells over a hundred feet deep were being hand dug near Baku, in what is now Azerbaijan.

Today's petroleum era began in 1846 at Baku, then a lonely spot in the Russian Empire. Baku lies on the windy Absheron Peninsula, at the foot of the Caucasus Mountains, on the western edge of the Caspian Sea. It was there that the first modern oil well was drilled—modern in the sense that the shovel and hand drill were discarded in favor of percussive hammers and other mechanized equipment.

What had begun in Russia arrived in America 13 years later, in Titusville, Pennsylvania, where Edwin Drake completed the first commercially successful U.S. well that had been drilled solely for oil. It reached a depth of 70 feet and produced 25 barrels per day.

Drake's well ran dry just two years later, but its discovery set off a fervid search for petroleum, one that quickly expanded beyond Pennsylvania and eventually stretched to the four corners of the earth.

At the time, petroleum was used as a lubricant or to produce kerosene, which was easy to handle and could be used for heat and light. Kerosene's primary by-product, gasoline, was far more volatile and was rightly seen as dangerous to handle. Demand was limited to users who were willing to deal with the risk of explosion. Attempts to use it in lamps often ended in fiery disaster.

The invention of the four-stroke internal combustion engine in 1876 changed everything for gasoline and hence for oil. Gasoline went from unloved to most popular and became the dominant term in the profit equation for petroleum refining. Soon, the fuel was on its way to the status of military necessity. An army that ran out of gasoline would be an army that had run out of chances.

Russia recognized oil's importance earlier than most. In the latter part of the nineteenth century, Baku was the most productive oil region in the world. After hundreds and possibly thousands of years of bucket gathering, mechanized techniques brought a 200-fold increase in production between 1875 and 1895.

Russia's czarist government welcomed foreign investment, and Baku's population grew faster than that of London, Paris, or even New York. Auctions of petroleum-rich land to investors, primarily European, began in 1872. From there, it was off to the races. By the turn of the twentieth century, Baku was producing nearly half the world's oil. Capitalists making fortunes in Baku included the Rothschild family and

Ludvig and Robert Nobel, who entered with financial backing from their brother Alfred, the inventor of dynamite.

At the same time, other Russian oil deposits were being tapped directly across the Caspian Sea, on the Cheleken Peninsula in what is now Turkmenistan, to the northwest on the Black Sea, in the Arctic, and on Sakhalin Island in Russia's Far East.

Though America's production overtook Russia's in the early years of the twentieth century, the Baku region remained prolific. At the end of World War I, it was producing 15 percent of the world's oil. For Hitler, a generation later, it was still a prize worth fighting for. He was sure that if the German Wehrmacht captured Russia's two black golds—oil from the Caucasus and the rich soil of Ukraine—the Third Reich would be self-sufficient and unstoppable. He gambled to make it happen.

The Pioneer

Drake's well in Titusville made news in 1859, but in the years that followed, only a few Americans had any notion of where its success might lead. One of those few was John D. Rockefeller, who in 1863 built an oil refinery in Cleveland with his partners.

Seven years later, at the age of 31, Rockefeller incorporated Standard Oil of Ohio and began building it into an integrated oil producing, transporting, refining, and marketing company. It came to dominate the oil products market. It developed the business trust as a structure for mergers and acquisitions. It streamlined production and logistics, lowered costs, undercut competitors, and became one of the earliest and largest multinational corporations. At its peak, Standard Oil controlled 90 percent of the U.S. oil industry.

In 1911, the Supreme Court sustained a ruling that Standard Oil was an illegal monopoly and ordered it broken up into 33 separate companies. At the time of the dissolution, Rockefeller was the richest man in the world. And he has remained the richest single human ever to walk the earth, with a net worth of $340 billion in today's dollars.

(That's if you don't count King Mansa Musa I, who ruled the Mali Empire from 1312 to 1337 and controlled half of the world's gold and salt production. His fortune is pegged at the modern equivalent of $400 billion, although when you go back that far, the reliability of estimates declines and the ambiguity of inflation adjustments increases. No numbers are found for Genghis Khan, who might have topped them all.)

Go Big

In the quarter-century following Rockefeller's first refinery in 1863, the oil industry had grown into big business, but it hadn't yet grown into a giant, world-shaping business. It couldn't do so when a major well might yield only 50 barrels a day.

Then everything changed.

In the early 1890s, a group of businessmen and amateur geologists became convinced that a giant pool of oil lay under a salt dome south of Beaumont, Texas. By 1899, several attempts to tap the pool had failed, so the early investors leased part of the land, a tract at Spindletop Hill, to mining engineer Andy Lucas, an immigrant from the Dalmatian coast of Croatia.[1] Lucas had financial support from Andrew and Richard Mellon, whose father had founded one of the nation's biggest banks in Pittsburgh.

Lucas represented a remarkable confluence of persistence, timing, and luck. He continued drilling, and on January 10, 1901, his derrick at Spindletop punctured the rock dome that had been holding down a sea of pressurized oil. A geyser of crude erupted toward the sky, the first oil gusher.

It must have been quite a sight. In Lucas's own words, set down a year later:

> After many difficulties, a layer of rock containing marine shells was reached, at the depth of 1,160 feet. . . . At this time there was about 600 ft. of 4-in. pipe, weighing at least 6 tons, in the well. . . . When the rock was penetrated the well "blew out," lifting the whole of the 4-in. pipe. . . . The pipe was shot into the air . . . to a height of 300 feet above the derrick, the upper works and heavy tackle of which it carried away. . . . The remaining 4-in. pipe, freed from the weight of the upper portion, followed with greater rapidity, and was shot through the top of the derrick. Simultaneously, the water which filled the well (being used to keep the pipe-lining clear by removing the debris of drilling) was expelled to a great height; and a column of gas, rock-fragments and

---

[1] To his mother, he was still Antun Lucic.

oil followed it, at first at the rate of about 250 barrels per hour, rapidly increased to 500, 1,000 barrels, etc., until on the third day the discharge (by that time carrying no solid matter and a diminished quantity of gas) was estimated by officials and engineers of the Standard Oil Co., who were naturally the most experienced judges, to be at least 3,000 42-gallon barrels of oil per hour, or about 75,000 barrels in 24 hours.[2]

After that, capping the well became the overriding problem. No one had any experience with such a monster, and the crew had to improvise on the fly. It took nine days to bring the well under control.

Spindletop signaled the advent of Texas's, and America's, mammoth oil industry. Beaumont became a "black gold" boomtown, its population tripling in three months. The town filled with oil workers, investors, merchants, and con men (earning it the nickname "Swindle-top"). Within a year, more than 285 wells were producing at Spindle-top, and some 500 oil and land companies were operating in the area, including forebears of today's Exxon, Texaco, and Mobil.

The new, super-size oil industry came to be dominated by a handful of companies eventually dubbed the Seven Sisters. These were the big go-to players for anything to do with oil and gas: exploration, development, production, refining, or marketing.

Unsurprisingly, three of the sisters were spin-offs from Rockefeller's original Standard Oil:

- Standard Oil of California (today's Chevron)
- Standard Oil of New Jersey (predecessor of Esso)
- Standard Oil of New York (predecessor of Mobil, which merged with Esso to become Exxon Mobil Corporation)

The other four were:

- Anglo-Persian Oil Company (predecessor of British Petroleum [BP], following a merger with Amoco)
- Gulf Oil (most assets later merged into Chevron)
- Royal Dutch Shell (which remains intact)
- Texaco (now merged with Chevron)

---

[2] Anthony F. Lucas, "The Great Oil Well near Beaumont Texas," *American Institute of Mining Engineers Transactions*, XXXI (1902), 362–374.

The Seven Sisters and their descendants were and are purely public companies. At one time, they controlled virtually all of the world's oil industry. But after World War II, governments that resented foreigners owning their resources began nationalizing domestic oil production.

The result today is a set of state-controlled oil companies, some of which are owned wholly by a government and some of which are owned partly by the public. Prominent among them are:

- Saudi Aramco in Saudi Arabia (the world's largest producer of crude oil and holder of the largest reserves)
- Iraq National Oil Company
- National Iranian Oil Company
- China National Petroleum Company
- Petroleos de Venezuela
- Petrobras in Brazil
- Rosneft in Russia (the biggest quasi-public producer)

The publicly owned international companies, powerful though they be, are small potatoes compared with these new giants. Today the six biggest private super-majors are responsible for just 13 percent of world oil production and hold a mere 3 percent of the world's oil and gas reserves. The comparable numbers for the seven listed state-controlled companies are 30 percent of production and 44 percent of reserves.

The shift to state ownership reduced American presence in the sector and diminished American influence on pricing.

Oil, War, and Peace

It is impossible to fight a modern war without oil. The outcome of World War II was determined largely by who had or could get the stuff. The United States was able to enter and win the war because it had an abundant domestic supply of petroleum for its planes, ships, and tanks.

Germany and Japan had little domestic supply, and much of their military effort was aimed at capturing foreign sources. Hitler attacked Russia in part because Germany needed Russia's oil and had to try to take it regardless of the risk. When Japan bombed Pearl Harbor, it wasn't to seize all the cool surfing spots. Japan wanted to keep the United States from interfering with its plans to seize the oil resources of the Dutch East Indies.

At war's end, the United States stood alone. It had oil and lots of it. Its infrastructure was intact, while the industrial centers of Europe and Asia lay in ruins. Its economy was poised for rapid growth as millions of returning soldiers set about building their careers.

The U.S. economy developed into such a juggernaut that domestic oil production couldn't keep up. In 1949, the United States crossed over from net oil exporter to net oil importer. From there, imports kept increasing, which increased U.S. reliance on supplies from unstable and unfriendly countries. By 1972, half the oil the United States consumed was imported.

Then, in October 1973, the Yom Kippur War led to a huge shock to the politics of oil.

The conflict itself—between Israel and a coalition of Arab states led by Egypt and Syria—lasted only three weeks. It began when the Arab coalition launched a surprise invasion of territories Israel had captured during the Six-Day War six years earlier. That was followed by massive resupply efforts by the United States for its Israeli ally and by the Soviet Union for the other side.

After initial success by the Arab armies, Israeli counteroffensives pushed the Arabs back into Syria and captured the Sinai. A ceasefire was reached on October 25, leaving Israel in possession of large stretches of hitherto Arab territory.

The war had far-reaching consequences. The Arab world had sustained another humiliating defeat at the hands of its despised enemy. For its part, Israel took heavy casualties and, despite its sweeping success on the battlefield, felt the beginnings of doubt that it could always dominate the Arab states militarily. Thus came negotiations that culminated in the 1978 Camp David Accords. Israel returned the Sinai to Egypt, and the two countries settled into a none-too-friendly peace.

A more immediate blowback from the war was retaliation by the Organization of Arab Petroleum Exporting Countries (OAPEC, consisting of the Arab members of the Organization of Petroleum Exporting Countries [OPEC] plus Egypt, Syria, and Tunisia). Furious with the West for resupplying Israel, OAPEC imposed an oil embargo against Canada, Japan, the Netherlands, the United Kingdom, and the United

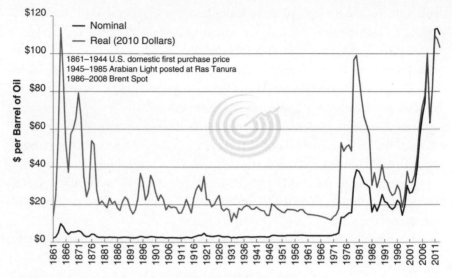

Figure 3.1   Nominal versus Real Price of Oil
SOURCE: Energy Information Administration. © Casey Research 2014.

States. It lasted from October 1973 to March 1974, and it hit hard. Everyone who was there remembers the gasoline shortages, rationing, and long lines at filling stations.

The embargo triggered a sharp increase in oil prices. For most of the preceding quarter-century, oil's price in U.S. dollars had risen by less than 2 percent per year. On October 16, 1973, OPEC raised its posted price by 70 percent, to $5.11 a barrel. Concurrently, oil ministers agreed to cut production by 5 percent and to continue cutting until their economic and political objectives were met. (See Figure 3.1.)

It takes time for consumers of a basic commodity like oil to adjust fully to a drop in supply. So the market's immediate response to even a modest drop in supply can be an oversized jump in price. In the case of OAPEC's announced production cuts, the market price of oil leapt from $3 per barrel to $12, setting the United States on a path of recession and ghastly high inflation that continued until the early 1980s.

Meanwhile, through self-inflicted wounds, the Soviet Union was setting itself up to lose the Cold War.

The narrative that the Soviet Union was somehow laid low by Ronald Reagan makes for a nice story, but it's largely myth. What brought the United States' erstwhile adversary to its knees was, yes, oil—or, more specifically, the way the Soviet Union fatally mishandled its vast petroleum resources.

Thanks to a rich natural endowment, oil and gas were profitable for the Soviets. Given that almost everything else in their centrally planned economy operated at a loss, the petroleum industry was the Soviets' lifeline. But they neglected that lifeline by failing to reinvest enough of the profits to increase or even maintain production rates. Instead, they diverted the revenue to support minimum living standards for the public.

Exploiting an oil field requires ongoing capital expenditures. Skimp on that spending, and production suffers. With so little capital going back into the oil fields—to drill new wells, maintain existing wells, and revitalize old wells with secondary production methods—the Soviet oil industry was withering. Of course, rising prices can offset declining production, but only as long as prices keep rising.

After the Arab oil embargo, as Soviet production continued to fall, the world price of oil plummeted. There was neither enough money to subsidize basic goods for the public nor enough to maintain the oil fields, so production was allowed to continue its slide.

The problem haunted the USSR's government for two decades. Oil production dwindled by 55 percent. Russia had long been a major producer, and now it couldn't even cover its own needs. Nor did it have the wherewithal to develop the new technologies that were driving the growth of Western economies.

The USSR's dependence on oil coupled with its failure to maintain its energy infrastructure left it brittle. The postembargo drop in world oil prices shattered it. That's the real reason the Soviet Union lost the Cold War, not Reagan's saber rattling. In 1989, the USSR broke apart.

And so the war ended. Fueled by cheap energy and control of the sector, and equipped with the intellectual capital that is a by-product of freedom, the United States emerged as the world's only superpower.

The First Nickel

At the end of World War II, unchallenged by anyone, the United States held a historically unique position to reconfigure international relations. The first order of business was to make its currency the world's currency.

Understanding how that was done and how the dollar eventually became linked to oil requires a brief look at money itself.

Money was invented independently in three different places at about the same time—in China, India, and the eastern Mediterranean, where gold, silver, copper, and bronze coins began appearing between about 700 BC and 500 BC. Because coins were made of metal that was both durable and valuable, they served as a way to store value. And because coins were portable and easy to recognize, they served as a medium of exchange. Store of value and medium of exchange—that's money.

Coins were a momentous social invention. Trading things for money and money for things is vastly more efficient than barter. But coins come with disadvantages, including their bulk and weight. More-over, they are interchangeable and belong to whoever has them—a plus, but also a problem. If yours are stolen, there's little chance of recover-ing them. In Europe, that shortcoming led to the use of guarded vaults, where coins and gold and silver bullion could be stored.

Goldsmiths kept private vaults and issued receipts that could be redeemed only by the depositor. That practice evolved into goldsmiths acting as bankers: lending gold at interest, issuing depository receipts that were negotiable (early paper money), and later issuing receipts for imaginary gold (the beginnings of fractional-reserve banking).

Paper money originated in China around the sixth century—it was one of the marvels Marco Polo wrote about in his *Travels*—but ban-knotes didn't appear in the West until 1661, when Johan Palmstruch's Stockholms Banco issued the first ones. The idea quickly caught on. Initially, any bank could print its own currency, and its value hinged upon the perceived trustworthiness of the institution. At one time in the United States, there were several thousand different currency issues circulating, some nationally, some only locally.

For most of their history, banknotes, like the early goldsmiths' receipts, had a precious-metal backing. They were, by the promise of the issuer, convertible into gold and/or silver according to their denom-ination. Of course, whether the metal would actually be there when you wanted it was another matter.

A bank, under the fractional-reserve principle, can create more money to lend out than has been deposited with it. So an unexpected run on a bank, with depositors demanding more gold than the bank had, could quickly render the bank insolvent. Such events were not rare. When they occurred as epidemics, hard times usually followed.

It didn't take long for governments, or their proxies, to recognize the advantage of being the sole producer of banknotes. The Bank of England was one of the earliest, establishing its monopoly in 1694; its American counterpart, the Federal Reserve, didn't arrive until 1913.

Convertibility continued after governments became the money issuers, but there were compromises. In 1933, Franklin Roosevelt outlawed the private ownership of gold by U.S. citizens. Dollars were still convertible for gold—but not if they were tendered by an American. The United States was on a path to a completely *fiat* currency (i.e., one that was not backed by anything). And as the United States would go, so eventually would the rest of the world.[3]

Everyone's Dollar

As the carnage of World War II was winding down, two things had become clear: The Allies were going to win, and after the war the United States would be the economic strongman. It had all the best cards to play.

For three weeks in July 1944, with the end of hostilities in Europe still nine months away, 730 delegates from all 44 allied governments gathered at the Mount Washington Hotel in Bretton Woods, New Hampshire, for the United Nations Monetary and Financial Conference—now simply referred to as the Bretton Woods Conference. They came to design the financial structure of the postwar world. At the end of the conference, all present signed an agreement with two key monetary provisions.

To promote ease of international trade and to help fund postwar reconstruction, each member state agreed to maintain a fixed exchange rate for its currency versus the U.S. dollar (and by implication, fixed exchange rates versus all other participating currencies). To that end, each signatory pledged to buy and sell U.S. dollars as needed to keep its currency within 1 percent of its agreed-upon exchange rate.

---

[3]U.S. dollar silver certificates, freely redeemable in that metal, hung around until the 1960s, but the writing was on the wall.

The United States, for its part, assured the solidity of the arrangement by pledging to deliver gold, at a price of $35 per ounce, to any foreigner who chose to tender its dollars (although this was later modified to honor redemptions only by foreign central banks). Because at the time the U.S. Treasury had an abundance of gold (a result of the deflationary Great Depression and then wartime trade surpluses and capital flight), it was an easy promise to make.

The Bretton Woods Agreement placed the United States at the center of international finance. Its allies may not have liked the new way of things, but in truth, they had little choice in the matter if they wanted to rebuild their countries. In signing, they ushered in the dollar's golden age. The dollar had become the world's reserve currency.

The promise of gold redeemability was honored for 27 years. It ended when U.S. trade deficits and creeping price inflation undermined confidence that the U.S. government would be able to live up to its promise much longer. To keep the open-market price of gold from rising more than pennies above $35, the United States and its partners in the London Gold Pool had to sell larger and larger quantities of the metal. That couldn't go on forever. In 1967, France withdrew from the effort and added the insult of repatriating the gold it had been storing with the Federal Reserve Bank of New York. Yellow bars flew to Paris.

The U.S. government continued to sell gold, in increasing quantities, to keep the open-market price near $35. Then, on August 15, 1971, President Richard Nixon "closed the gold window," ending the convertibility of dollars into gold by anyone and eliminating the need for further sales to suppress the open-market price. He referred to the default on America's pledge as a measure to stop "international money speculators."

The dollar was still the world's reserve currency, but it had become fiat money. And since other major currencies were convertible only into dollars, they too became fiat money. With narrow exceptions, all the world's currencies were untethered from gold.

The new regime allowed governments to pull unlimited currency units from thin air. Inflation became a fact of life everywhere, including in the United States. Since 1971, money creation by an unfettered Federal Reserve has cost the dollar nearly 80 percent of its purchasing power.

Thank You, Mr. Nixon

With gold no longer part of the system, something had to be done to maintain the dollar's preeminence as the world's reserve currency.

Washington might have sought to ease the country's trade deficit (the counterpart of which is a buildup of dollars in foreign hands), but that would have required a slowdown in the printing of new dollars. So, of course, it didn't take that approach. Quite the opposite. It sought a way to gain a grip on the global financial system that would be so strong it would protect the dollar's status as the world's reserve currency even as the flood of new fiat dollars continued.

The power to pass off ever more units of the world's reserve currency made everything produced outside the United States both cheap and plentiful for U.S. consumers. A failure to keep that system running would mean a drop in Americans' living standards and political death for whoever got the blame.

Conveniently, an opportunity for protecting the dollar's status was ready and waiting. It came from a commodity far more important to the world economy than gold: oil. Though rightly disdained for much of what he did, Richard Nixon underwrote his country's dominance for decades to come by devising the petrodollar system.

After closing the gold window, Nixon dispatched Secretary of State Henry Kissinger to Saudi Arabia to offer the ruling House of Saud a four-part deal. The U.S. government would provide military protection for Saudi Arabia and its oil fields. It would sell the Saudis any weapons they needed. It would guarantee protection from Israel and any other Middle Eastern state, such as Iran, that might attempt to destabilize the kingdom. And it would secure the Saud family's place as rulers of the country in perpetuity.

That last point was the clincher.

In return, the Saudis would do two things. They would make oil sales in U.S. dollars only. And they would invest their surplus oil proceeds in U.S. Treasuries.

Saudi Arabia was (and remains) a sparsely populated country with enormous riches. It is stuck in a historical twilight zone between the Dark Ages and the modern world. It sits in a bad neighborhood, where religious imperatives readily evolve into imperatives for slaughter. It faces

a pair of much larger and inherently stronger neighbors that are waiting for a chance to eat it. No surprise that its rulers felt vulnerable and
welcomed a powerful protector.

To the ruling family, Kissinger's proposition was a sweet deal.

Saudi Arabia signed on in 1974, and as Nixon and Kissinger had
calculated, the other members of OPEC quickly fell in line. By 1975,
all of them had embraced the petrodollar system.

It was a brilliant maneuver. The world's demand for U.S. dollars would soar with the world's increasing demand for oil. For the
United States, the new "dollars for oil" system was even better than the
Bretton Woods "dollars for gold" system. There was no pesky redemp-
tion promise, so it imposed no constraint on the creation of more and
more dollars to pay for imports.

It was quite a feat, and with knock-on effects. Everyone needed oil.
Since it could be purchased only in dollars, countries needed to stockpile
them, which meant more demand for currency units that the Federal
Reserve could produce at zero cost.

Nixon's petrodollar system kept the United States at the top of the
global economic heap for decades. But the Great Game wasn't over.
At the beginning of the twenty-first century, on the eastern fringe of
Europe, a master player was at work, rebuilding his shattered country
and preparing it to return to the playing field.

Chapter 4

The Slavic Warrior

I've already detailed how Vladimir Putin, using the letter of the law and exploiting a powerful legacy of state worship, was able to install himself as the new Russian strongman, a nouveau czar for a resurgent Russia. The people loved the images he projected—weapon-firing warrior, tough-guy pilot, shirtless horseman. After the long, painful years with an ineffectual and often drunk Boris Yeltsin, this was exactly the kind of leader they yearned for.

Moreover, it wasn't just showmanship. Putin not only talked the talk, he walked the walk: He crushed the Chechen revolt, destroyed the hated oligarchs (selected friends spared), and took no back talk from anyone.

For the United States, Putin's popularity in Russia all comes down to this: What does he want? The answer is far more complicated than most Americans—from politicians to the mainstream media and to Joe Sixpack—imagine. Failure to appreciate Putin's vision and his complexities has been, and will continue to be, the United States' Achilles' heel.

This book tries to blow away some of the fog that hides the real Russian leader from us, so that we in the West can see him as he is, not as he's being painted in the press; not as we might wish (or fear) he is, but as he really is. Only then can we find out what he wants.

Little Boy Putin

Vladimir Putin hails from St. Petersburg, or Leningrad as it was known when he was born there in 1952. That was less than a year before the passing of Stalin and the end of his decades-long rule by terror and the 20 million deaths it brought.

The St. Petersburg connection is fitting for Putin. First, the city was founded by Peter the Great at the dawn of the eighteenth century, after he seized control of the port from Russia's archrival, the Swedish Empire. Peter was decisive, fearless, and dedicated to the glory of Mother Russia. The powerful czar is the historical figure Putin strives to emulate.

Second, St. Petersburg has long been Russia's "window to Europe." It sits directly across the Baltic Sea from Stockholm, on the delta of the Neva River. Although Russia stretches from there to the Pacific, Putin considers the motherland as first and foremost a European country, and that its rightful place is at the head of the European nations.

Putin's mother was a factory worker and his father a Soviet Navy conscript. His parents raised him in a rat-infested communal apartment where four adults and two children shared a single, 200-square-foot room without hot water or even a bathtub for the cold water. The toilet was outside, on a landing, which made for brutally painful trips during the long Russian winters.

Yet despite his poor upbringing, Putin was exposed to the ways of the Soviet elite at a young age, through a man destined to have a profound effect on his character: his paternal grandfather, Spiridon Ivanovich Putin. Young Vladimir learned all about war and revolution at the feet of a granddad who had lived through both. He also received an early education in Russian politics.

The elder Putin, born in 1879, came from peasant stock in the Volga basin, about a hundred miles southeast of Moscow. At the age of 15, he left home for St. Petersburg, where he was trained as a cook and once served the infamous Grigory Rasputin, who noted the similarity in their names and was so impressed with the cuisine that he left a 10-ruble gold coin as a tip.

After World War I and the Communist revolution, Spiridon moved to Moscow where, given his culinary reputation, he was hired to cook at Lenin's dacha at Gorki. After Lenin's death in 1924, Spiridon continued to serve the family and later became a cook for Stalin. His connection to Lenin, who had been highly critical of Stalin, apparently did him no harm. Unlike many of Stalin's intimates, whom the dictator killed off or banished to forced-labor camps, Spiridon survived all the purges. He even managed to outlive the tyrant he fed so well.

This was no small feat; it required sensitive political instincts and nimble balancing. In St. Petersburg and late in his life, he passed what he had learned to a grandson eager to hear of such things. And, intriguingly, he may also have initiated Vladimir into some of the arcana of the spy game. There are indications that Spiridon had been trained by the NKVD, the secret-police predecessor of the KGB. He died when his grandson was 13.

By his own account, Vladimir Putin was a mischievous child at best. He thirsted for autonomy and power. He was bossy and impulsive, a schoolyard punk prone to violence. He was a poor student. Once he was hauled before a neighborhood "comrades' court" for acts of petty delinquency.

Hostility toward Jews has a long and unlovely history in Russia, but whatever the reason, Putin seems not to have absorbed that sentiment. He grew up with and befriended Jewish neighbors. His early German-language teacher was a Jew, and in her later years, he acknowledged her influence in his life by giving her an apartment in Tel Aviv. Dodging anti-Semitism has worked to Putin's advantage. It has left him free to seek political support from the Jews among Russia's oligarchs, and, as we'll see, it has allowed him to deal dispassionately with Israel as a potential ally in the Middle East.

Big Boy Putin

As has happened for many street toughs, sports rerouted his life. Around the age of 12, while his grandfather was still alive, Putin started boxing and then moved on to judo, karate, and the Soviet martial art sambo.

He would go on to become the citywide sambo champion and at one point actually take down the world judo champion in a sambo match.

It was the physical and spiritual demands that attracted the young Putin to martial arts. They were the way of the warrior, a role he coveted for himself. He also learned he would have to compensate for his slight physical frame, which was common among children whose mothers had battled starvation during the Nazi siege of Leningrad. He was strong for his size. But judo taught him that he would also need to be smart, cunning, and, above all, tightly disciplined.

With the new passion for martial arts came a transformation into a top student.

As an adolescent, Putin loved the spy stories he found in books, on TV, and in the movies. In comic book tales promoted by the KGB, agents of the Soviet secret services were portrayed in heroic roles fighting Nazi Germany. A 16-year-old Putin was fascinated with the 1968 film *The Shield and the Sword*, a James Bond–style movie depicting a double agent who infiltrated Germany to thwart the Nazis' war plans.

Putin began to dream of a life as a Russian spy. But unlike other kids with such fantasies, he acted on his. In the ninth grade, he initiated a meeting at the office of the KGB Directorate to find out how to get a job. He was told that law school was one way into the KGB. He also was told never to contact the agency again.

After that, Putin pursued the law with singular determination, despite it being a low-paying and low-prestige field in Soviet Russia. Against the wishes of his parents, who saw him as an engineer, he enrolled in the law department of Leningrad State University in 1970. He never did have to contact the KGB again. They came to him instead, in the fourth of his planned five years of college. In 1975, at the age of 22, he was recruited as an agent.

Putin at Work

Over the next 16 years, Putin worked as a self-described "specialist in human relations." Fluent in German and able to pass for Nordic, he was posted to Dresden in the German Democratic Republic (East Germany) in 1985 and spent five years there under cover. He apparently was good at his job, because he was promoted three times, yet he remained a minor functionary.

Like any Soviet intelligence officer who managed to stay employed and alive, he was expert at reading and manipulating people and was unfazed by violence. These were indispensable qualities for anyone out to make his way to the top of the Russian political pile.

With the fall of the Berlin Wall and the unraveling of the German Democratic Republic, Putin's communications line to Moscow went silent, leaving him to make decisions on his own. It was a pivotal episode in his life. As he later recalled, "It seemed to me as if our country no longer existed. It became clear that the Soviet Union was in a diseased condition, that of a fatal and incurable paralysis: the paralysis of power." Years later, he would vow that no such paralysis would ever take hold on his watch.

He understood that he was in danger and had to flee the German Democratic Republic. But before doing so, with his office under siege by an angry mob, he destroyed and burned many files. Then, carrying the most sensitive material with him, he stepped out the front door and slipped away unnoticed, like a ghost.

He formally resigned from the KGB in 1991, by which time he had returned to the university to finish his PhD. In his doctoral thesis, he argued that Russian economic success would depend on properly exploiting energy resources.

After college, Putin entered politics in St. Petersburg, where he fostered relationships with Dmitry Medvedev and Igor Ivanovich Sechin, who would remain his closest associates through the years.

A portrait of Peter the Great—not Boris Yeltsin, whom most of Putin's contemporaries honored—hung in Putin's office. The picture, which showed the early Romanov czar in his prime, was a fitting symbol for Putin's ambitions. When Peter came to power at the end of the seventeenth century, Russia was an isolated country untouched by the scientific and technological developments of the European Renaissance. The powerful Russian Orthodox Church was still steeped in medieval superstition, and Russia's culture remained cut off from the rest of Europe.

Despite strong pushback from the Russian aristocracy, Peter reformed the military and reorganized the government. He built a formidable navy, secured access to the Black Sea through battles with the Ottoman Empire, and expanded Russian territory into the Baltics. In addition to modernizing the Russian alphabet, starting the first Russian newspaper, secularizing schools, and bringing Western-style dress into vogue, Peter recruited European experts to introduce Russian students to the world of technology.

Peter's farsighted reforms revolutionized the Russian economy and equipped Russia to function internationally as a modern country. To produce such extraordinary results, however, Peter ruled as a tyrant who dragged his people into modernity whether they wanted to go or not—a model that appealed to Putin's heart. The economic and political derangement Putin would inherit would seem to him like a reappearance of the disordered nation Peter had transformed into a global power. When Putin's turn came, he knew what to do.

Hands off Georgia

Yeltsin's selection of Putin as his successor surprised many Kremlin watchers. Putin's rise to power may have seemed meteoric, even inexplicable. But it fit a plan laid out years before Putin entered national politics. Putin had a vision of what Russia should be and an unwavering belief in the rightness of that vision. Now he was in the driver's seat, surrounded by competent people he could trust. He had the ability to diagnose and solve problems. And he didn't give a tinker's damn what anyone thought of him.

We now know he was lucky to have popped into his position at the top at just the right time; arriving even a few years earlier or later would have made his rise far more difficult, if not impossible. But he always knew what he wanted and the best path to get it.

As we have seen, Putin moved early to define himself in the eyes of the public with his no-nonsense handling of Chechnya. Then he showed who was boss in Russia by taking down some of the previously untouchable oligarchs and domesticating the others. In doing so, he also took charge of Russia's energy sector, according to plan. It was the base upon which he intended to build the modern counterpart of Peter's empire. He seized control of the oil fields by digesting Yukos and placing Rosneft, Gazprom, and other energy companies in the hands of his loyalists.

It was in his long-term interest to maintain close ties with (if not domination of) many of the former Soviet states as well, since they held so much of the energy and infrastructure assets that were needed for his plan.

Georgia in particular had always been a thorn in Russia's side. In past centuries, it had repeatedly entangled Russia in conflicts with Iranians and Ottomans. More recently, it pursued an energy policy that conflicted with Russia's and sought membership in the North Atlantic Treaty Organization (NATO). In 1991, Russia recognized Georgia's independence, which it had gained through the demise of the Soviet Union. But within the Georgian Republic, there was friction over Abkhazia and South Ossetia, two autonomous zones whose populations had long been cordial to Russia and did not speak the Georgian language, and whose forebears had fought against Georgians for centuries. They wanted to break away and be recognized as sovereign states.

In 2003 came the Rose Revolution, which deposed the autocratic Eduard Shevardnadze (a Georgian native and formerly Soviet foreign minister under Mikhail Gorbachev) as president of Georgia.

Shevardnadze's administration had been strongly pro-Western. The country accepted financial and military aid from the United States, signed a strategic partnership with NATO, and declared an ambition to join both NATO and the European Union. Notably, Shevardnadze made a $3 billion deal with Western investors to build a pipeline to carry oil from Azerbaijan to Turkey, in competition with portions of the Russian pipeline network.

There had been several attempts on Shevardnadze's life, and some people blamed at least one of them on Russia. They may have been right. Not only was Moscow offended by Shevardnadze's ties to the United States—which welcomed him as a counterbalance to Russian influence in the Transcaucasus region—but the Russians also believed he had supported terrorists in neighboring Chechnya while Russia had been at war in that region.

Throughout Shevardnadze's reign, Georgia suffered from an epidemic of common crime and rampant corruption, especially among senior officials and politicians. His closest advisers, including several members of his family, were accumulating enormous wealth; the inner circle may have controlled as much as 70 percent of the economy.

While Shevardnadze himself was not accused of profiteering, many Georgians held him guilty of shielding corrupt supporters and of abusing his powers of patronage. Add in stories of rigged elections, and Georgia became a brand name for dirty deeds.

Eventually, Shevardnadze's erstwhile benefactors in the United States grew tired of pouring money down a rat hole. Not only did they give up caring whether he stayed or went, but they also began pushing for greater democracy and honest elections. For once, Moscow and Washington were more or less aligned.

Shevardnadze went. But the Rose Revolution was anything but a march of the flower children. It was largely orchestrated by nongovernmental organizations (NGOs), which play a large political role in this part of the world.

Georgia's 1997 Civil Code had made the registration of NGOs relatively easy, and they operated with few restrictions. Not surprisingly, they proliferated. By the end of 2000, the number of NGOs in Georgia was estimated at 4,000. Not all of them were political, of course. But those that were political had strong financial backing from outside the country—as Western support shifted from the regime to the opposition—and a significant number had leverage with parliament. Though few members of the public directly participated in them, NGOs were instrumental in rallying the people to challenge Shevardnadze.

The showdown came after the parliamentary elections on November 2, 2003. The following day, protestors in the capital of Tbilisi cried fraud and labeled the new parliament illegitimate. The crowd slowly grew to over 100,000 demonstrators (3 percent of the country's entire population) demanding Shevardnadze's resignation. It all ended 20 days later, on November 23, when Shevardnadze stepped down.

Nearly everyone had something to celebrate, because the Rose Revolution had come without bloodshed. Even though Shevardnadze had sent soldiers into the streets, they had refused to shoot anyone.

Notably, Putin declined to intervene, despite Georgia being a close neighbor and despite the ongoing tension over Abkhazia and South Ossetia.

Without question, his Soviet predecessors would have moved in quickly to squash the first sign of dissent. Not Putin. He's hardly reluctant to project military force, but the decision always comes from calculation and never from reflex. He carefully calculates the costs and risk of acting, and weighs them against the likely benefit to the homeland. He's also constrained by a genuine, if not absolute, respect for the law; he prefers to act within it, or at least within his interpretation of it. Thus, unless there is a compelling need to intervene, he'll stand aside and let matters play out.

Nevertheless, it is best not to poke him in the eye, as Georgia found out four and a half years later.

Hands on Georgia

Conflict began, unsurprisingly, over Abkhazia and South Ossetia. The two would-be countries—mindful of the recognition given Kosovo after its own declaration of independence—had submitted requests to Russia and other countries, and to international organizations, asking to be treated similarly.

In April 2008, Putin (then prime minister under President Medvedev, but still pulling all the strings) announced that Russia would consider recognizing Abkhazia and South Ossetia. Violence escalated through the summer, as separatists in the two regions fought for independence, bolstered by Russian military support, while Georgia, which wished to join NATO, received aid from the West.

It was yet another proxy war, but with this kicker: Gazprom was considering the construction of a gas pipeline to Abkhazia.

In any event, Russia recognized the two countries in August 2008, and that precipitated the Russo-Georgian War. Georgia sent troops to South Ossetia to reclaim its territory. Russia sent troops to oppose them and launched airstrikes the next day.

It was a brief conflict, ending in a ceasefire after just 12 days. Casualties were few, although hundreds of thousands of civilians were displaced. Georgia lost nearly one-fifth of its territory and 6 percent of its population, and Abkhazia and South Ossetia continued on their way as Russian-recognized sovereign countries.

Note that Putin didn't commit to full-scale war, nor did he try to annex Abkhazia or South Ossetia. He merely maintained the status quo through a measured military response.

Postwar, he (through then-President Medvedev) worked to replace confrontation with cooperation. Despite lingering bad feelings, in November 2011, Georgia and Russia agreed to a Swiss-mediated proposal for monitoring the trade between them. It was good fence-mending, with a bonus for Russia. Smoothing relations with Georgia allowed Russia to join the World Trade Organization (WTO). Membership in the WTO requires a consensus, and Russia needed an "Aye" from Georgia.

Chapter 5

Ukraine

Russia and Ukraine go back a very long, complicated, and bloody way.

At one time, Ukraine *was* Russia. Kievan Rus, the first East Slavic state, was established by the Varangians in the ninth century. It attained considerable power during the Middle Ages but broke apart in the twelfth century. The territory and its inhabitants have been fought over ever since. At the end of the eighteenth century, Ukraine was partitioned, with a small slice going to Austria/Hungary and the rest to the Russian Empire.

The second decade of the twentieth century was as chaotic for Ukraine as it was for the rest of Europe. Civil war raged from 1917 to 1921, with a host of factions vying for control of the government of the newly proclaimed Ukrainian Republic. That sovereign state proved to be short-lived.

Even as Ukraine was asserting its independence in 1918 with its capital in Kiev, Russia was setting up a rival republic with Kharkov as its capital. The fighting and killing rolled on. By 1922, the Russians had overpowered the outmanned Ukrainian army and established the Ukrainian Soviet Socialist Republic, one of the founding republics of the nascent Soviet Union.

However, conflict between Russia and Ukraine continued, and under Stalin's rule the Ukrainian people were tormented mercilessly. The most terrible episode was the Holodomor of 1932–1933, a contrived catastrophe that translates as "extermination by hunger." Many claim that Stalin engineered the mass starvation to force Ukrainian farmers into collectivization.

While there is some debate as to how the Holodomor came about, there is no doubt about it being a massive human disaster. Soldiers confiscated grain from farmers; a famine followed, which Russia did nothing to alleviate. Deaths from starvation were at least 2.5 million and perhaps as many as 7 million. Some survived only through cannibalism.

The country's misery continued during World War II, when the Ukrainian Insurgent Army tried to reestablish independence. It fought both Nazi Germany and the Soviet Union. But for many Ukrainians the memory of the Holodomor was all too fresh, and a significant number, driven by fear and hatred of Russia, collaborated with the Nazis. Echoes of Nazism can still be heard from some Ukrainian political parties today.

World War II was an unmitigated horror for Ukraine. In 1941, it was occupied by Germany, and millions of Ukrainians were taken to Germany as forced laborers or prisoners of war. Others were used as cannon fodder to distract and busy the Soviet Army, for the tactical advantage of the Germans. One of every six Ukrainians died in the conflict. The country remained under Nazi rule until 1944, when it was recaptured by the USSR.

In 1954, Soviet Premier Nikita Khrushchev oversaw the transfer of the Crimea, then Russian territory, to Ukraine. Ostensibly, it was done in celebration of the 300th anniversary of the country's unification with Russia. But it was also the case that Ukraine was Khrushchev's favorite republic. He'd been born in a border town and after World War II had spent much time trying to help rebuild the country.

Additionally, Khrushchev had set out to delegitimize the cult of Stalin, and handing over Crimea was a way of demonstrating regret over his predecessor's atrocities and hence of publicly highlighting them.

What Putin Wants in Ukraine

Since the fall of the USSR, Ukraine has again been caught in the middle, with some forces pulling it toward the European Union (EU) and others toward Russia. The country is no prize. Nonetheless, Putin's Russia is very interested. The interests are:

- Ukraine should accommodate the movement of natural gas produced in Russia to buyers in Europe.
- The Russian Navy should be secure in the use of the port at Sebastopol (on the Crimean Peninsula, in the Black Sea).
- The government in Moscow should be seen as the protector of all Russian people, of whom 8 million, about 18 percent of Ukraine's population, live in the eastern part of the country.
- Ukraine should serve as a buffer that keeps NATO at a distance.

Gas Transport

Ukraine is one of Europe's most extravagant energy users, consuming four times more energy in relation to its gross domestic product (GDP) than the EU average. I've seen an example. When I arrived at my hotel room in Kiev, I found the air-conditioning running full blast and the bathroom heater toasting away.

Half of Russia's gas exports to the European Union (which cover 25 percent of the EU's consumption) pass through Ukraine. For years, Ukraine charged little for the accommodation, and in return Russia gave Ukraine a generous price break on the gas it bought for its own use. The arrangement used to mean *very* cheap gas relative to the price in Europe, and that cheap gas drove Ukraine's economy and provided, among other things, cheap electricity.

All in all, cheap is good, but it does encourage wasteful habits. Ukraine became one of the world's largest gas importers and one of its least energy-efficient countries.

Then, when relations with Russia soured in 2005 and Russia ratcheted up the gas price, Ukrainians struggled to afford the electricity they used to take for granted.

Disputes with Russia over gas debts and nonpayment started almost immediately after the Soviet Union collapsed. Ukraine worsened the conflict by stealing gas intended for Europe. The disputes were more than talking wars. Russia repeatedly suspended exports to Ukraine, several times leaving much of the country without heat or electricity in the depth of winter. Gazprom even closed the pipelines to Europe to keep Ukraine from taking more without paying up, leading to shortages in Europe in 2006 and again in 2009.

In mid-2010, a Stockholm arbitration court ruled that Ukraine's state-owned Naftogaz must return 430 billion cubic feet of gas it stole in 2009. Ukraine responded that the return would "not be quick."

To gain an alternative route for delivering gas to Europe, Russia is building the South Stream pipeline, which will run beneath the Black Sea. It is doing so despite Ukraine's insistence that it would be cheaper to modernize its existing pipeline.

For Russia, the topic of gas and Ukraine is both business and politics. Russia wants the revenue from keeping Europe warm in the winter. That means keeping the gas flowing through Ukraine at a tolerable cost in theft and price concessions to Ukrainian customers. Russia also wants the political leverage that comes with the power to shut off gas deliveries to Europe, an option that can be rendered ambiguous by the power of Ukrainians to push Russia to shut it off by simply not paying their bill. From Russia's point of view, a docile government in Kiev would be both a business and a political plus.

Sevastopol

A presence in Crimea is critical to Russia's security.

Russia's Black Sea fleet has always been based in Sevastopol's natural harbor, for access to the Balkans, Mediterranean, and Middle East. After Khrushchev's 1954 transfer of the region to Ukraine, Russia leased back part of Crimea to ensure the continued use of the naval base. That lease is scheduled to run to 2042, and it authorizes Russia to station 25,000 troops.

There is an energy connection as well. Russia's South Stream pipeline passes through what formerly were Ukrainian waters, close to

Crimea. And there may be oil nearby, under the Black Sea, but that's a detail.

Protecting Russians

Every government is a protection racket. Citizens pay taxes and satisfy other conditions imposed by the government, and the government promises to protect them from other governments and from all the small-time entrepreneurs in the theft and intimidation industries (common criminals). Protecting noncitizens who share the country's race, ethnicity, religion, or other group traits is a common government sideline. It's a marketing program; governments do it because it reinforces their legitimacy in the eyes of their own citizens.

For 15 million Ukrainians, about one-third of the population, Russian is the first language. They are concentrated in the eastern parts of the country, and in some areas, including Crimea, they are a majority. (See Figure 5.1.) They are conspicuous candidates for protection by the Russian government.

The catastrophes that visited Ukraine in the twentieth century touched the Ukrainian-speaking population and the Russian-speaking population differently. The Holodomor, which killed millions, is remembered as an export from Russia. Collaboration with the Nazis, who accounted for more millions of deaths, was concentrated among Ukrainian speakers. Thus the possibility of mob violence or even civil war between Ukrainian and Russian speakers is at least plausible. The country has been getting a taste of such trouble since late 2013.

In politics, plausible is all it takes. The plausibility of intramural violence is enough to make it awkward for Putin to ignore pleas for help from Russian-speaking Ukrainians who claim they are under attack. That same plausibility is enough to provide propaganda cover for anything Putin might choose to do in the Russian-speaking areas, including an invasion.

The Buffer

It may seem fantastic to a North American reader that in 2014 Russia would fear an invasion by Western forces. The European countries are

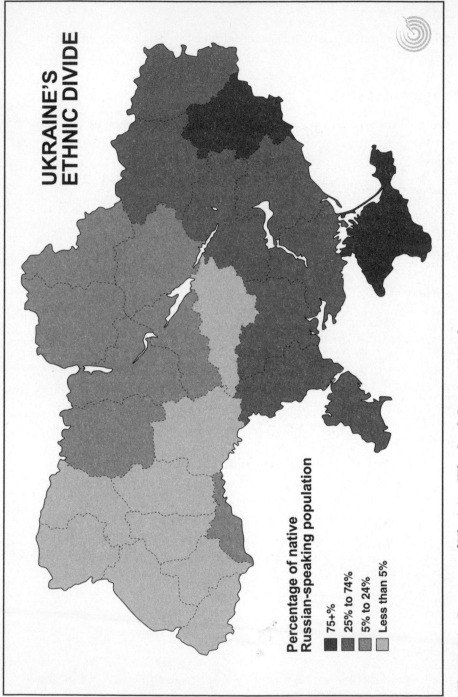

Figure 5.1 Percentage of Ukrainians Who Speak Russian Natively

SOURCE: Statistics Service of Ukraine (2001 census data).

largely demilitarized, and their populations are focused on enjoying risk-free lives as beneficiaries of the state. None of them has an appetite for combat at any level higher than a soccer riot. And the Americans, although they often seem careless about joining wars, never did come to direct blows with the Soviet Union, even when it was a mortal threat.

Call it historical post-traumatic stress syndrome. Twenty million Russians (one in eight of the total population at the time) died in World War II, and that wasn't the country's first experience with armies from Western Europe. Reasonable or not, the Russians want neutral countries on their border, countries that are aligned with no one (except perhaps Russia) and that are keen only about not giving offense. Topography adds special sensitivity to Ukraine's status; the country is an open plain for any force heading toward Moscow.

Russia doesn't want another country with strong ties to the West on its border that might join the EU or even become a missile-hosting member of NATO. Instead, Russia wants a Ukraine with strong ties to the East that serves as a buffer state.

After the USSR

An independent Ukraine emerged in 1991, after the dissolution of the Soviet Union. From day one, the country was plagued by corruption and political intrigue. The citizenry were fiercely divided between aligning with the West with an eye to joining the EU or, alternatively, aligning with Russia.

The rapid transition from communism brought severe unemployment and other dislocations that continued for the rest of the decade. Measured GDP dropped 60 percent from 1991 to 1998, leaving most Ukrainians struggling to get by. Widespread shortages forced the government to free the prices of most goods, but it continued to feed subsidies to state-run agricultural and industrial operations.

A loose monetary policy led to hyperinflation. In 1993, prices rose more than a hundredfold. After Kiev introduced a new currency, the hryvnia, in 1996, the economy slowly mended. By 2000, the economy was growing 7 percent annually. Then the global recession of 2008 brought progress to a halt. In November of that year, the International

Monetary Fund (IMF) provided a $16.5 billion stand-by loan for the country.

The breadbasket of Europe had become a basket case.

The history of Russia's transition to a market economy holds the clue as to how that happened. Until 1991, Ukraine's economy was modeled after Soviet Russia's: central planning, central control, and state ownership of industry and resources—an enervating regime of disincentives for individual initiative.

Ukraine's unwinding of state ownership and control spawned the same kind of oligarchs and provided the same rich opportunities for corruption as the transition in Russia. A few well-positioned and shrewd individuals snatched up the country's mining, metals, chemical production, and energy distribution assets on the very cheap. The big difference vis-à-vis Russia was that Ukraine didn't have a Putin to impose limits on the looting. So it continued.

For two decades, Ukraine's oligarchs benefited from cozy relations with government officials, who would accept rich kickbacks to turn a blind eye to the oligarchs' often Mafia-like activities. It has been great for the oligarchs and their political allies, but not so good for anyone else.

Don't Forget to Vote

Going into the 2004 election, the incumbent president and the man with his hands on the levers of state power was the Russian-leaning Viktor Yanukovych. He was being challenged by, among others, Viktor Yushchenko, a popular West-leaning politician who had, just a few months earlier, survived an attempt to poison him with dioxin. The election progressed to a runoff between the two Viktors. A victory claim by incumbent Yanukovych was met with cries of voter intimidation and electoral fraud, complaints that were confirmed by several domestic and foreign election monitors.

In November 2004, thousands of Yushchenko supporters (generally Ukrainian speakers oriented more toward Europe than toward Russia) took to the streets in protest and ensnarled Kiev in a campaign of civil resistance. It was the beginning of the Orange Revolution. Protests spread across the country but remained nonviolent, with the emphasis on civil disobedience, sit–ins, and general strikes. Much of the organizing for the protests was funded by Western money sent through NGOs.

The protestors got what they wanted. In late December, Ukraine's Supreme Court ordered a revote. The balloting was closely watched by domestic and international observers, who by and large pronounced the second runoff "fair and free." The earlier result was reversed, and the West-leaning Yushchenko assumed office.

Through the Orange Revolution and the unseating of a Russian-leaning president, Putin remained true to his publicly professed credo of noninterference in the affairs of other sovereign countries. But it must have tried his patience that the so-called people's Orange Revolution was financed by Western money and largely orchestrated by the NGOs handling that money.

Yushchenko served a full six-year term without drawing active opposition from Moscow.

By the time of the next election, in 2010, President Yushchenko had fallen out with an important ally and leader in the Orange Revolution, former Prime Minister Yulia Tymoshenko, who had developed presidential aspirations of her own. She entered a three-way contest with Yushchenko and the reappearing Yanukovych, which split the pro-Western vote. Yanukovych received a plurality in the first round and then a majority in a runoff against Tymoshenko.

A Moscow-friendly president was back in office. It was up to him to deal with the sorry state of Ukraine's economy. He pleaded and negotiated for help from the West, and he pleaded and negotiated for help from Russia. He vacillated between aligning the country politically with one and then the other. He was gambling that beggars *could* be choosers.

Yanukovych was still fishing for the best deal when his government came under attack at the end of 2013. Demonstrations in Kiev's Maidan Square protesting a proposed agreement with Russia turned violent and then turned into a violent insurrection. In the end, Yanukovych was pushed out and a West-leaning government was installed.

Maidan Up Close

The Maidan Revolution played in American media as an uprising of people weary of rule by a despot luxuriating in Sun King splendor while the citizenry scrabbled for their daily bread. Those ordinary citizens hoped for a better future as newcomers to the EU and feared the grasp of their neighbor to the east. All of which is true enough, as far as it goes.

Yanukovych was, in fact, a despot who made the most of his time at the top of the food chain. He gorged himself on state assets, on taxes paid by the public, and on money given by foreign governments. The leftovers went to his buddies.

It's also true that many Ukrainians wanted closer ties with the EU. In 2011, Yanukovych angered them by rejecting $2.4 billion of loans from the International Monetary Fund (IMF) and the World Bank. But accepting the loans would have poisoned relations with Russia and tied Ukraine to the West. And there were loan conditions, including deep cuts in pensions for retired government employees and the elderly.

Yanukovych hoped to get a better deal from Russia. Then he all but gave up on Russia, until a Russian offer changed his mind.

After turning down the IMF and the World Bank in 2011, Yanukovych began drifting toward the West. Two years later, he was close to turning his back on Russia and embracing the European Union.

Help from the EU would come with conditions, however. IMF Managing Director Christiane Lagarde called for a "profound transformation," especially of Ukraine's fiscal, monetary, and energy policies. Yanukovych understood and seemingly accepted this. In September 2013, the chairman of Ukraine's parliament assured Yanukovych that the laws the EU required would be passed. Except for the Communist Party, all factions in the parliament were on board.

There were some sticking points, to be sure. A big one was an EU demand for the release of the jailed Yulia Tymoshenko, whom Yanukovych had defeated for the presidency in 2010 and who later had been convicted of embezzlement on a $100 million scale.

And the up-front money wasn't all that generous. Prime Minister Mykola Azarov had told the EU that Ukraine needed $27 billion just to begin to get back on its feet. But the EU was offering only $838 million in loans, which might have been beneath consideration had the country not been at the brink of a nasty precipice.

Ukraine was up to its eyeballs in debt and close to exhausting its foreign currency reserves. The national currency, the hryvnia, had plummeted in value. Fitch Ratings, an international credit rating service, had downgraded the country's sovereign debt from B– to CCC (from junk debt to junkier debt). Without money from someone, Ukraine literally wouldn't be able to keep the lights on.

In November 2013, an Association Agreement with the EU was awaiting signing at an upcoming summit in Lithuania. Yanukovych seemed just a signature away from committing to the West.

"I would like to emphasize that Ukraine has no alternative to reforms and European integration," he said at the time.

Then came two meetings.

First was a public one in St. Petersburg between Ukraine's foreign minister and the government heads of other Commonwealth of Independent States (CIS) members. The topic was trade, and Moscow used the occasion to demonstrate its openness for economic cooperation and its willingness to extend debt payments and resume cut-price gas sales to Ukraine—provided the government would suspend its negotiations with the EU.

Soon after the St. Petersburg meeting, Russia sweetened its proposal to include a $15 billion purchase of Ukrainian government bonds. This offer came with no requirements for internal reforms, a point that carried great importance for a government as systemically corrupt as Ukraine's. It meant "No oligarch left behind."

Getting a pass on mandated reforms was the carrot, and a big one. But Russia was also wielding a stick. In August, the Customs Service of the Russian Federation had put everything originating in Ukraine on its list of potentially dangerous goods. Ukraine was shut out of the Russian market. Of course, should Ukraine choose to join the Common Economic Space (CES), the Putin-designed customs union of Russia, Belarus, and Kazakhstan, the flow of commerce could resume.

What transpired in a second, secret meeting between Yanukovych and Putin is still unknown, but you can be sure they weren't talking about flower arranging.

In any event, it was followed by a stunning about-face by Yanukovych. At the last minute, he announced that Ukraine would turn its back on the EU and embrace the Common Economic Space. It was deeply embarrassing for an EU that was all set to throw Ukraine a grand welcoming party.

The defeat was unacceptable for the West, and it set in motion the events leading to the Maidan Revolution, aka the "Orange Crush."

With the coming of the Maidan uprising came the propaganda. Fed to the American people by its government was a tale of spontaneous revolt by courageous, unarmed pro-democracy citizens against an unpopular tyrant. Tyrant he was, true, and unpopular. But he had in fact been elected by the voters, and the people didn't all of a sudden decide to rise up and smite their hated ruler because he took an eastward turn.

The United States and EU had been working for years to pull Ukraine away from Russia. Accomplishing that and placing an antagonist state on Russia's border would be a foreign-policy triumph. So, ultimately, the United States would end up spending $5 billion in Ukraine to persuade and then to destabilize.

That's not a figure invented by the "blame America" crowd. It comes from Victoria Nuland, who at the time was U.S. assistant secretary of state for Europe and Eurasia. In mid-December 2013, she boasted that the United States had "invested" not only the billions of dollars but also "five years' worth of work and preparation" to help "build democratic skills and institutions" and achieve what she called Ukraine's "European aspirations."

She reported on a two-hour "tough conversation" with President Yanukovych during which she made it "absolutely clear" that the United States required him to take "immediate steps" to "get back into conversation with Europe and the IMF."

Or else ... what?

Washington hadn't gotten what it wanted, so it supported a coup against the elected government. It was easy. All the elements were in place. The president of the European Commission announced in late November 2013 that the EU would "not accept Russia's veto" of the EU's agreement with Ukraine. Protestors streamed into the streets of Kiev, egged on by Hromadske.TV, an online television outlet funded by American money.

Crowds in Kiev grew into the hundreds of thousands and clashed with police. A movement that began as a call for the president to return to a pro-EU policy morphed into one bent on regime change. People died, some from sniper fire directed at both sides, apparently to stoke the conflict. Eventually, the insurgents seized government buildings. Yanukovych fled in February 2014, and a new interim government was formed. It promptly appointed candy magnate Petro Poroshenko, "Ukraine's Willy Wonka," as president.

The Ukrainian revolution wasn't just about Ukraine. It was a proxy struggle between Russia and the West. And much about it fits badly into U.S. officialdom's standard "white hat versus black hat" narrative.

The Ukrainian revolution was a coup that overthrew a democratically elected president—normally not the sort of thing the United States likes to be seen encouraging.

The insurgents who drove Yanukovych out of office and out of the country were depicted in Western media as noble fighters risking death to oust an autocrat and build a democracy—which is roughly half of the truth. The ranks of the so-called freedom fighters included some unsavory characters indeed, among them members of the Svoboda Party, an organization whose story line is told in the vocabulary of 1930s-style anti-Semitism. Its leadership includes the founder of the Joseph Goebbels Political Research Center.

Washington downplayed the neo-Nazi involvement, of course. But Senator John McCain's ill-advised December 2013 visit to Ukraine didn't help. He found himself sharing the stage with Svoboda leader Oleh Tyahnybok—a man who is quick with a Nazi salute, has urged his countrymen to fight against the "Muscovite-Jewish mafia," and has called on the government to halt the "criminal activities" of "organized Jewry."

The U.S. government saw the neo-Nazis as an asset to be used but contained and kept out of view. Victoria Nuland, presumably as part of her effort to "build democratic skills and institutions," collaborated closely with Tyahnybok in planning the revolution. Later, leaked phone conversations found her wondering what to do with him. Best, she said, to keep him "on the outside" but in close consultation with the new, U.S.-approved president "four times a week."

While the mainstream media mostly ignored this shameful aspect of the story—*Time* magazine, for one, maintaining that nowhere in Ukraine "has the uprising involved neo-Nazi groups"—*Salon* corrected the record with a piece on February 25, 2014:

> As the EuroMaidan protests … culminated this week, displays of open fascism and neo-Nazi extremism became too glaring to ignore. Since demonstrators filled the downtown square to battle Ukrainian riot

police and demand the ouster of the corruption-stained, pro-Russian President Viktor Yanukovich, it has been filled with far-right street fighting men pledging to defend their country's ethnic purity.

White supremacist banners and Confederate flags were draped inside Kiev's occupied City Hall, and demonstrators have hoisted Nazi SS and white power symbols over a toppled memorial to V.I. Lenin. After Yanukovich fled his palatial estate by helicopter, EuroMaidan protesters destroyed a memorial to Ukrainians who died battling German occupation during World War II. *Sieg heil* salutes and the Nazi Wolfsangel symbol have become an increasingly common sight in Maidan Square, and neo-Nazi forces have established "autonomous zones" in and around Kiev.[1]

The Svoboda Party was handed four positions in the interim government—deputy prime minister, minister for agriculture, minister for environmental matters, and prosecutor general.

Despite the EU's 2013 demands for internal reforms, Ukraine's oligarchs are still open for business. Commerce between people who steal money and people who steal power won't end just because the new government tilts toward Brussels.

The interim government has already placed oligarchs in positions of power. Serhiy Taruta, the sixteenth-richest man in Ukraine, is now governor of the Donetsk region. Petro Poroshenko, the first post-Yanukovych president and billionaire owner of Ukraine's largest candy company, made his initial fortune picking up state assets at extraordinarily buyer-friendly auctions during Ukraine's privatization era. He's not a guy who is going to lead the "profound transformation" that the IMF's Lagarde called for.

Ukrainian journalist Andriy Skumin wrote of Poroshenko:

European circles, blindly searching for any adequate Western-thinking individuals within Ukraine's establishment, have a favorable opinion of Poroshenko as a person who is reliable, [and] can be charged with introducing changes in Ukraine and ending the deadlock in EU–Ukraine relations … but the preservation of the monopolistic oligarchy will not allow for any European integration or even domestic

---

[1] Max Blumenthal, "Is the US backing neo-Nazis in Ukraine?" *Salon*, February 25, 2014, www.salon.com/2014/02/25/is_the_us_backing_neo_nazis_in_ukraine_partner.

transformations using European patterns. The only thing that could be done is perhaps [to give] an outward European appearance.[2]

Crimea Comes Home

In 1954, when Khrushchev handed the Crimean Peninsula to Ukraine, the transfer was considered a mere gesture, since no one imagined the USSR might one day come apart at the seams.

What Khrushchev did was, strictly speaking, illegal, since under Soviet law the matter should have been debated in the Presidium of the Supreme Council of the Soviet Union and then submitted to a referendum. The Supreme Council did approve the transfer by unanimous vote, but it did so without a quorum present. Those legal defects would be cited by Putin 60 years later.

Putin had reason for mixed feelings about the Maidan Revolution. On one hand, the possibility of NATO moving closer was certainly unwelcome. On the other hand, Ukraine was a money pit he wouldn't mind leaving for someone else to fill.

After the coup, Russia quickly eliminated Ukraine as a cost center. Gazprom called in its debt, and Russia terminated its gas subsidies, leaving the price of gas to double overnight. Now Ukraine would be paying Russia for fully priced energy with money from Western Europe.

What Putin could not tolerate, however, was any risk to the naval base in Crimea. Keeping it under Russian control was imperative. To protect it, he first put the Russian troops already stationed there on alert. Next, according to some but denied by Putin, he moved more combat-ready soldiers to the area. Then, nodding to a resolution by Crimea's parliament to secede from Ukraine, he publicly welcomed a plebiscite to decide the matter.

Unsurprisingly, the region's largely Russian population, whose sympathies have always reached eastward, voted to join the Russian Federation. The alternative was to accept a coup co-ventured by the United States and fascist throwbacks. The voters had reason to fear a new

---

[2]Andriy Skumin, "The Return of the Prodigal Son, Who Never Left Home," *Ukranian Week*, March 30, 2012, http://ukrainianweek.com/Politics/46136.

government that included elements who so disliked ethnic Russians that they executed dozens of them during the uprising in Kiev. Joining Russia was an easy choice.

The process was remarkably quick and peaceful. Unlike what happened in Kiev, not a drop of blood was shed.

The howling in the West did nothing to slow Putin in welcoming Crimea into the Russian Federation. No amount of scorn, sanctioning, or isolation will turn him from acting in what he believes are the interests of his country.

What happens next in Ukraine is anyone's guess. But it's not likely to be pretty. The coup leaders, with U.S. and other Western backing, have stirred the pot by appointing two oligarchs as governors of the ethnically Russian regions of Donetsk and Dnepropetrovsk, two hotbeds of separatist sentiment. Many there want to follow Crimea in joining Russia. If they do, Putin may give them a reluctant welcome, even though he has discouraged further plebiscites to avoid inheriting more populations with economic troubles.

He has said he won't intervene militarily, but with a caveat: He will act to protect the Russian population of eastern Ukraine if it is threatened.

No one wants the Colder War to turn hot. However, that's not the only danger from U.S. involvement in Ukraine. Continuing to provoke Putin will only add urgency to his plan for the demise of the petrodollar.

Ukraine's Energy Resources

In energy matters, Ukraine is best known for two things: its quarrels with Russia over its natural gas bill and its history as ground zero for the Chernobyl nuclear disaster. But there's a lot more to the Ukrainian natural resources sector.

Ukraine has substantial natural gas reserves waiting to be exploited by conventional techniques. In addition, there might be sizable shale gas deposits that could be developed with the fracking methods now being used in the United States.

At the moment, neighboring Poland is experiencing a boom in shale gas exploration. Potential reserves in the Lublin Basin, which may turn Poland into a net exporter of natural gas, have been estimated at 50 trillion cubic feet (about $400 billion worth at current European prices). And that's just on the Polish side. The Lublin Basin extends into Ukraine, where a like amount could be waiting.

Developing its own resources would lessen Ukraine's dependence on Russia, but so far exploration for shale gas has languished. The country is competing for exploration dollars with Poland, and Poland is far more hospitable and holds less political risk. In Ukraine, foreign start-ups face court challenges over licenses to produce gas and then price ceilings on sales. It's easier to explore in Poland, where registering for a concession and getting an exploration license is a three-month exercise involving a single Ministry of Energy. In Ukraine, the same process involves several ministries and departments and can take a year or more. Many players, including larger ones like Marathon Oil, have already come and gone in Ukraine.

And shale gas is not even Ukraine's primary unexploited resource. The country has vast deposits of coal: 34 billion metric tons, the sixth-largest coal reserves in the world. But as with gas, the regulatory tangle repels investors.

Ukraine's existing coal mines are famously inefficient. The few privately owned mines are profitable, but most of the industry loses money on every subsidized ton extracted from government-owned mines. Perversely, Ukraine is a net coal importer.

Coal Bed Methane

With so much coal, the country is also endowed with a coal bed methane (CBM) reserve of 105 to 125 trillion cubic feet.

(Continued)

Producing the CBM would move Ukraine a long way toward energy independence.

Capturing the methane, which is explosive, also would also make the coal mines safer and reduce the fatality rate among miners, which has been averaging 317 deaths per year, second only to China. And it would spare the mines from the slowdowns and shutdowns that high methane levels sometimes necessitate.

Another CBM opportunity is that methane is a greenhouse gas (considerably more potent than CO_2), and 3 billion cubic meters of it escapes from Ukraine's coal mines every year. Capturing that gas could be a valuable source of carbon credits.

Of course, yet again, investor unfriendliness retards any such development.

However, in 2009, after years of discussing the country's CBM potential, Kiev did set out rules for CBM exploration and production. The law covers licensing, permitting, safety, and environmental protection. There are tax incentives and state guarantees to encourage CBM exploration and production, including an income tax holiday stretching until 2020.

First to step up to the plate? You guessed it: Russia. Its gas giant, Gazprom, quickly signed an agreement for a CBM joint venture with Ukraine's Naftogaz.

Chapter 6

Putin the Statesman

Playing hardball comes naturally to Putin, but there's another side to his foreign policy (call it Nice Putin) that eschews confrontation and strife.

Putin's model for how nations should associate with one another is the Common Economic Space (CES), a free-trade zone that currently includes Russia, Kazakhstan, and Belarus. Putin called its formation "without exaggeration, a historic milestone for all three countries and for the broader post-Soviet space."

Here are more comments from Putin on the CES, as published in *Izvestia*. It reveals much about what makes the guy tick.

We are making [CES] integration a comprehensible, sustainable, and long-term project, attractive to both individuals and businesses that operate independently from fluctuations in the current political environment or any other circumstances.

Later, this framework will also include common visa and migration policies, allowing border controls between our states to be lifted.

[New] conditions … will foster trans-border cooperation. For the general public, the lifting of migration, border and other barriers, including what are known as labor quotas, will mean that they have a free choice about where to live, study, or work, [thereby creating] a civilized environment for labor migration.

Broad swathes of opportunities will also open up for businesses. I am referring here to new dynamic markets governed by unified standards and regulations for goods and services—in most cases consistent with European standards.…

I am convinced that in economic terms the commonwealth must be firmly founded in extensive trade liberalization.

[The CES will create] real jurisdiction competition for entrepreneurs. All Russian, Kazakh, and Belarusian entrepreneurs will be able to choose in which of the three countries to register their companies, where they want to do business. … This will be a serious incentive for national administrative systems to start improving their market institutions, administrative procedures and their business and investment climate. Taken as a whole, these systems will be forced to address their inadequacies and all the lacunae they have never addressed before, and advance their legislation in line with best European and global practices.

[It] is highly important for us that the general public and business communities in all three countries perceive the integration project not as some kind of wheeze orchestrated by the top bureaucracy but as a living organism, and as a good opportunity to implement initiatives and succeed. [It will] be guided by the basic requirements to minimize bureaucracy and heed people's actual interests.

Is the ex–KGB officer really a champion of free and open markets? If his words can be believed, it would appear so.

And there is more.

[We] are setting ourselves an ambitious goal: to move to the next, even higher level of integration, to a Eurasian Union.

The result, in his words, would be a "full-fledged economic union," capable of rivaling the European Union and China.

To make that happen, he proposes extending the CES customs union to Tajikistan and Kyrgyzstan, both of which have sought aid from Moscow. Kyrgyzstan is likely to join in 2015, as is Armenia.

Putin is also courting Azerbaijan and Moldova, although in competition with the European Union. The possibility of pulling Uzbekistan, Turkmenistan, and Tajikistan away from Chinese influence is being explored, although those three are wary of bringing Moscow back into their lives.

Note that Azerbaijan has lots of oil, while Turkmenistan and Uzbekistan are rich in both minerals and energy reserves. All would be plums for Putin's CES.

If the Eurasian Union seems like the resurrection of the USSR, well, that's the way most influential Washingtonians tend to see it, too. Putin, though, consistently downplays that notion.

In the *Izvestia* article, he insisted that "none of this entails any kind of revival of the Soviet Union. It would be naive to try to revive or emulate something that has been consigned to history. But these times call for close integration based on new values and a new political and economic foundation."

Beyond the Common Economic Space

The man does not think small: "We are proposing a model of a powerful supranational association that is capable of becoming one of the poles of the modern world and, within that, to play an effective linking role between Europe and the dynamic Asia–Pacific region...."

Putin always likes to stress cooperation. In this instance, he argued that the Eurasian Union would actually grow to become a partner for the European Union. "Membership in the Eurasian Union, apart from direct economic benefits, will enable its members to integrate into Europe faster and from a much stronger position."

There are many people, especially in Washington, who would like to dismiss this as empty rhetoric. That would be a mistake. Putin may or may not be a dedicated free-market proponent. But his words are probably sincere for one very pragmatic reason: To the extent that agreements

like this strengthen Russia—economically, politically, and militarily—
they support Putin's grand vision.

The proposal for the Eurasian Union, however, will play out on a
tricky part of the Great Game board. Maybe no amount of pressure from
the Kremlin will persuade some of the target states, especially Ukraine
and Azerbaijan, to join the new union. And providing financial incentives to coax a slew of cash-strapped dictator states into an economic and
political partnership poses a high cost for Russia.

Moreover, the open-borders aspect of Putin's Eurasian plan could
draw resistance from the Russian people. While they love their Slavic
warrior president, they won't welcome an influx of low-wage migrants,
many of them Muslim, into Russian cities already hostile to Islam.

So perhaps the "new USSR" will never happen, nor even its ram-
bunctious stepchild, the Eurasian Union. But neither is critical to Putin's
plan. He has a lot of geopolitical alternatives bubbling on other burners.

One is the Shanghai Cooperation Organization (SCO), whose
members are Russia, China, Kazakhstan, Tajikistan, Kyrgyzstan, and
Uzbekistan. The group was formed ostensibly to oppose extremism and
enhance border security, but it's really a counterorganization to NATO,
a point the SCO doesn't deny. Its official motto is nonalignment, non-
confrontation, and noninterference in other countries' affairs. But the
members do conduct joint military exercises.

The SCO is a work in progress: Putin wants to add Pakistan. China
wants Iran in. If both join, it will be a geopolitical game changer.
Russia, China, Iran, and Pakistan would be coordinating both in economic matters and in security matters.

Of course there are energy implications as well. With Iran in the
club, members of the SCO would control half of the world's natural gas
reserves. Development of the pipeline network would become a matter
of Asian integration, not Eurasian integration.

The United States and Europe are shadows of their former selves,
leaving the balance of global power up for grabs. The battle of the Colder
War, fought with oil and gas, uranium and coal, pipelines and ports, will
determine where that balance tilts. Putin has been preparing for the fight
for a decade already and is in it for however long it takes.

Russia is set on her course. The Putinization of the world is not only
coming; it has already started.

Much depends upon how the West responds.

Here's why: Despite Putin's pronouncements about cooperation among the world's peoples, he always puts his own country first. His overriding goal is to secure Russia a position at the head of the table whenever nations gather. And achieving this involves concentrating his efforts on natural resources, to which everything else is tied, and on diminishing the strength and influence of the United States.

Just read the following excerpt from Putin's Candidate of Science dissertation in economics, defended in 1997 when his country's economy was in tatters, and titled "Mineral and Raw Materials Resources and the Development Strategy for the Russian Economy":

> In conclusion, one should note that the existing socio-economic pre-conditions, as well as the strategy *for Russia to emerge from its deep crisis and attain its previous might at a qualitatively new level* show that the condition of the mineral and raw materials complex of the country will remain the most important factor in the development of the country in the near term. The speed with which the crisis phenomena in the country are overcome; the creation of the material-technical base for the production of high-technology and science-intensive products, including durable goods; the solution of food supply problems, including ensuring Russia's state security in the area of food products; changing the structure of foreign trade to correspond with the exchange of goods in the world's developed countries; the solution of many social problems and a whole range of factors which determine the future of the Russian Federation depend overwhelmingly on the level of rational, well-considered responsibility and the scale of the use of natural wealth potential. (Emphasis added.)

If the end is for Russia to recover its previous might at a "qualitatively new level," then the means, in Putin's eyes, is to focus on three critical sectors in which he would like the country to rise to global dominance: oil, gas, and nuclear power.

Here We Go Again

In the early years of the new millennium, any political analyst who said that a hand from Russia was preparing itself to reach westward to seize

Europe in a cold, greedy grip would have been regarded as a terrible analyst and maybe a bit goofy. Most people would have discarded the message as stale propaganda left over from the Cold War. And who needed that? The Cold War was finished, and the West had won. In the aftermath, the Russians were too busy crying in their vodka to prepare to do anything.

Yet in fact a new, Colder War was developing. Its weapons would be oil wells, gas fields, uranium mines, energy processing plants, pipelines, and ports. Again, Europe would be the primary zone of engagement even though the United States would be the primary opponent. (See Figure 6.1.)

Russia's vast resource wealth and China's massive bank account were readily available to found a new coalition that could include former Soviet client states and countries along the Eurasian divide and in the Far East. The coalition might also attract countries in Africa and Latin America that just didn't like the way the United States had been comporting itself on the world stage.

And Vladimir Putin has presented himself as the leader of that emerging bloc.

In matters of foreign policy, it has never been a secret that Putin despises the United States' self-appointed role as global policeman and holds Europe equally at fault for cooperating with U.S. foreign policy. As for the U.S. presidents who have stood beside Putin in world affairs, just a mention of the names Bush and Obama are enough to evoke his contempt.

Putin believes a leader should be both strong and flexible, as circumstances dictate. The past two American presidents have been neither. To Putin, Bush was a slow-witted, bull-headed man under the sway of his neoconservative advisers and war drum beaters. Obama is just not up to the task—a geopolitical lightweight who was easily outmaneuvered in Syria and Iran.

For Putin, military force, when it is clearly necessary, should be swift and unforgiving, as he demonstrated in Chechnya. But an unprovoked invasion is a losing move. Why confront another nation with soldiers when you can build cooperative relations that will serve your interests so much better in the long run?

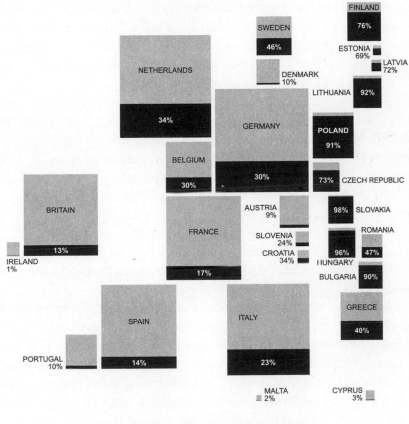

- Square size represents the total energy imports into each country (excluding intra-EU trade).
- Black area represents percentage **from Russia**.

Figure 6.1   How Much Europe Depends on Russian Energy
Source: Eurostat as published by Global Trade Information Services.

The long run is what matters. Putin's scorn for the American political process and American indifference to anything beyond the next election is boundless.

For a long while, the U.S. government could go about its business regardless of what Russia said or did in the United Nations Security

Council. If a Russian veto tried to interfere, the United States would proceed with its plans through NATO or some "coalition of the willing," or even go it alone if no one else would come along. Washington snubbed Moscow at every turn, quite intentionally making the point that Russian opinion didn't matter.

Could the United States have gotten along with Putin by being slower to confront and quicker to cooperate? Perhaps, or perhaps not. Animosity and mistrust between the two countries run deep. But the question is a moot one. One thing is certain: Putin was never going to accept the part of playing the United States' tagalong.

Nor did he need to consider taking on such a role. Russia is home to immense resource wealth. Per square mile, it has a far richer endowment of natural resources than most other countries. It is the largest country in the world by square miles, nearly twice the size of second-place Canada, the planet's big warehouse of oil, gas, coal, uranium, gold, silver, and much else.

Natural gas abounds. In 1999, Europe was already beholden to Russia for much of its supply. Then Putin lengthened Russia's list of gas customers through new pipelines and through contracts with China. He also worked to corner the uranium market; his country now controls 40 percent of global uranium enrichment capacity, the lion's share of the world's downblending facilities, and a fair chunk of the world's in-ground resources. On top of that, Russian nuclear-power giant Rosatom builds more nuclear-power plants than any other company in the world, with international deals for 21 reactors currently on the books.

These are all important factors, as we'll see. But as always in the modern world, in the end everything comes down to oil. The era of Putinization began with oil, so let's take a look there first.

Chapter 7

The Putinization of Oil

Most of Russia's oil production today comes from western Siberia, but at the turn of the century, the fields there were in rough shape. As noted in Chapter 3, the industry entered a death spiral in the 1970s. Output declined straight through to the last days of the Soviet Union and the economic and political struggles of the 1990s.

Production had already started to pick up when Putin came into power in 1999, and he supported the oil industry wherever and however he could by encouraging the larger companies to absorb the successful small ones, thus giving risk takers a potential exit route. Since 2007, a staggering $160 billion has been spent consolidating Russian oil companies.

As a payoff, Russia's oil output climbed from 6 million barrels per day (bpd) in 1998 to 10 million bpd a decade later. In 2009, Russia surpassed Saudi Arabia to become the world's top producer. In 2012, the country's wells were yielding 11 million bpd. (See Figure 7.1.) Domestic consumption has changed very little over the past 20 years, so Russia is now exporting almost 8 million barrels of oil every day.

Oil Production

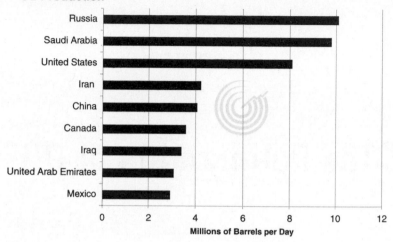

Figure 7.1   Worldwide Oil Production
SOURCE: Energy Information Administration. © Casey Research 2014.

That means nearly a billion dollars per day moving to Russia from the rest of the world.

It also means that Russia is a big factor in keeping the planet going. In 2012 the world consumed 85 million bpd, of which 55 million were traded internationally. That means Russia produced 13 percent of the world's oil and 15 percent of the oil moving in world markets.

The country is an oil giant.

Moreover, not only does it *produce* a lot of oil, but it also hosts vast untapped reserves. It is difficult to put a hard number on Russia's oil potential, but big is too small a word. Proven reserves range from 60 billion to 77 billion barrels (depending on who is making the estimates), representing about 5 percent of the world total.

Oil Talk

Crude Oil

Crude oil is a soup of chemicals produced from organic debris (primarily dead zooplankton and algae) through the action of heat and pressure applied over millions of years. The composition varies from deposit to deposit, but it is primarily hydrocarbons with small amounts of sulfur, nitrogen, and oxygen compounds.

Hydrocarbons are a family of chemicals whose members are built exclusively out of atoms of hydrogen and carbon. The varieties with just a few carbon atoms tend to be more free-flowing than the varieties with more carbon atoms. A molecule of octane (an ingredient in commercial gasoline), for example, has eight carbon atoms, whereas paraffin wax consists of molecules with 25 or more carbon atoms.

Sweet versus Sour Crude

The sulfur in crude oil must be removed during refining in order to yield clean-burning products. Removal is costly, depending on the amount of sulfur present.

"Sweet" crude refers to oil with a low sulfur content. Being cheaper to refine, it trades at a premium to "sour" crude (with a high sulfur content). Brent crude (from the North Sea oil fields) and West Texas Intermediate (WTI) contain no more than 0.5 percent sulfur and are classified as sweet, whereas oil from Saudi Arabia, with a sulfur content of 1.7 percent, and Mexican Maya crude, with 3.5 percent sulfur, are classified as sour. In the U.S. market, the price of West Texas Intermediate is usually $6 to $12 per barrel higher than the price of Mexican Maya.

Heavy versus Light Oil

In "light" crude oil, the ratio of hydrogen to carbon is higher than in "heavy" crude oil. Barrel for barrel, light crude is richer in energy than heavy oil and commands a higher price. Both Brent and West Texas Intermediate are considered light oils.

(Continued)

Crude from Venezuela's Orinoco oil belt is heavy oil. Saudi crude is an intermediate oil, between heavy and light.

Tar

Tar is a mix of large-molecule hydrocarbons. Asphalt, for example, consists of molecules with 35 or more carbon atoms.

What Are Condensates?

Condensates are high API gravity liquid hydrocarbon (above 50 degrees) with low density that generally occur in association with natural gas production. The term "wet gas" comes from natural gas production that is associated with liquid condensates.

Refining

Crude oil refining is a multistep process.

Step 1 is distillation. Crude oil is boiled, and as the resulting vapor cools, each type of hydrocarbon condenses to a liquid at its distinct temperature (its boiling point).

Step 2 is cracking. Heat, steam, and added chemicals are applied to break larger hydrocarbon molecules into small ones (i.e., to turn viscous material into free-flowing fuels). The cracking process can be tuned to control the composition of the output, depending on what types of petroleum products are most in demand at the time.

Natural Oil Temperature

Most oil comes out of the ground at a temperature between 100 and 170 degrees Fahrenheit. Oil from some offshore deposits comes out cooler than 100 degrees.

Finding Oil

The earliest oil wells were dug where oil was seen seeping out of the ground. But all those obvious opportunities have been exploited.

Oil originates in sediments containing organic material, so today the place to search for large pools of oil is in sedimentary rock near continental rifts and basins. Sedimentary rock with a high level of porosity is especially attractive, since if oil is present, it will be easier to pump out than oil trapped in harder rock formations.

After finding a sedimentary rock formation, the next step is a seismic survey (essentially a series of sonograms) to produce a picture of what lies below the surface. If the picture is promising, the company that has been paying for the search may decide to risk the additional, perhaps much larger, cost of drilling an exploratory well. Even if the well fails to produce oil, it will produce valuable information in the form of rock samples that can be examined for oil staining, porosity, and other clues.

Arctic Oil

The estimates of Russian oil reserves don't even count Arctic or shale oil deposits, which taken together should easily increase Russia's reserves to over *200 billion* barrels—or over 10 percent of the world total.

It's true that there are competing claims on Arctic resources, with Canada, the United States, Norway, and even Denmark (via Greenland) all elbowing for a share of the undersea treasures. But in March 2014, Russia pushed to the head of the pack.

After 13 years of wrangling, the UN's Commission on the Limits of the Continental Shelf awarded Russia jurisdiction over a 20,000-square-mile area in the Sea of Okhotsk. Putin wants as much of the Arctic as he can get. In April 2014, he announced the formation of a "united system of naval bases for ships and next-generation submarines in the Arctic," to defend Russia's interests there. He also suggested "strengthening of the naval component of the FSB."

Exploring for and developing oil in the Arctic are about as heavy as heavy industry gets. But Russia has already proven that it is up to the challenge. In 2014, it began production at the Prirazlomnaya oil field in the Pechora Sea, where 40 wells are being drilled to tap into a 530-million-barrel pool.

The command center for the project, a massive offshore platform, is an engineering marvel—the first platform built in the Arctic. It's designed for extreme conditions and to withstand high winds and ice loads. The special alloys used in its construction are resistant to salt corrosion, low temperatures, and constant wetness. The platform's own weight (500,000 tons, including a stone berm that protects against scouring by drifting ice) anchors the entire structure to the seabed. A high-strength deflector shields the platform from waves and drifting ice.

Prirazlomnaya is also designed to preclude oil spills. All the wellheads are situated inside the platform perimeter, so the platform's foundation stands between the wellheads and the open sea.

Putin is open to cooperating with the West. In 2009 his pet company, Rosneft, signed a deal with Exxon Mobil for joint ventures in Arctic oil exploration. For Exxon, it was a 180-degree turn from five years earlier, when the company fled Russia after Putin's takedown of Mikhail Khodorkovsky (detailed in Chapter 2). The deal was renewed in 2011 and again in 2013, despite the war of words between Putin and Obama over human rights and the extradition of Edward Snowden.

The two companies agreed to develop wells in the Kara Sea (potential reserves of 36 billion barrels) with construction of 15 sea platforms costing $300 billion. They also planned to cooperate in fracking shale fields in Siberia, drilling in the Black Sea (8.6 billion barrels in reserves), and building a terminal in Russia's Far East to export liquefied natural gas.

Under a separate 2009 deal, Rosneft gained a 30 percent stake in Exxon Mobil projects in the United States, the Gulf of Mexico, and Canada.

Nor is Russia put off by political instability. The Mideast division of another Russian company, Lukoil, recently began production at its 75 percent owned West Quma-2 property in Iraq. West Quma-2 hosts

14 billion barrels of oil reserves; Lukoil's production goal is 1.2 million bpd for 20 years.

European Market

Europe is Russia's richest customer. The European Union has a modern, energy-eating economy but very little domestic oil production. There is the North Sea, largely the province of Norway and Great Britain, and that's about it. And North Sea reserves are dwindling.

Today, with so much Russian oil available for export and with the country located next door to Europe (Putin would say "in Europe"), many EU members now rely heavily on Russian oil. Piping it from Russia is more economical than getting it from the Middle East, and doing so sidesteps that region's uncertainties.

Finland and Hungary get almost all their oil from Russia; Poland more than 75 percent; Sweden, the Czech Republic, and Belgium about 50 percent; Germany and the Netherlands upwards of 40 percent.

Between 2002 and 2010, Russia's share of the overall European oil market grew from 29 percent to 34 percent. Exports to Europe from members in Russia's Commonwealth of Independent States rose as well. Kazakhstan's share jumped from 2 percent to 6 percent, and Azerbaijan's increased from 1 percent to 4 percent.

This quasi-dependence gives Putin a strong hand in dealing with the European Union. None of those countries is going to risk its supply by interfering with any of his policies, no matter how irritated the United States gets over Russia's geopolitical maneuvering. And the numbers in Putin's Oil = Power equation are going to keep getting bigger as Russia's control and output of energy continue to grow and as Europe's supply from other sources dwindles. From 2002 to 2010, Norway's share of the European oil market dropped from 19 percent to 14 percent, and Saudi Arabia's shrank from 10 percent to 6 percent.

Sure, most European countries would dearly love to wean themselves off Russian oil. But what are they going to do? The list of alternatives is short:

- Venture outside the continent for oil
- Drill within their own borders

That's it. Concerning the first choice, large oil deposits are harder and more expensive to find than ever, and many regions that may still harbor such elephants—Arctic deposits come to mind—can be so difficult to operate in that they're economically out of reach for most countries. To make things worse, Europe would have to compete with China and India, two nations whose governments have gone all-in in the race to secure deposits that will yield long-term supplies.

That leaves the second choice. The problem is, there is very little in the way of conventional oil deposits in Europe. There may not be much unconventional oil, either, but if there is, no one will get it out of the ground in France, which has banned fracking. The Netherlands may soon follow suit. And Germany's tight environmental regulations preclude fracking for natural gas. So, although conventional drilling in Europe is increasing—from just over 80 rigs in 2009 to nearly 140 today—it's not even close to being enough.

Europe will still have to deal with Putin.

Rosneft

At the center of Putin's oil plans is the colossus Rosneft.

Rosneft was a bit player when Putin assumed the presidency in 2000, but he adopted it as his baby and worked to bring it to a robust adulthood. He began building up the company with a forced buyout of minority investors. Next, he appointed Rosneft to be the government's representative in projects based on production sharing, a move that generated deal flow for the company.

With development of its domestic properties on track, Rosneft was ready to expand outside Russia, beginning with projects in Algeria and Kazakhstan. In four years, its production increased 50 percent, to 400,000 bpd in 2004. That was still small potatoes, though; at one point Rosneft had to fight a takeover by fellow Russian enterprise Gazprom.

Putin was in a hurry to show that his state company of choice was a force to be reckoned with and that anyone foolish enough to challenge it was risking a bloody nose. But it was taking far too long for internal growth to turn Rosneft into a dominant player. In 2004, Putin put Igor

Sechin in charge of Rosneft, and together they boosted the company to the top of the global energy heap.

Sechin is one of the "St. Petersburg boys," a trusted old confidant who followed Putin to Moscow. Known as tough, ruthless, and secretive, Sechin is thought to have worked as a spy in Africa and as the Soviet Union's primary arms smuggler for Latin America and the Middle East. With his background and his ties to Putin, he is the de facto leader of the Kremlin's *siloviki* faction, a sort of higher-level inner cabinet. They are a cadre of dedicated statists, for the most part former officers of the KGB, Chief Intelligence Directorate (GRU), and FSB. Their loyalty to Sechin may contribute to his considerable influence with Putin.

In any event, Sechin's purely political work—for 10 years he was deputy chief of the Putin administration—is likely less consequential than his economic accomplishments. As CEO since July 2004, he built the Rosneft we know today.

In July 2006, he took Rosneft "public" with an initial public offering (IPO) in London. I use quotation marks because only a quarter of the company was offered to outside investors; the rest of it stayed with or close to the Russian government, which is to say under Putin's control. Moreover, anyone holding publicly traded shares became instantly wealthy. It can't be proven, but it is widely suspected that Putin and Sechin are among those who got very, very rich.

Over the years, Rosneft frequently gobbled up small competitors and then moved on to a big target, TNK-BP, a vertically integrated company until 2012 owned by BP (formerly British Petroleum) and a consortium of Russian billionaires known as AAR. At the time, it was the second-largest oil producer in Russia and among the top 10 in the world.

TNK-BP had been a financial dream come true, paying billions in dividends to its owners—but it was also a business relations nightmare. The partners fought chronically. In 2008, Russian authorities arrested two British TNK-BP managers amid a dispute over strategy that forced then-CEO Bob Dudley to flee Russia—and that was just one of many partnership scandals.

The writing had been on the wall for TNK-BP since 2011, when one of the AAR billionaires quit as CEO of the venture and declared that the relationship with BP had run its course. After that, speculation was rife over who might buy in to take his place, but in retrospect the answer seems obvious: Rosneft, which might as well be called PutinOil. And the answer Rosneft provided was far bigger than the question.

It was a two-part deal. In the first part, Rosneft acquired BP's 50 percent share of the joint venture for cash plus Rosneft stock worth $27 billion. That gave BP nearly a 20 percent stake in Rosneft.

Why did BP go along? While Russia had been profitable for the British firm, management got tired of the drama within TNK-BP but still wanted to participate in developing the country's energy resources. The cash-and-shares deal gave BP a nice ownership stake in Rosneft— the best way to profit from Russia's immense untapped oil potential, because Putin will ensure that Rosneft has first dibs on all the juiciest opportunities.

In addition, the change placed BP personnel in regular, direct contact with Igor Sechin, Rosneft's CEO and Putin's trusted ally with a significant say in Russian energy policy. Anyone who wants to operate in Mother Russia has to have an inside track to the Kremlin. Otherwise, you are likely to find yourself kicked to the curb.

For his part, Putin knew he couldn't nationalize all of Russia's resources and go it alone. Extracting oil is difficult. Russia simply didn't have enough native oil and gas expertise. He needed BP.

Putin understood what the Saudis learned the hard way. When Saudi Arabia kicked out the foreigners and nationalized its oil industry in 1980, the country was producing more than 10 million bpd. Within five years, production had fallen to 4 million bpd.

So BP was encouraged to stick around and help Rosneft with technology to tap Russia's huge reserves of unconventional tight oil and shale gas. There was one further benefit: Having BP as a significant shareholder also lets Putin claim that Rosneft is not simply an arm of the government (and that he is not leading the country back into communism).

With BP accommodated, Rosneft could proceed with part two of the deal. It bought the other half of TNK-BP from the AAR group for $28 billion in cash. The oligarchs of AAR were motivated to sell, rather than stay in a joint venture with Rosneft. They'd had ringside seats for the Khodorkovsky/Yukos affair, and they knew they could easily meet the same fate if they tried to partner with Rosneft as equals. Why run that risk? Better to take the money and go.

In the end, it was the richest deal in the oil industry since Exxon bought Mobil in 1999. Rosneft emerged as the biggest (somewhat) publicly traded oil producer in the world.

Rosneft's rise to dominance of the Russian oil space has been spectacular. In 1998, the company produced a paltry 4 percent of the country's petroleum, with Lukoil the top dog at 17 percent and a crowd of small companies claiming the rest. Just 15 years later, in 2013, Lukoil remained healthy at 16 percent, but most of the little guys were gone, swallowed by Rosneft, which now accounts for 43 percent of Russia's production.

It would be hard to exaggerate Rosneft's position in the world. For perspective, this one company produces more oil than all of China and twice as much as Nigeria.

It's a state corporation with Putin's favor behind it, so Rosneft has vast potential for raising capital and enjoys an exalted place in the "too big to fail" category. It can continue to seek growth via acquisitions, either domestically or internationally, as well as organic growth from its operations across Russia and the Arctic shelf.

Rosneft combines the discipline of a publicly traded company with the backing of a powerful government. It has rich exploration potential to complement its immense production base. And it has the cash to gobble up oil assets when they come on the market anywhere in the world.

It's the perfect cornerstone for the grand plan to consolidate power in the hands of Russia's supreme ruler. Through Rosneft, Russia will gain the discretion to turn supply on and off and to raise and lower prices. Then Putin can play energy-needy countries against one another and squeeze Europeans to accept long-term, high-price contracts as the only way to secure reliable supplies. (See Figure 7.2.)

Further, with Rosneft's acquisition capabilities, Putin has a tool to enhance Russia's influence in countries with resource potential that currently depend on Russian oil. Acquiring oil and gas reserves in such a country would let Russia dominate the customer's internal development as well as the flow of oil into or out of it.

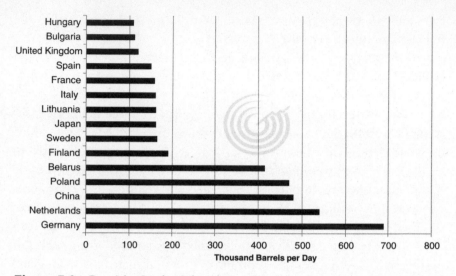

Figure 7.2   Russia's Crude Oil and Condensate Main Export Destinations, 2012

SOURCE: Global Trade Atlas, Energy Information Administration. © Casey Research 2014.

Winking at OPEC

Beyond that, we can speculate about what might be next: an alliance with the Organization of Petroleum Exporting Countries (OPEC)? That would be the United States' and Europe's worst nightmare. Such a consortium would produce 56 percent of the world's oil and hold most of its spare capacity. Such an ultra-OPEC could name its price for oil, and the rest of the world would simply have to pay—at least for a period of years. And any offer from its leader on any matter would be hard for any country to refuse.

As already mentioned, Europe has steadily increased its reliance on Russian oil.

The United States is in a better position, enjoying the highest domestic oil production numbers in years, and its dependence on imports has fallen dramatically. In 2005, it depended on imported oil for 60 percent of its consumption, but in 2013 for only 32 percent—a remarkable improvement. However, about one-sixth of its oil still comes from Russia and OPEC.

Would OPEC welcome Russia into its fraternity? Perhaps. On the one hand, some of its leaders have been courting Putin for years. Russian representatives frequently attend OPEC meetings, and on occasion the country has pledged to cooperate with OPEC production cuts. On the other hand, Russia has a history of reneging on its promises and has repeatedly tried to undermine OPEC's price setting.

So far, Putin hasn't shown any interest in joining the cartel. Giving up control over the pricing of Russian resources is not his way.

Nor does he believe higher oil prices are always good for the producer. His concern is that excessively high prices would boomerang on the Russian economy by raising domestic energy costs.

Rosneft CEO Igor Sechin also weighed in on the topic, in an interview with the *Wall Street Journal*. "It would be irresponsible for Russia to join OPEC," he said, "because we can't directly regulate the activity of our companies," which he noted are nearly all privately owned, as opposed to the state ownership in OPEC.

Still, never say never. Once, when asked about the possibility, Putin stated flatly, "Russia is not going to join OPEC." However, he added, "We are a comfortable partner for OPEC," without explaining what Russian partnering with OPEC would entail.

Dmitry Medvedev, while Russian president, went further (presumably with Putin's blessing). When oil prices plunged during the recession of 2008, he said:

> We are prepared for [joining OPEC]. We must defend ourselves, since this is our revenue base, both from oil and gas. These kinds of defensive measures could be tied to lowering oil production, and participating in the existing suppliers' organization, and participating in new organizations, if we can come to an agreement beforehand, so to speak.
>
> I believe that we can't exclude any options for ourselves. Let me say this again: this is an issue of our country's revenue base, an issue of her development, and we cannot be ruled by any abstract criteria, by recommendations of other international organizations, and so forth. These are our national interests. We will proceed as we see fit.[1]

---

[1] "Medvedev: Russia May Join OPEC, Cut Crude Output," *The Other Russia*, December 12, 2008, www.theotherrussia.org/2008/12/12/medvedev-russia-may-join-opec-cut-crude-output.

Oil Pipelines

Meanwhile, Putin has moved quickly on export infrastructure. When he came to power, he couldn't help but see room for improvement, and he immediately set to work on pipelines and ports.

One big accomplishment was the East Siberian Pacific Ocean (ESPO) pipeline, which began operating early in 2010. In its first phase, with a capacity of 600,000 bpd, the pipe linked oil fields in eastern Siberia with the city of Skovorodino, near the border with China. From there, 300,000 barrels were sent into China each day via a connecting line, under a 20-year contract with China National Petroleum Company (CNPC). The other 300,000 bpd were taken by rail to the new export terminal at Kozmino (on the Pacific Coast), to be sold on the spot market.

The second stage of ESPO increased daily capacity to 1 million barrels and extended the pipe to the terminal at Kozmino, which eliminated the need for rail transport. It was completed in 2012, two years ahead of schedule. With ESPO, Russia gained a direct oil line to Asia and considerable clout in the growing Chinese market, one of the keys to Putin's overall strategy. There will undoubtedly be more such connections, especially if Exxon and Rosneft succeed in tapping the vast oil reserves beneath Russia's Arctic seas.

Putin also built a port for exporting oil, his answer to a pipeline transit dispute. Ukraine may be the most famous pipeline squabbler, but it's not the only one.

In this instance it was Belarus, at odds with Moscow over the Druzhba pipeline. Druzhba is the longest pipeline in the world, carrying 1 million barrels of Russian oil every day across Belarus to refiners in Poland, Germany, the Czech Republic, Slovakia, and Hungary. Belarus wanted a bigger cut of the profits.

Putin's response was the port of Ust-Luga, which opened in March 2012. It's on Russia's Baltic coast, at the Gulf of Finland, at the end of the Baltic Pipeline System that brings oil south from the Timan-Pechora and West Siberian basins. Now instead of having to send all of its northern oil through the Druzhba pipeline and across Belarus, Russia can load some of it directly onto tankers and set sail.

The port also helps Putin in another of his oil quests, which is to promote the predominant type of Russian crude, called Urals, as an international standard. Ust-Luga reduces concern over disruptions in the supply of Urals by providing a reliable export route, and that increases traders' confidence in the blend's steady availability. To give Urals even more vigor, Russia constructed a $1 billion storage facility and terminal in the busy trading port of Rotterdam dedicated to Urals oil.

I'll have a lot more to say about pipeline issues, especially regarding natural gas, in the chapters that follow. They've played a key role in the geopolitics of recent years.

The point for now is that here, once again, Putin showed his energy savvy and creativity, peacefully turning a source of friction into a resource advantage for Russia.

Chapter 8

The Putinization of Gas

Oil is the essential fuel of every modern economy, but it isn't the only hydrocarbon that's important to Russia or its neighbors. And being the biggest player in the oil patch isn't enough by itself to give Russia the power to squeeze world energy supplies that Putin wants.

After oil, there's also the fuel you can't see: natural gas.

The gas fields of Siberia have been yielding over 50 billion cubic feet (Bcf) per day of natural gas for the past two decades. In 2014, production rates are approaching 60 Bcf per day. At current European prices, that's more than $100 billion worth per year.

Cheap gas from Russia was one of the glues that held the old Soviet Union together, and today much of Europe, as well as the USSR's former satellites, depends on Russia to keep delivering. Selling gas means revenue for Russia, of course, but Putin is focused on the glue factor, the political leverage that comes from being a customer's irreplaceable source of energy.

The European Union as a whole relies on Russia for a third of its natural gas. Several countries, including Poland, Finland, Romania, Bulgaria, and Serbia, depend on Russia for well over half their supply.

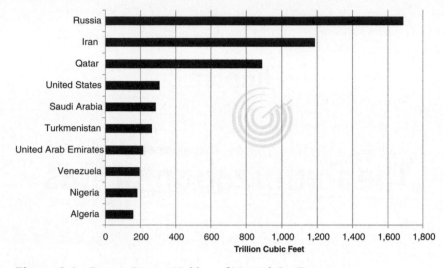

Figure 8.1 Largest Proven Holders of Natural Gas Reserves
SOURCE: Energy Information Administration. © Casey Research 2014.

The strong production so far is only the start of what Russia can do. The country sits on 1,600 trillion cubic feet (Tcf) of natural gas, roughly one-quarter of the world's known reserves and five times what Russia has produced in the past 20 years. And those big numbers don't include stores of unconventional gas. All told, Russia may well control as much as one-third of the world's natural gas. (See Figure 8.1.)

Delivery infrastructure is the make-or-break factor in the natural gas market. Unlike oil, which can move by truck or railcar, natural gas goes nowhere except by specialized, dedicated facilities.

Two infrastructure strategies are positioning Russia to dominate the Eurasian gas market. First, build pipelines that bypass unreliable countries, to ensure Russia's ability to deliver gas to customers in Europe and Asia. Second, build facilities on the coasts of the Pacific Ocean and the North Sea to handle liquefied natural gas (LNG), which can go where pipelines can't.

The pipeline system Putin inherited from the USSR was big and dumb. Many key lines crossed countries that just couldn't find a reason to stop demanding higher transit fees. Some would take "No" as an excuse for siphoning off gas intended for other customers. For Russia, it was one headache after another.

And the pipelines were concentrated in Russia's west—good for reaching customers in Europe but useless for delivering to buyers in Asia.

Measuring What You Can't See

Btu stands for British thermal unit.

MMBtu stands for 1 million British thermal units and is equal to 1,000 cubic feet of gas.

As a matter of industry practice, the size of a natural gas deposit is usually stated as the number of cubic feet the gas would occupy at the standard conditions of 60 degrees Fahrenheit and a pressure of 14.7 pounds per square inch (which is atmospheric pressure at sea level). The customary abbreviations are:

Mcf: 1,000 cubic feet of gas

MMcf: 1 million cubic feet of gas

Bcf: 1 billion cubic feet of gas

Tcf: 1 trillion cubic feet of gas

An Mcf (1,000 cubic feet of gas) will meet the needs of most households that burn natural gas for heating and cooking for three or four days.

Natural gas is predominantly methane, but the actual composition—and the heat content per cubic foot—varies somewhat from source to source. Accordingly, natural gas is usually priced not in cubic feet but in British thermal units, or Btu. As of August 2014, the price of natural gas in the United States was approximately $3.90 per MMBtu and in Europe $6.50 per MMBtu.

A cubic foot of natural gas provides about 1,000 Btu, depending on the field it came from and on how it has been processed. Thus a Tcf of natural gas contains about a quadrillion Btu, also known as a quad.

The energy content of a barrel of crude oil is roughly equal to the energy content of 5.8 Mcf of natural gas.

Better Pipes

Putin has made the system bigger and smarter.

Some of the new pipelines lead to Europe, but, unlike older lines, they skirt troublesome countries. Other new lines run eastward, directly to growing, energy-hungry markets across Asia and to feed Russia's existing or planned LNG plants.

For many years, most Russian gas heading toward Europe flowed through a 930-mile-long, 40-inch pipe buried in Ukrainian soil. The original deal paid Ukraine a modest fee for allowing the gas to pass beneath the country's fields and plains, and as a sweetener, Russia sold gas to Ukraine for local use at below-market prices.

Many countries could have made such a win-win arrangement work nicely for both parties, but not that pair. Things quickly soured. Russia raised its prices. Ukraine stopped paying for the gas it used and started just helping itself to as much as it wanted. Russia pressed its neighbor to cede parts of its pipeline infrastructure as payment for what it owed.

The matter became so contentious that three times—in January 2006, March 2008, and January 2009—Russia slowed or stopped pumping gas into the pipelines running through Ukraine. On each occasion, Ukraine, along with 18 other European countries, suffered painful shortages in the dead of winter.

Putin tired of the headache of dealing with an antagonistic country. It has taken time, but Russia has come far in developing alternatives that work around the Ukraine problem.

"We are at the beginning of a long road of redirecting transit gas volumes from Ukrainian territory to our subsidiary Beltransgaz and our new undersea export routes," Gazprom spokesman Sergei Kupriyanov said in 2012 after Gazprom slashed export volumes through Ukraine by 50 percent for a day, in a stark warning to Kiev.

Beltransgaz owns a pipeline running from the gas fields of northwest Siberia through Belarus and on to Western Europe. Russia gained control of the pipeline in 2013 by buying Beltransgaz for $2.5 billion from the government of Belarus. (The bankrupt state had sought help from the International Monetary Fund and had just been turned away.) Russia is also financing a $10 billion nuclear power plant in Belarus, and it is selling gas to the country at less than half the standard price for European deliveries.

Putin traded reliance on Ukraine for reliance on Belarus. It was a trade up, because the latter isn't a troublemaker. There is no historical baggage of the kind that still burdens Russia's relationship with Ukraine. And Belarus is tied to Russia in ways that Ukraine is not. In particular, being a charter member of the CES customs union discussed in Chapter 4, Belarus is Russia's partner.

The new undersea route that Kupriyanov referred to is the Nord Stream pipeline. Nord Stream takes gas from Russia to Germany via a 759-mile segment along the floor of the Baltic Sea (the longest undersea pipeline in the world). It cost $20 billion to build and went fully operational in late 2012. It moves just under 1 Tcf of gas annually to Russia's European customers.

With Nord Stream completed and Beltransgaz in Russian hands, Putin had realized his dream of a secure, untroubled path for delivering Russian gas to Europe. It was time to get on with things in Asia. Pipelines and LNG ports to the east would enable Russia to enroll all the energy-hungry nations of Asia as paying customers and eventually as dependent customers.

The long arm for the planned reach into Asia was the proposed Altai pipeline, which would run from western Siberia through Russia's Far East and into China. The plan was stalled for years while the two countries dickered over details. The negotiations ended in a mammoth gas agreement in May 2014 (more about that later). The infrastructure build-out to move gas from Russia to China and money from China to Russia is now running at full speed.

Altai will link up with the Sakhalin-Khabarovsk-Vladivostok gas pipeline that Putin commissioned in 2011. And there's another possible linkup at Altai's eastern end: a spur through North Korea to deliver gas to South Korea. While the Korean line is just in the concept stage, North Korea seems open to the idea and to the $100 million per year it could earn in transit fees. Getting a big check can be more fun than pretending to be crazy.

Liquefied Natural Gas

Then there's the cold stuff, LNG.

The global market for natural gas is expanding almost as rapidly as the product does when it's not kept refrigerated. Driving the LNG industry are the growing preference for clean energy (gas is far cleaner than oil and far, far cleaner than the cleanest coal), the discovery of huge volumes of natural gas during the past decade, and new technology that cuts the cost of turning gas from a well into LNG and moving it from producer to user.

LNG has been around for a long time. The first patent was filed in 1914, and commercial production began three years later. The steps are: Purify the gas coming out of the ground to at least 90 percent methane. Reduce the temperature of the purified gas to minus 265°F, at which point it condenses to a liquid with just 1/600th the volume of the original gas. Then do something with it—which today means putting it on a ship heading toward a market that pipelines alone can't reach.

Liquefying flammable gas on an industrial scale is a hazardous process, and it consumes a lot of energy (equal to about 35 to 50 percent of the gas's energy value). Building a facility to do the job safely and efficiently is expensive—the bill for a terminal being built in Louisiana, for example, is approaching $10 billion. LNG is not an industry for small players.

Storing the finished product requires cryogenic tanks, which also are expensive. So most LNG isn't stored for long. It's moved, first by ship and then, when the ship reaches port, through a plant that gently warms and regasifies the product and sends it to users by pipeline.

LNG progressed from a big idea in 1914 to a big and fast-growing industry today because of technologies developed early in this century. The new methods cut the cost of building plants to produce LNG, terminals to receive and regasify it, and the specialized ships needed to move LNG between the two.

In 1990, global production capacity was 50 million tonnes (metric tons) per year. In 2013, it was five times that. Even with that growth, the industry still isn't mature. Only 19 countries currently are exporting LNG, and only 17 countries have facilities to receive it. Japan is by far the biggest importer, especially after the Fukushima disaster paralyzed its nuclear power industry. In 2013, the country imported 88 million metric tons of LNG, about a third of world production. South Korea is the second-biggest buyer.

Putin sees Russia playing a big role in this growing market, especially with so much demand for gas from areas in Asia that can't be reached economically with pipelines alone. To help speed things along, he has enticed international and domestic investors with tax incentives for LNG production and development.

There's already an LNG plant that condenses gas from the Sakhalin II project into 10 million tonnes of LNG per year, for sale to China, Japan, and South Korea. Putin aims to add 60 million tonnes of LNG capacity by 2020, starting with plants in the Primorye Territory and the Leningrad region.

The Shtokman Giant

Waiting in the far north is the behemoth offshore Shtokman field, owned 75 percent by Gazprom and 25 percent by France's Total S.A. It holds an estimated 137 Tcf of natural gas, making it one of the largest gas fields in the world.

The gas would move via a 600-kilometer undersea pipeline to south of Murmansk and then into Nord Stream. Some of it could go to feed an LNG plant proposed for the village of Teriberka, about 100 kilometers northeast of Murmansk.

Shtokman would be a *major* challenge to develop. Norway's Statoil was a 24 percent partner at one time, but in 2012 got cold feet, so to speak, and handed its shares back to Gazprom. The deposit lies 550 kilometers offshore, beneath the Barents Sea, in a neighborhood where conditions are as cold, icy, windy, and rough as they get. Because of the hostile environment, development costs could top $40 billion, so for now Shtokman is on hold, where it likely will remain until the price of gas in Europe rises above $12 per MMBtu.

European Burners

But wait, you may argue, isn't Europe's reliance on Russian gas on the wane?

It certainly seems that way if you look only at aggregate figures. In 2002, Russian gas imports met 45 percent of Europe's needs, a number that has receded to near 30 percent today. Much of the difference was picked up by Qatar, Libya, and Nigeria, sources not in the picture earlier.

The decline can be attributed in part to new LNG facilities in the United Kingdom, Netherlands, and Italy, which have increased the number of sources that can sell gas to Europeans. However, the macro numbers don't tell the entire story. LNG is available only to countries with an LNG regasification terminal, and to have a terminal, a country needs to lay out the capital to build it and also must have a workable coastal spot to build it on. Thus the number of LNG-enabled countries is limited.

Those that can't make use of LNG remain near or at total dependency on pipeline gas, and for now that means Russia. Finland and Slovakia get 100 percent of their gas from Russia, with Poland and the Czech Republic near 90 percent. Even Germany still sits at 40 percent. For those countries, Russia's importance as a natural gas supplier is little changed in this century.

Gazprom

And the company keeping gas flowing to Europe? It's Gazprom, the natural gas counterpart to oil giant Rosneft. (See Figure 8.2.) Together they give Putin a solid one-two punch of oil and gas supremacy in Europe.

Like Rosneft, Gazprom was a bit player at the start of the Yeltsin era. Then it was gutted by oligarchs during the shark-bite privatization period of the 1990s. Putin took a chewed-up Gazprom under his protection and transformed it from carcass to global player.

A history of Gazprom reveals a lot about Vladimir Vladimirovich.

When the USSR Ministry of Gas Industry was reorganized in 1989 (the same year the Berlin Wall fell), Gazovaya Promyshlennost ("gas industry" in Russian), or Gazprom for short, was born. But it was a state entity only briefly. A year after the breakup of the Soviet Union in 1991, the government decreed that the company would be privatized.

Gazprom had the advantage of inheriting all of Russia's assets in the former centrally controlled gas industry. It stormed out of the gates in 1993, producing more than twice the combined Russian natural gas of Chevron, British Petroleum (BP), Exxon Mobil, and Royal Dutch Shell. It looked like Gazprom was already in the big leagues.

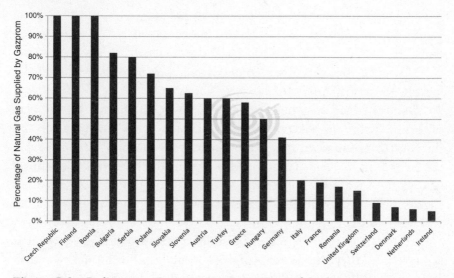

Figure 8.2 Reliance on Gazprom as a Percentage of Consumption
SOURCE: Energy Information Administration. © Casey Research 2014.

It wasn't. It was in a big swamp.

Gazprom had trouble collecting bills from hard-up customers, many of them old, Soviet-era utilities unused to competing in the marketplace. In many cases, to make the best of a bad account, Gazprom accepted in-kind payments. Unfortunately, textile factories and vacation excursions for employees couldn't pay for the maintenance and expansion Gazprom really needed.

To make matters worse, several former Soviet republics—most conspicuously Ukraine—had trouble paying for their natural gas imports or just outright refused. Things got so bad that in 1994, despite producing far more gas than Exxon, Gazprom collected only one-eighth as much revenue.

In 1996 Gazprom registered American depositary receipts (ADRs)[1] for its shares, so that they could be traded publicly in the United States. It also obtained a $2.5 billion loan from international investors on market terms. That gave it some breathing room and time to negotiate

---

[1] An American depositary receipt (ADR) is a receipt issued by a custodian in the United States to evidence ownership of stock in a foreign company that has not retained a stock transfer agent in the United States.

several lucrative contracts with foreign companies. It survived the 1998 Russian financial crisis, even slightly increasing its production during that year.

However, the company then nearly succumbed to the menace from within—its management.

Gazprom had long been evading taxes, with the occasional help of Prime Minister Viktor Chernomyrdin, a Yeltsin appointee and the longest-serving prime minister in Russian history. When Yeltsin removed him in 1998, Chernomyrdin returned to his old job as head of Gazprom, where he turned to full-on asset stripping. Board members eagerly went about parceling out Gazprom's properties to their buddies and relatives.

In one particularly egregious example, Gazprom sold a 32 percent stake in subsidiary Purgaz, valued at $400 million, for a total consideration of $1,200 (yes, one thousand two hundred dollars). Gazprom also lent $850 million to favored third parties at low rates while borrowing money at market rates. In total, between 1997 and 2000, Gazprom "sold" assets worth nearly $6 billion for just $325 million. After that, there wasn't much production left.

Enter Putin.

Almost immediately, the company's fortunes picked up. As he had in the oil sector, he moved early to rein in the Yeltsin-era oligarchs and disable them politically. Chernomyrdin got the boot in June 2000, 12 weeks after Putin was elected president. He was replaced by Dmitry Medvedev, one of the St. Petersburg boys and the man who would later inherit the presidency from Putin.

The next month, Putin replaced CEO Rem Vyahkirev with the little-known Alexei Miller, another longtime ally. Under Medvedev and Miller, the looting ended and the company set about recovering what it had lost. In one instance, they forced a competitor to sell back a 51 percent stake in Sibneftgaz—at a below-market price—by disconnecting the company from Gazprom's pipeline network.

Slowly, Gazprom regained its strength, and with that came better access to financing from abroad. At home, Gazprom entered the financial sector directly by establishing Gazprombank, now the country's third-largest bank (board chairman: the same Alexei Miller). An improving balance sheet enabled it to acquire more resource assets, modernize old facilities, and build new ones. In 2005, Russian state ownership rose past 50 percent.

In recent years, Gazprom has begun to see more competition within Russia from smaller firms as well as from foreign companies with production-sharing contracts. But Gazprom has made acquisitions of its own and is developing exploration projects in the Arctic that could host tens or perhaps hundreds of trillions of cubic feet of natural gas.

Gazprom has also staked out a position in the LNG market through its involvement with Sakhalin-II (on Sakhalin Island, north of Japan), one of the largest integrated oil and gas projects in the world.

Then there's shale gas. This is the stuff that used to be an uneconomic resource but now can be recovered profitably by fracking horizontal wells. Unconventional recovery has transformed the economies of areas that sit above large shale gas deposits, such as in North Dakota. Shale gas has moved the United States from net importer status to gas self-sufficiency.

And it's another resource in which Russia is rich, or likely so. Because the country has so much oil and gas waiting for conventional drilling, little attention has been given to measuring the unconventionally recoverable shale gas in the gigantic Bazenhov Formation in Siberia (at surface, an area as big as Texas and the Gulf of Mexico put together). A recent drive-by estimate put the recoverable resource at 285 Tcf and 350 million barrels of oil.

Gazprom has remained nearly mum on the subject, and what little the company has to say about the economic viability of shale gas is negative. That has led to criticism that Gazprom is behind the times in the unconventional game.

Or it may be slyly ahead of the game. I take the don't-need-no-shale comments as talk for public consumption, to discourage Europe's development of shale gas while the company quietly explores the opportunities. Like Putin, Gazprom's management and technical teams are far from stupid, and again like Putin, they're capable of a little deception to advance their purposes.

Gazprom is also expanding its delivery system with the South Stream pipeline.

South Stream was conceived in 2007, partly as a response to the European Union's Nabucco pipeline. Nabucco, envisioned back in

2002, would have carried gas from Azerbaijan all the way to Austria. It was intended to lessen Europe's dependence on both Russian gas and Russian pipelines. The plan, however, was abandoned in 2013, for both political and economic reasons.

Something similar may still come to pass, though. The Trans Anatolian Pipeline (TANAP), funded by Azerbaijan and Turkey to move gas to Turkey, should open by 2019. From there, a proposed Trans Adriatic Pipeline (TAP) would continue on through Greece and Albania and under the Adriatic Sea to southern Italy.

Although the TANAP/TAP line would reduce Europe's dependence on Russian gas, its capacity of 570 Bcf per year is only a third of what was planned for Nabucco and only 25 percent of what South Stream will deliver. It would cover just 1 percent of Europe's total consumption. And while Nabucco was a joint European project, TANAP/TAP would operate at the discretion of Turkey and Azerbaijan.

South Stream is progressing. It will run under the Black Sea and through Bulgaria and should come on line in 2018. Total cost: over $23 billion. It'll immediately be a big factor on the continent, delivering 2.3 Tcf of gas per year, or more than 6 percent of Europe's usage. And it will give Russia another route that bypasses Ukraine. The Russians intend to double its capacity by 2028.

With all that's going on in Europe, and with Russia already a major gas exporter, you might think that Putin would have little to no interest in developing production in Africa. But you'd be wrong.

Beyond Europe and Back

Quietly—over the past decade and even more so in recent months—Russia has been ramping up natural gas exploration and production in Nigeria, Egypt, Mozambique, and especially Algeria.

Russia and Algeria have a long history of close ties. Russia was the first to recognize Algeria's independence from France in the 1960s. Algeria was one of Russia's closest allies during the Cold War. The arms trade between them remains brisk. From 2003 to 2012, Algeria spent $54 billion abroad on military supplies, with over 90 percent of the money going to Russia. Those purchases accounted for 10 percent of Russia's total arms exports and made Algeria its third-biggest customer, after only China and India.

Whether out of gratitude or not, Gazprom was the first foreign company invited to participate in Algeria's petroleum industry, in 2006. The arrangement was recently extended to 2039. Their joint venture will explore and develop more than 30 prospective hydrocarbon deposits spread over an estimated 20 percent of Algeria's territory.

So what's going on here?

It's simple. Africa is the third-largest supplier of natural gas to the European Union, and by 2015 Moscow will control nearly half of Africa's production. That will put Moscow's hand on nearly 40 percent of Europe's gas supply. Moreover, Southern European countries like Italy and Spain, which don't depend on Russian pipelines but draw much of their natural gas from North Africa, would join the list of those sensitive to nudges from Putin.

Once again, Putin is thinking long term. When the infrastructure to process Africa's output is in place, nearly all of Europe will begin sliding into deep dependence on Russian-controlled gas. With Russia to the east and Africa to the south, the European Union will sit in an energy pincer that Putin can squeeze at any time for any reason.

Putin understands that being top dog in Europe isn't enough to be top dog in a world where European economies are stagnating and Asian economies are booming. Thus, while Gazprom seeks to heighten its influence in Europe, it's moving to expand its presence in the Far East as well.

The big prize there is, of course, the voracious energy market in China. (See Figure 8.3.) And by a big margin, there is no better source for the gas China needs than Russia. Perhaps because of centuries of mistrust between Russia and China, or perhaps because of the enormous size of the mutual benefit that was waiting for the two countries to come to terms, reaching a deal was a tortured process.

The sticking point was the pricing structure, which must protect both parties from market unknowns for a period of three decades. The two sides haggled for 11 long years. The agreement they finally reached and then signed in May 2014 derives prices for the gas from a formula driven by market prices of oil and oil products.

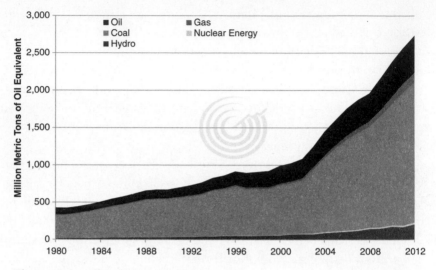

Figure 8.3   China's Energy Consumption
SOURCE: Energy Information Administration. © Casey Research 2014.

What finally brought the two parties to terms was perhaps the shared fun of demonstrating that U.S. participation in the great matters of the day isn't needed anymore. Beyond that, China wanted to clean up the coal-choked air of its coastal cities and avoid an approaching "airpocalypse." Replacing coal with gas to fuel electric generation plants would help. Putin wanted to open the Asian markets, which are natural consumers for its Siberian gas fields. It was a marriage made in Eurasia.

The 30-year agreement is huge. Gazprom will supply China National Petroleum Corporation with 1.3 Tcf of gas annually, about a quarter of China's current gas consumption. The contract is worth around $400 billion. Gas will begin flowing to China by 2019, perhaps in 2018.

To make it all happen, Russia will invest $55 billion and China will invest at least $20 billion, according to Putin. Plans call for building the long-delayed pipeline to link China's northeast to a line that carries gas from western Siberia to the Pacific port of Vladivostok. Developing a gas center there will also support Russian exports to Japan and South Korea.

"Without any overstatement, this will be the world's biggest construction project for the next four years," Putin said.

There was jubilation in Moscow. Putin's visit constituted a "major step toward a strategic partnership of the two nations," said Mikhail Margelov, head of the foreign affairs committee in the upper house of the Russian parliament.

Alexei Pushkov, head of the international affairs committee of the parliament's lower house, jabbed at the United States, adding, "The 30-year gas contract with China is of strategic significance. Obama should give up the policy of isolating Russia. It will not work."

With all the talk, the aspect of the deal that is most important for the United States never came up: What currency will be used in the gas transactions? Doing it all in rubles and yuan would be a damaging blow to dollar supremacy in the energy sector.

More on that later.

Chapter 9

The Putinization
of Uranium

On Friday, March 11, 2011, nature struck.

A monster, magnitude 9.0 earthquake grabbed the seabed 40 miles northeast of Honshu, in Japan. It tossed the entire island eight feet eastward and shifted the earth's axis by more than four inches. The shock generated tsunami waves that reached elevations of 130 feet and inundated areas six miles inland. Hundreds of thousands of people fled. Nearly 16,000 bodies were recovered and another 2,500 still are missing.

Lying in the tsunami's path were generators that fed the Fukushima Daiichi nuclear power plant's cooling system. They were disabled, and the cooling system stopped. Reactor core meltdowns followed. On the International Nuclear and Radiological Event Scale, it was a Level 7 disaster, matched only by Chernobyl.

In the aftermath of Fukushima—whose cleanup will take decades—the spot price of uranium yellowcake has dropped more than 60 percent, to $28 per pound (see Figure 9.1), and the stock prices of uranium miners

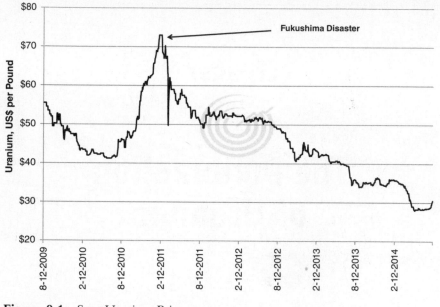

Figure 9.1   Spot Uranium Price
SOURCE: S&P Capital IQ. © Casey Research 2014.

have plunged between 60 and 85 percent. Japan shut down all 52 of its other reactors for safety evaluations. South Korea followed suit for its 23 reactors—although most have now been returned to service.

Fukushima rousted antinuclear protestors out of bed around the world. For them, the earthquake revealed nuclear power to the world for the terrible idea it had been all along. Germany announced it would shut down all 17 of its reactors, permanently, by 2022. It seemed that many other countries—perhaps all of them—would be closing their nuclear power plants as well.

Well, not so fast.

No one followed Germany's lead. Today, no fewer than 71 new plants are under construction, in more than a dozen countries, with another 163 planned and 329 proposed. (See Figure 9.2.) Many countries without nuclear power soon will build their first reactor, including Turkey, Kazakhstan, Indonesia, Vietnam, Egypt, Saudi Arabia, and several of the Gulf emirates.

While many countries with nuclear power plants declared a time-out to reassess safety practices, almost all are staying with what they have. Uranium is still the only fuel that can produce base-load electricity

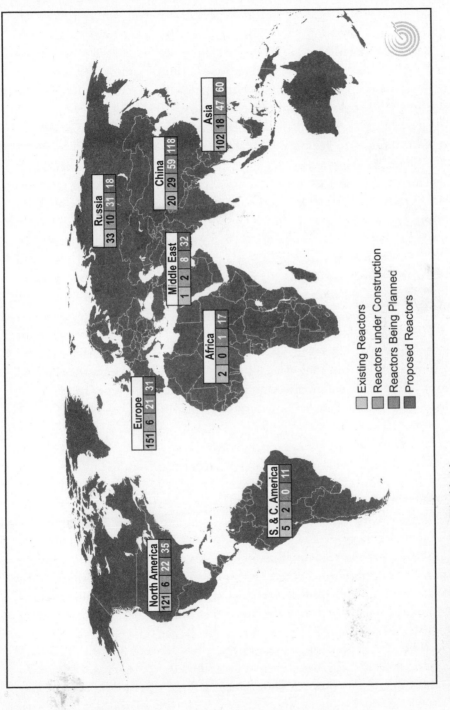

Figure 9.2 Nuclear Reactors Worldwide

economically and without exhaling greenhouse gases and other unwelcome hydrocarbons.

In the United States, which hasn't opened a nuclear power plant since 1977, six new units are scheduled to come online by 2020, four from license applications made since mid-2007. The country is the world's biggest producer of nuclear energy, accounting for more than 30 percent of the worldwide total. Its 65 nuclear plants (housing just over 100 reactors) generate 20 percent of U.S. electricity.

France is the country most dependent on uranium; 75 percent of its electricity comes from nuclear power. China, whose urban residents are choking on pollution from coal-fired plants, is now on a nuclear-construction fast track. It already has 17 reactors in operation, and 29 more are being built. The country wants a fourfold capacity increase by 2020. India has 20 plants and is adding seven more. Several countries in Africa, where more than 90 percent of the population goes without electricity, have begun to explore the possibility.

New facilities are going to be safer, too, especially after Fukushima exposed the vulnerabilities of older designs. Though the containment systems at Fukushima were far more robust than the buckets that held the Chernobyl reactors, they were 40 years old, several generations behind today's containment engineering and materials. Fukushima would soon have been a candidate for decommissioning.

Long-Term Shortage

While Germany *may* be able to get by without nuclear power plants (although its carbon footprint is spreading, and it's already fudging by importing nuclear-generated electricity from France), none of the other countries using or readying for nuclear power can. There's just no alternative. That means the demand for uranium will rise as both the world's economy and its discomfort over fossil fuels grow. And that means profits and political leverage for any country that might dominate the uranium industry.

The World Nuclear Association predicts demand growth of 33 percent from 2010 to 2020 and similar growth in the 10 years that follow. In 2011, the world consumed 160 million pounds of yellowcake uranium.

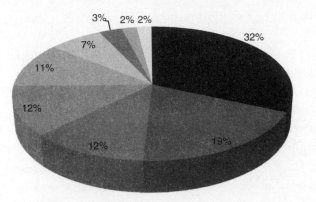

Figure 9.3   EU-27 Sources of Uranium, 2010
Source: Energy Information Administration. © Casey Research 2012.

By 2024, just 10 years from now, it will be chewing through 200 million pounds annually—if it's available.

At the same time, a supply crunch is building. In 2012, the world consumed 25 percent more uranium than came out of its mines, a shortfall of 40 million pounds (at current long-term prices, about $1.8 billion worth). The deficit is likely to rise to 55 million pounds by 2020. Uranium mines are few and far between. Only 20 countries have even one, and half of global production comes from just 10 mines in six countries. (Sources for the European Union are shown in Figure 9.3.)

In the United States, 100 reactors are burning fuel from 43 million pounds of uranium per year to produce electricity. Supply from U.S. mines is about 4 million pounds, or only 9 percent of what's needed to keep those plants running.

Here's another way of looking at it: The estimated needs of U.S. nuclear power plants between now and 2021 come in at around 275 million pounds of yellowcake. *The country's entire inventory* amounts to only 120 million pounds.

In the long run, more mining is the only answer. But a new uranium mine is more difficult to bring into production than any other kind of resource. Given the engineering challenges, environmental and safety requirements, and strict permitting, it takes 10 years, minimum, to get from decision to production. New mines are not coming online quickly enough to meet expected growth in consumption. And the world *already* is using more than it digs out of the ground. In fact, it has been doing so for the past 20 years.

If every uranium mine proposed in the past decade were approved, built, and commissioned on schedule, supplies *might* be able to keep up. But current uranium prices are too low to entice any company to build those potential mines, and any risk taker that might decide to gamble on rising prices would face the separate risk of regulatory delay. Getting the permits to build a uranium mine is not like standing in line for an hour at the Department of Motor Vehicles. You have to stand in many lines for many years while you wait for decision makers to find the courage to confront the radiation bogeyman.

A shortage is coming, and Putin is preparing to turn it into a cash register and also into a tool of geopolitics. Controlling in-the-ground resources is just part of Putin's plan. Understanding the whole plan requires a brief detour.

Science Lesson

The uranium fuel cycle starts with digging uranium-bearing ore out of the ground and then subjecting it to a chemical process that extracts the uranium oxides (chiefly U_3O_8). The dried product is a powder called yellowcake. You can guess the color.

Of the uranium atoms in a pile of yellowcake, more than 99 percent are U-238, a barely radioactive isotope that cannot sustain a chain reaction for a power plant, bomb, or any other purpose. Virtually all the rest of the uranium atoms, about 0.7 percent, are U-235 (the number difference indicating three fewer neutrons), which is a somewhat more radioactive isotope that in quantities of just a few pounds can sustain a chain reaction. U-235 has that capability because when an atom of the stuff splits, it flings out neutrons with just the right velocity for splitting any other U-235 atoms they encounter. It's like one drunk starting a fight that spreads through an entire barroom.

To turn the yellowcake into something useful, enough of the U-238 must be separated out so that the concentration of U-235 in the remaining material is:

- 3 to 10 percent for use in a commercial nuclear power plant
- 20 percent for use in certain types of research and medical reactors

- 20 to 90 percent for use in the compact power plants of submarines
- 90 percent for use in weapons

Moving from the 0.7 percent U-235 concentration provided by nature to something higher begins with introducing fluorine to the uranium oxides. That produces uranium hexafluoride (UF_6), which at room temperature is a gas.

Next, the uranium hexafluoride gas is pumped through a system that exploits the slight weight difference between an atom of U-235 and an atom of U-238 (whose greater weight comes from its three additional neutrons). There are half a dozen clever techniques for doing this, but only two are in commercial use. One is to spin the gas through a series of ultra-high-speed centrifuges. The other is to pump the gas through a series of ultrafine filters.

With either technique, each step in the series yields two streams of gas, one slightly higher in U-235 and one slightly lower in U-235 than the gas that went into the step. After the gas has passed through many centrifuges or through many filters, the process ends with two tanks of uranium hexafluoride. One contains the desired concentration of U-235, and one contains U-238 with traces of U-235 well below nature's 0.7 percent. The contents of that second tank are referred to as tails. For easier long-term storage, the tail gas may be reconverted to a uranium oxide.

For fuel, the final step is fabrication. The enriched gas (with the desired concentration of U-235) is chemically processed into uranium dioxide powder. The powder is compressed into pellets, heated until it coalesces into a ceramic, and then bundled into rod-shaped fuel assemblies tailored for a particular kind of reactor.

The current uranium enrichment capacities of several nations is shown in Figure 9.4.

Short-Term Fixes

An adequate supply of uranium is available today to fuel the world's reactors only because a secondary supply is filling the gap between usage and primary supply from mines. Most of that secondary supply involves Russia.

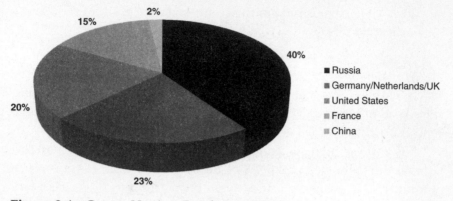

Figure 9.4 Current Uranium Enrichment Capacity
© Casey Research 2014.

When the USSR collapsed, Russia inherited over 2 million pounds of weapons-grade uranium and vast, underused facilities for handling and fabricating the material. Starting in 1993, the two were brought together under the Megatons to Megawatts agreement between Russia and the United States. Over the 20 years that followed, 1.1 million pounds of Russian warhead-grade uranium (90 percent U-235), equivalent to 20,000 nuclear warheads, was blended down to 33 million pounds of reactor-grade uranium (3 percent U-235) by diluting it with tails—enrichment in reverse. The resulting product was sold to the United States.

Megatons to Megawatts helped to fill the supply gap for two decades but now is history. Its expiration in November 2013 marked the end to 24 million pounds of annual uranium supply, 55 percent of what the United States had been using.

During the Megatons to Megawatts period, Russia operated a separate stream of secondary production. It put its excess enrichment capacity to work on other people's tails. In the 1990s and early 2000s, Russia accepted boatloads of ready-to-process tails from major players like Areva (Canadian) and Urenco (a European consortium). Today that sideline also is history.

The United States now contributes to secondary supply in a modest way. During the Megatons era, the United States also was converting unwanted warhead material to fuel. But only one American company,

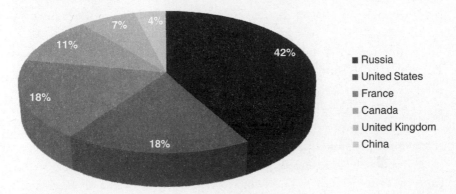

Figure 9.5 Uranium Conversion Capacity
© Casey Research 2014.

WesDyne International, has facilities for downblending weapons-grade uranium to fuel grade, and its capacity is less than 18,000 pounds per year. (Russia's capacity is more than five times that.) (See Figure 9.5.)

So while the United States has plenty of warhead uranium to feed downblending plants, it doesn't have much plant capacity to feed it into. To speed things up, it would have to send the material to Russia for conversion to fuel. Imagine the screaming if any U.S. politician proposed handing nuclear warhead material to Mr. Putin.

Today Russia is producing enriched uranium from its own stockpile of tails, in addition to enriching the output from Russian mines. As a producer of uranium ore, Russia is in sixth place; however, when the former Soviet states combine their production, Kazakhstan, Uzbekistan, and Russia make up almost half the global uranium production. As a producer of enriched uranium, Russia is number one. It supplies over 40 percent of the world's enriched uranium, mostly to power plants.

Putin's Uranium Superstore

Russia now ranks sixth in the world for mine production of uranium. On top of that, Putin carries a lot of clout in neighboring Kazakhstan, a member of the Common Economic Space (CES) customs union and the world's top primary uranium producer, with 38 percent of the total.

So Russia already has its hands on 47 percent of the world's primary production.

Control over so much capacity for mining and enrichment makes Putin the go-to source for countries desperate to secure long-term supplies of reactor fuel. In 2012, for example, Russia signed an agreement with Japan—which, despite Fukushima, can't afford to give up on nuclear power—that guarantees the availability of uranium enrichment services for Japanese utilities.

Russia will continue supplying the United States as well, but this time on Russian terms. The Megatons agreement didn't let Russia sell directly to American utilities—only to the U.S. Enrichment Corporation (USEC), at a set, below-market price. And the only product eligible was downblended warhead uranium—nothing from new mine production. It was because of those and other restrictions that Russia made no effort to extend Megatons past 2013.

In 2012, Tenex, Russia's nuclear fuel exporter, reached six-year deals to supply more than $1 billion worth of reactor fuel to four American utilities. It has also contracted to provide enrichment services to USEC for nine years. Annual deliveries under the USEC contract should be about half of those under Megatons. There is no price ceiling, and there are no conditions on where the uranium comes from.

Putin has also captured long-term customers for Russian uranium in countries where Rosatom, Russia's state nuclear utility, is building reactors.

Rosatom is a giant in the global nuclear sector. The company builds more nuclear power plants worldwide than anyone else, with construction currently under way in China, Vietnam, India, and Turkey. The 21 projects now on Rosatom's order book are worth $50 billion. Iran plans to buy at least eight new nuclear reactors, and the Russians are ready to build and operate the projects *and* supply the fuel. While the United States dithers over Ukraine, Putin is cementing more long-term contracts into place.

Moreover, many of those new facilities come with a life-of-plant fuel supply contract, such as the one Rosatom recently signed with Bangladesh for its first nuclear power plant. Putin understands the meaning of "full-service provider."

Rosatom also handles $3 billion per year of Russian uranium exports to other customers. One-fifth of the material goes to the Asia-Pacific region, a market growing so quickly that Rosatom is building a new uranium products transportation hub at Vladivostok, Russia's largest Pacific port.

The Ultimate Source

Putin has been locking up mine production outside of Russia. In mid-2010, AtomRedMetZoloto (ARMZ, an arm of state-owned Rosatom) boosted its stake in Uranium One, one of the largest publicly traded uranium producers in the world, from 17 percent to 51 percent. At the time, ARMZ wanted to use Uranium One as a public vehicle to attract investors for its expansion plans.

That notion evaporated when Fukushima killed investor interest in uranium. Thus, in 2013, it acquired all of the remaining shares in Uranium One for $1.3 billion and took the company private at over 100 percent premium to the market price of the shares at the time. The timing was right.

Uranium One is a major producer, with 16 million pounds per year. Through the acquisition, Russia picked up mining operations in Australia, Canada, Kazakhstan, South Africa, Tanzania, and even the United States, where it will now produce more uranium each year than all American mining companies combined.

Russia has signed uranium exploration and development agreements with Japan, France, India, South Korea, and Canada. ARMZ is already involved in joint production projects with Kazakhstan's state-owned Kazatomprom, the world's largest producer of uranium.

Russia has also been courting Namibia, which possesses 5 percent of the world's known uranium reserves. It is already a big producer and is expected to become the number two yellowcake exporter by 2018, after Kazakhstan.

Egypt has a place in Putin's plan as well. After a 2013 meeting with then-President Mohamed Morsi, it was announced that the two countries would "resume cooperation in peaceful nuclear projects," including construction of nuclear power plants. Cairo wants 4 gigawatts of nuclear generating capacity by 2025, enough to power about 3 million homes. Egypt also invited Moscow to cooperate in the joint development of uranium mines. Given the benefits to Egypt, the agreements are likely to survive Morsi's overthrow.

Going to School in Mongolia

Russia is willing to go pretty far to get what it wants. Though Putin shies away from waging war over resources—preferring to let other countries do the dirty work, then step in for a share of the spoils, as in Iraq—he's not shy about economic warfare. Consider events in Mongolia, one of those bordering nations, like Ukraine, that Russia proprietarily considers part of its "near-beyond."

Russia was the first developer of Mongolia's 7,500-acre Dornod deposit. The Soviets and then the Russians mined it from 1988 to 1995, with a workforce that peaked near 10,000. Russia spent $150 million on developing the site but then abandoned it in 1995, during the turbulent time when the money supply from Moscow had all but dried up.

Despite leaving, Russia never lost its sense of entitlement for Dornod.

The project sat idle until 2003. Then the Mongolian government opened it to Western mining interests. It was snapped up by a small Canadian company, Khan Resources, which took a majority stake and also took on the Mongolian government as a partner.

Then Khan got clipped by Putin.

In January 2009, Russia and Mongolia announced a joint venture for uranium extraction. Next, in January 2010, the Mongolian parliament bestowed upon the Mongolian government a 51 percent share in every project in which the Mongolian government had an investment. That included Dornod. Thus Khan lost control of the project through a no-compensation expropriation; that is, they were robbed.

The matter is now entombed in international litigation. Whatever Khan recovers in the legal fight, if anything, will go to the lawyers—another dead client for dinner.

There is no question that the impetus for squeezing out Khan came from Moscow. The focus of then-Prime Minister Putin's July 2009 visit to Mongolia was uranium. And it was no coincidence that then-President Medvedev would show up in Ulaanbaatar a month later, bringing ARMZ's president with him. Guess what they were there to discuss.

Relations between the Russian leadership and Mongolia's President Tsakhiagiin Elbegdorj seemed to turn chilly over the course of 2010. That's when the economic screws were beginning to turn. During the summer of 2011, there was an unexplained interruption of Russian diesel fuel deliveries, which threatened Mongolia's harvest. The message to Elbegdorj seemed clear: Toe the line on uranium or face unpleasant consequences.

As Russia has been consolidating its position in Mongolia, U.S. efforts in the country have crashed and burned. In 2011, the Mongolian government was in secret negotiations with Japan and the United States over "nuclear fuel lease contracts," under which it would process uranium into nuclear fuel and export it. In return, Mongolia would agree to take back spent nuclear fuel from its foreign customers.

The United States was deeply involved in the talks. Both the supply and disposal features were very appealing. And Mongolia (with U.S. support) had a lot to gain. First, the country would establish itself as an accredited dump for nuclear waste. Then it would sell nuclear fuel with a commitment to take it back when it was spent—like an old-time milkman who would pick up the empty bottles. Mongolia would immediately become an important, not to mention independent, player in the worldwide uranium fuel business.

In September 2011, President Elbegdorj abruptly pulled the plug. The ostensible reason, as he described it, was that the nuclear waste of other countries is a "snake grown up in another body. ... Receiving back the nuclear waste after exploiting and exporting uranium must not be, as I think this is, a pressure from foreign superpowers, and we must throw out this delusion." So a law was passed banning the importation, transit, or storage of nuclear waste.

Perhaps Elbegdorj's concerns were genuine. But many would see the hand of Vladimir Putin once more at work.

Today Mongolia finds itself in the unenviable position of being down to just one partner for developing its uranium industry: Russia. And apparently Mongolia will have but a single role: provider of feedstock to ARMZ. Russia is now firmly entrenched at Dornod, and Mongolia—its uranium supplies for commercial purposes largely in Putin's hands—will join Kazakhstan as an obedient foreign client.

Toward the Endgame

With all of this going on, Rosatom's head honcho Sergei Kiriyenko was bursting with enthusiasm when he spoke with Putin at a January 2014 meeting. He predicted that Russia's recent production rate of six and a half million pounds of uranium annually would soon almost triple. "In 2015, we will reach 8,400 tons [a year], and the prime cost will be completely different," Kiriyenko said. That's 18.5 million pounds.

It wasn't empty talk. Rosatom puts Russia's uranium reserves at 1.2 billion pounds of yellowcake, which would be the second largest in the world; the company is quite capable of mining 40 million pounds per year by 2020. Add in Russia's foreign projects in Kazakhstan, Ukraine, Uzbekistan, and Mongolia, and annual production in 2020 jumps to more than 63 million pounds. Include all of Russia's sphere of influence, and production easily could amount to more than 140 million pounds per year by 2020.

No other country has a uranium mining plan nearly this ambitious. By 2020, Russia itself could be producing a third of all yellowcake. With Kazakhstan chipping in another 25 percent, Russia would have effective control of more than half of the world's supply.

Russian dominance doesn't stop there.

Globally, there are a fair number of facilities for fabricating fuel rods. Not so with conversion plants (uranium oxide to uranium hexafluoride) or enrichment plants (isolating the U-235). The world leader in conversion and enrichment is … a country where people speak Russian.

Russia's main conversion facility, in Angarsk, in the Irkutsk region of Russia, turns out 44 million pounds of uranium hexafluoride per year, with a smaller facility, in Seversk, in the Tomsk region, contributing another 22 million. All told, Russia has one-third of all uranium conversion capacity. The United States is in second place, with 18 percent. Russia's share is projected to rise, assuming Rosatom proceeds with a new conversion plant planned for 2015.

Similarly, Russia owns 40 percent of the world's enrichment capacity. Planned expansion of the existing facilities will push that share close to 50 percent.

While yellowcake production is important for controlling the market, it's not the critical element. Kazakhstan increased uranium production fivefold in a decade. Other countries, such as Russia, Namibia, and Mongolia, are capable of matching that production growth rate. But owning all the yellowcake on the planet won't help you one bit without the ability to turn it into something a nuclear reactor can use.

The choke point in the whole process isn't in the mines but in the conversion and enrichment facilities that turn yellowcake into nuclear fuel.

That's Putin's goal: to corner the conversion and enrichment markets. It's a smart strategy, too—control those, and you control the availability and pricing of a product whose demand will be rising for decades. And that control will tighten, because the barrier to entry for either function is very high. Building new conversion or enrichment facilities is too costly for most countries, and it is difficult in the West due to the influence of the NIMBY (not in my backyard) crowd.

Here's where Russia stands: on track to control 58 percent of global yellowcake production, currently responsible for a third of yellowcake-to-uranium-hexafluoride conversion, and soon to hold half of all global enrichment capacity.

There's a word for this: stranglehold.

The Transient Surplus

Putin's plan has required patience because, despite the inevitability of rising demand, the uranium market has been in the doldrums since the Fukushima meltdown in 2011. No one I know predicted that a single event would swamp the effect of all the billions of dollars spent in the past decade on reactor development. But that's what happened.

Post-Fukushima, the price of yellowcake dropped more than 60 percent, from $72 per pound before the event to around $28, its nine-year low. Share prices of uranium producers have been hammered. They've been losing money, so they're shutting mines.

As noted, though, Fukushima didn't scare the world away from atomic energy. So what are the reasons for the price drop?

First and foremost, there's Japan hitting the pause button for its entire nuclear industry. The country accounted for 13 percent of global nuclear power generation, and since Fukushima, all 50 of its plants have been shut. Most will come back into operation, but it will take time, with only the first half-dozen or so expected to return to service by 2015. That's a big blow to the demand side of the uranium market.

And there's selling from stockpiles. Japanese utilities were holding three years of uranium inventory when the plants went down, and they have since received a further two years of supplies they had committed to buy under long-term contracts. Rather than sit on it all, the Japanese dumped much of it on the spot market (delivery now for payment now).

That had a big impact, because normally the spot market accounts for only 10 percent of all uranium transactions. The other 90 percent is sold under long-term contracts, at prices that generally work out to be 45 percent or so above spot. Utilities use long-term contracts, with their higher expected prices, to ensure delivery of uranium years ahead. The alternative would be to gamble on the volatile spot market.

The sellers—Japan and South Korea, the latter of which had put some of its own inventory on the market while its reactors were shut—took a beating, since they had bought at higher prices. But one man's loss is another's gain. Buyers were able to build up their own stockpiles on the cheap. Japan hasn't named the countries it sold to, but I believe Russia was one of the big buyers. Russia would be content to hold it for years, awaiting the inevitable rebound.

All around the world, Fukushima accelerated the retirement of several older reactors, adding to the one-time sales of uranium in the spot market. The hurried-up decommissioning of the San Onofre nuclear plant in California, for example, released about 10 million pounds.

A second price hit came from the U.S. Department of Energy. In 2013, ConverDyn—the only U.S. plant for conversion of yellowcake to uranium hexafluoride gas—was shut down for most of the year, for planned maintenance. Without a conversion plant, supplies of yellow-cake were building up. So what did the Department of Energy, the largest warehouser of both yellowcake and uranium hexafluoride in the United States, do? It began selling both forms of uranium in quantity.

Further, in July 2013, the agency released a new plan for "excess uranium inventory." An earlier plan, adopted in 2008, capped sales at 10 percent of the total annual fuel requirements of all U.S. nuclear plants. The new plan has no such cap. How much the Department of Energy will sell isn't known, but 7 to 10 million pounds per year wouldn't be surprising.

Finally, as noted earlier, low-cost U-235 from tails (Russian, naturally) is flooding the market. That will continue until about 2018, at which time all the cheap uranium will be gone, and primary production will return as the driving factor.

Sure, the present supply glut keeps prices depressed, which in itself seems bad for a big producer like Russia—but not if the big producer is as smart and future-focused as Russia is. While it has been waiting for higher prices, the country has disposed of surplus tails, stockpiled physical uranium, and picked up distressed assets (like Uranium One) at rock-bottom prices.

Russia has set itself up for muscular influence over everything related to uranium, especially in Europe, where Russia itself provides 32 percent of the uranium entering the EU, and Kazakhstan and Uzbekistan provide another 19 percent.

So, just as Europe relies on Russia for its natural gas, it is even more dependent on Russia for uranium.

Nuclear power has been the world's fastest-growing source of industrial-scale energy in every decade since the 1950s. That's not going to change, however loudly the green drums pound in Germany. Putin sees the payoff for winning the race for uranium. He has already given Russia a significant head start, and he's still running faster than anyone else. No one in the United States or Europe has even entered the race.

Chapter 10

The Middle East: Oil, Wars, and the Great Game

A cross the world, oil drives machines. In the Middle East, it drives history as well, and it has been doing so since the early twentieth century. That's true not just of the three dominant producers—Iraq, Iran, and Saudi Arabia—but of every country in the region, including those with no oil at all.

The Middle East is a rough and noisy neighborhood. For an outsider, the turmoil is less bewildering if you notice a critical fact: In the Middle East, nation-states are the exception. Egypt—where most people (90 percent or so) share an ethnicity (Arab), a religion (Sunni Islam), and historical circumstance (dependence on a great river)—is the region's only country that's nearly monolithic. Iran, which is united by its own language (Farsi) and religion (93 percent Shi'a Muslim), is also a nation-state; although only 65 percent of the population share the primary ethnicity (Persian), none of the other ethnic groups are able to compete for control of the country. (See Figure 10.1.)

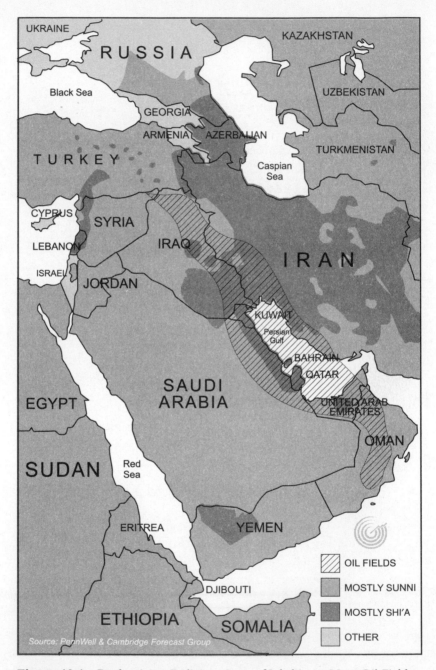

Figure 10.1   Predominant Religious Sects of Inhabitants Near Oil Fields
SOURCE: Pew Research Center, U.S. Department of State.

Iraq, in contrast, is divided along a Shi'a majority and a Sunni minority that at times dominates. It is also divided on a separate axis between Arabs and a Kurdish minority with its own language, its own local oil treasure, and the pull of large Kurdish minorities in Turkey, Syria, and Iran.

Syria is primarily Arab but, as you now know, has a sizable Kurdish population. Religious affiliation in Syria is predominately Sunni, but the government has long been controlled by Alawites, whose religion is an offshoot of Shi'a Islam. Syria also has a sizable Christian minority and houses a living museum of ancient religions, all of whose adherents, together with the Christians, tend toward political alliance with the Alawites.

Lebanon has all of the above and more, including an autonomous military organization that is deeply indebted to Iran for money and weapons and that shares Iran's hostility toward Israel.

Libya, although simply Arab and simply Sunni, is a collection of tribes, not a nation and only intermittently a state.

Turkey is all Sunni, but it is the rump of a long-gone empire, is conflicted between an Islamic heritage and an infatuation with Europe, and is home to a Kurdish minority whose fertility is pushing the Kurds toward majority status, perhaps within a generation or two.

Vladimir Putin's plan to undo the petrodollar and elbow the United States out of the way in world affairs rests on the energy resources of the Middle East. Turmoil there is his best friend, which is reason enough for a careful look at the recent histories of the region's three big oil producers (which pump 20 percent of the world's oil) and their neighbors.

Religion is a divider that can unite Middle Easterners living under different governments in the important business of attacking their own countrymen. Conflict between Shi'a and Sunni in one country induces conflict between the same two groups in other countries. It happens easily, almost unavoidably, because the differences between the two traditions are not details, like the differences between one-button Baptists and two-button Baptists. The differences are absolutes. No one has found any room, even in principle, for reconciling them. The career of any would-be ecumenical, should one appear, would likely be brief.

What separates Sunni from Shi'a is a succession dispute that erupted after the death of Mohammed in 632 AD. Those who accepted Abu Bakr, Mohammed's father-in-law, as the rightful successor became known as Sunnis. Those who believed that Ali, Mohammed's son-in-law, was properly the successor became known as Shi'ites. They've been fighting ever since.

Worldwide, about 85 percent of all Muslims are Sunni. However, in two of the Middle East's three biggest oil-producing countries, Iran and Iraq, they are outnumbered by a Shi'a majority. The third, Saudi Arabia, is overwhelmingly Sunni—although its restless Shi'a minority is concentrated inconveniently in the country's oil-producing east.

Iran: Sanctions, Coups, and Revolutions

Let's start with a known name, Winston Churchill.

Churchill is remembered by most as England's World War II prime minister, but there is much else to remember about him. At the time he was rallying his countrymen to oppose the Nazis, he was already in his sixties. Three decades earlier, in 1911, before World War I, he was First Lord of the Admiralty, with responsibility for the Royal Navy. Being more a visionary than a functionary, he set out to bring the Royal Navy's aging fleet into the twentieth century.

The Royal Navy still dominated the oceans of the world, but it was in danger of falling behind the Americans and, more ominously, the Germans. To keep up, Britain needed ships with the efficiencies that oil had made possible.

Most ships of the Royal Navy still burned coal, which Britain had in abundance but which was not nearly as well suited for warships as oil was proving to be. A pound or a cubic foot of the new stuff, oil, yielded far more energy, more go-power, than the same amount of coal. Oil burned without need for heavy, space-eating furnaces and required less shipboard manpower for handling. The economies of space and weight for carrying the fuel, for burning the fuel, and for feeding and berthing fuel handlers made oil essential for ships that could win wars.

Building oil-fueled naval ships would be expensive but in no way difficult for Britain. The difficulty was the oil: The British Isles didn't have any. So securing a reliable supply of oil became a matter of paramount importance to Churchill.

He also considered how technology would change ground warfare. It was still the business of armies to establish lines, dig trenches, lay barbed wire, and mass troops to attack an enemy that was doing the same things with trenches, wire, and troops. Churchill saw beyond that. He encouraged the development of armed, armored vehicles powered by internal combustion engines, vehicles that could push through barbed wire, roll over trenches, and annihilate enemy troops. Tanks (as they came to be called from British disinformation that they were water carriers) would need still more oil.

But where to get it?

The Americans were in their first oil rushes in Texas and California. That was one possible source, but American oil was an ocean away. Russia? It was a big producer but was also a rival empire, and its output was controlled by the Rothschilds, who couldn't be relied upon.

The ambitions of a Briton, William K. D'Arcy, found what Churchill was looking for. In 1900 D'Arcy, whose interest had been attracted by Persia's natural oil seeps, paid the ruler, Mozaffar al-Din Shah Qajar, £20,000 for a 60-year concession to explore for oil in an area of 480,000 square miles, which was the entire country save for five provinces in the north. The Persian government reserved a royalty of 16 percent of the oil company's profit.

After exhausting his personal fortune in exploring the area, D'Arcy farmed out most of the concession to Burmah Oil, which spent another £500,000 on exploration. In 1908, on the last hole their budget could cover, Burmah drilled into a major oil reserve. The following year, to exploit the mammoth opportunity the well had proven, Burmah Oil formed a subsidiary, Anglo-Persian Oil Company (APOC), which would later become the British supermajor BP.

Developing an oil field takes capital, especially in a land short on modern infrastructure. So APOC needed to raise money. In May 1914, at Churchill's urging, the British government provided the money in exchange for 51 percent of the company and the right to appoint directors to the board who would have controlling authority on any question relating to the British national interest. Additionally, the Royal Navy was guaranteed a 30-year oil supply at a fixed price.

It was a brilliant bit of maneuvering by Churchill. Britain had beaten the Germans to the first great Middle Eastern oil reservoir, and they would draw on it to win the war that started three months later.

After World War I, Reza Khan, an officer in the Persian Cossack Brigade, made himself indispensable to the shah by suppressing rebellions, establishing order, and driving out British and Soviet occupations. He became the most powerful man in the country. In 1925, he deposed Ahmad Shah Qajar and installed a compliant Majles (parliament) that declared him the head of a constitutional monarchy. Reza Khan, who had adopted the surname Pahlavi, became the new shah. The Pahlavi family would rule Persia—in 1935 renamed the Imperial State of Iran— for the next 54 years.

Reza Shah intended to be a modernizer. He planned to develop highways, railways, and a national public education system—everything needed to support large-scale industry. He would reform the judiciary and introduce European medical care. And to do all that, he needed a strong, centralized government with educated personnel. So he sent hundreds of Iranians, including his son, to Europe for schooling.

His project was costly. Reza Khan recognized that only oil revenue would carry Iran into the modern world, and that without it just keeping his personal power would be difficult. But under the D'Arcy deal, most of the enormous oil profits were going to foreigners. The shah wanted a new agreement, but the British, understandably, were in no hurry.

Reza Khan was running short of cash. By 1931, price inflation in Iran's local currency (the rial) was topping 45 percent. The government needed £5,000,000 to complete the railway, hospitals, and schools APOC had promised but had failed to deliver. And, of course, Reza Khan needed money to maintain the loyalty of his army.

So he threatened to terminate the original concession unless APOC (1) gave the Iranian government a 25 percent share of the company, (2) paid a production royalty, and (3) relinquished more than half of the concession's original territory.

APOC refused. The shah then made good on this threat to cancel the concession, but it wasn't the end of the matter; it was a negotiating tactic. The shah was more than willing to grant a new concession to APOC, and APOC wanted to stay in the game. They needed each other.

In mid-1933, the two parties agreed to a new, 60-year concession. From the shah's point of view, the terms were much improved. APOC would give the government:

- An immediate payment of £1,000,000
- A 20 percent share of the company
- An oil production royalty, in gold, of four cents per ton
- A tax of 4 percent on net profits from operations in Iran, subject to an annual minimum of £750,000

In addition, APOC would:

- Accept government-appointed corporate directors
- Subsidize petroleum products for local consumption
- Give up parts of the original concession area
- Give up the exclusive right to transport oil in Iran

The new deal made room for Iran to invite other companies to help develop the country's oil resources, which could mean more revenue and certainly meant an end to dependence on APOC. But whom to invite?

The Soviets offered to jump in, but Reza Khan didn't trust them. The Germans were eager to get their foot in the door, and politically they would be a counterbalance to the British. They had the technology and the money, and they were open to a 50–50 deal.

In 1935, though, he chose the Americans. The United States was a rising power, and the shah saw it as a better political proposition than the country that had just lost World War I. Hedging a little, however, the shah allowed German petroleum technicians to stay.

U.S. oil companies, including Standard Oil of New Jersey (later Exxon) and Standard Oil of California (later Chevron), were itching to get into Iran. They wanted the newly opened lands, and they planned to build pipelines to ports on the Gulf of Oman and the Persian Gulf, which would cut out the Germans and the Russians.

With all the aggressive jockeying for position within their country, Iranians built up a lot of resentment toward Britain and the United States. Nearly all the high-paying jobs went to foreigners, and almost none of the benefits the shah had led the public to expect from the oil industry materialized. With the shah's blessing, Iranian politicians stoked the resentment, painting the foreigners as thieves stealing from the people by paying so little for the oil, and as fraudsters who promised hospitals and schools they never built. But at bottom, the government was desperate for the money foreigners could deliver.

In 1939, just before the start of World War II, the British government agreed to lend the then-needy shah £5,000,000, to be repaid out of future oil production.

The British government also had declared an exchange rate for gold different from the rate in the free market. Thus the promised "four cents" in gold per ton of oil production resulted in less gold for the Iranian government.

Reza Khan could see that he was being shortchanged by the British. So he rejected the British loan offer and canceled the concessions from which the Anglo-Iranian Oil Company (AIOC, the successor to APOC) derived its oil.

It was a bold move, and a shrewd one, because Germany was preparing for another war. More accommodation from the British was coming. Winston Churchill regarded Iranian oil as essential in any conflict with the Germans. So in October 1939, a month into World War II, Churchill began advocating a policy of giving the shah whatever he wanted.

As the war heated up, though, problems developed. Even though Britain kept agreeing to the increasing royalties the shah was demanding, the British government had doubts that the shah would deliver the oil Britain was bargaining for. In addition, Britain and its new ally, the USSR, wanted to use the just-opened Trans-Iranian Railway to move supplies from the Persian Gulf to the Soviet Union and the Eastern front, a proposal that the shah resisted.

Reza Khan was sympathetic to the Nazis, and at the outbreak of World War II, he had proclaimed neutrality for Iran. But Britain insisted that the German engineers and technicians who were still there were spies and saboteurs and a threat to British oil facilities. London demanded that Iran send them home, but the shah refused.

In August 1941—citing Reza Khan's refusal to expel German nationals—Britain and the Soviet Union invaded Iran, arrested the shah, and exiled him to South Africa. The following year, the United States sent in a military force, ostensibly to help keep the Trans-Iranian Railway running. Over the next few months, the British, the Soviets, and the Americans took control of the railway and of Iran's oil industry.

In September 1941, Reza Khan's son, Mohammad Reza Pahlavi, was allowed to accede to the throne and appoint a government congenial to the British and the Americans. He was a convenient choice, only 22 years of age, and his attitudes were secular and very pro-Western. Like his father, he planned to use oil revenue to modernize his country.

The new shah's Western leanings disturbed much of the country, especially Iranians averse to modernization. After the war, there were protests against the shah's government, and an anti-Western movement—which among other things advocated nationalizing the oil fields—gained strength.

Meanwhile, neighboring Azerbaijan broke with Iran and became a Soviet republic.

The young shah remained loyal to the British and American governments that had installed him and that he believed would protect him from this new threat on his northwestern border. He resisted all proposals to amend the oil concessions to Iran's advantage. Despite his vow to act as a constitutional monarch deferring to the parliament, through the 1940s he increasingly sought to dominate parliament. He concentrated on reviving the army and ensuring its loyalty to the monarchy.

His primary postwar opponent was the nationalist parliamentarian Mohammad Mosaddegh.

Mosaddegh was the scion of a wealthy family and the first Iranian to obtain a PhD in law from a European university. He imagined Iran as a fully sovereign, modern democracy with control of its own resources, including its vast oil fields, its export facilities, and the giant Abadan refinery. He saw oil revenue as the key to eliminating poverty and restoring the country to greatness. While studying in Paris, he absorbed the French disdain for the British, an attitude that reinforced his differences with the shah.

Mosaddegh became popular with the Iranian people, who saw him as a liberator. In 1951, the parliament chose him to be prime minister. He promptly resigned, complaining that the shah had denied him authority to appoint the minister of war and other senior officials. Public protests followed, and the shah quickly reinstated him to his post, with all the powers he had demanded.

Mosaddegh set about nationalizing the oil industry, to pull Iran free from Britain and the United States. The shah opposed him, fearing that the West would respond with an oil embargo that would leave Iran in economic ruins.

But Mosaddegh pressed on, with the parliament's near-unanimous approval. When the shah tried to replace him, much of the public— seeing the hand of foreigners in their politics— joined in riots. Fearing a mutiny in the lower ranks if he ordered the army to suppress the riots, the shah fled the country, but he had not abandoned his throne nor his confidence that the British and Americans would stand by him to protect their oil interests.

Events proved the shah correct. The British government shut down the Abadan refinery, where all oil from Iran's fields was processed. Concurrently, Britain and the United States began a boycott of Iranian oil and pressed their allies to join. With no buyers, production soon stopped, as did the cash flow.

As if that weren't enough, the British and Americans shut the Strait of Hormuz. That hindered all seagoing trade with Iran. The economy was crippled.

The U.S. government was interested in more than the dollars and cents of the oil. It was the height of the Cold War. Mosaddegh's program of nationalization and interference in markets and his attempt to rule by decree invited the picture of a proto-Communist who might align with the bear. So for political as well as economic reasons, he had to go.

Britain and the United States plotted how to get what they wanted in a country bordering the Soviet Union without starting World War III. They decided on a coup, rather than an invasion. It seemed the best course for several reasons.

First, if the British invaded Iran, the Soviets likely would respond by invading the northern provinces. That could lead to a shooting war in which the Soviets would have a huge logistical advantage. They might push the British and Americans to the south and possibly out of Iran, and that would position the Red Army to directly threaten neighboring Turkey. The Soviets also would gain direct access to the Persian Gulf, something Russians had dreamed of since Peter the Great. From there, the Soviet navy could enter the Indian Ocean.

However, a coup that returned the shah to his throne would be much less of a provocation to the Russians. And a grateful shah could be expected to yield further concessions to American oil companies.

And finally, though the Western powers would deny any involvement in the coup, other Middle Eastern governments would know whodunit. The show of U.S. strength and cunning would help keep those governments oriented toward the West.

Given CIA assurances of his safety, the shah returned to Iran, and the United States set about organizing and funding supposedly spontaneous demonstrations against Mosaddegh. They paid clergy, politicians, army officers, and even street thugs to join in the campaign of protest. Given the hardships brought on by Iran's economic isolation, protests were easily pumped up into riots.

The coup came in August 1953, but despite all the planning, it didn't come smoothly.

The shah dispatched the military to the prime minister's residence to take Mosaddegh into custody. But the Imperial Guard colonel attempting to carry out the arrest was himself arrested by supporters of Mosaddegh. However, the CIA had already hired a string of Tehran mobsters to incite pro-shah riots. Other CIA-financed men were brought into Tehran in buses and trucks and took to the streets. Between 300 and 800 people died in clashes between them and Mosaddegh supporters.

A pro-shah mob paid by the CIA marched on Mosaddegh's residence and succeeded in arresting him. He was tried and convicted of treason by the shah's military court. In December 1953, he was sentenced to three years in prison, after which he was placed under house arrest, where he remained until his death 14 years later, in 1967. Other Mosaddegh supporters were imprisoned, and several were executed.

For decades, both the CIA and MI6 refused to admit they'd been involved.

Having saved Britain's bacon in Iran, the United States pressed AIOC to share its rights to the oil fields, mostly with American companies. British ownership was reduced to 40 percent, and American ownership was set at 40 percent. Royal Dutch Shell received 14 percent, and the French company Total S.A. got 6 percent. The Iranians were granted a 50 percent cut of the profits, but no rights of ownership to the fields.

Post-coup, the shah grew increasingly authoritarian. More and more of the oil revenue went into his own pocket, leaving less for the projects he'd promised. And there was friction with the big oil companies. The shah's government accused them of lowballing their reported earnings, to understate the profits to be shared with Iran.

The forces that had made Mosaddegh their point man hadn't dissipated with his removal. Resentment of the shah's rule—and of secularization and modernization in general—continued to build. In 1979, it boiled over as an Islamic revolution. The Shi'a clergy took power and allowed a student faction to seize the U.S. embassy and take 52 Americans hostage. Oil was about to be nationalized once again.

The U.S. government judged it futile to try to reinstate a pro-Western regime. So it turned its back on the shah and encouraged an invasion of Iran by Iraq. Saddam Hussein, the secular Iraqi dictator, went to war against his neighbor, supported by money and weapons courtesy of the United States.

American reasoning was straightforward. Washington decided that the best strategy for ensuring the flow of oil from the region was to encourage conflicts that tended to neutralize the parties. If Iraq and Iran were at each other's throats, they wouldn't be able to trouble Saudi Arabia, the United States' principal oil supplier.

The plan worked—for a while.

Once Shi'a fundamentalists gained the upper hand in Iran, conflict with neighboring Iraq was probably inevitable. Although Iraq is majority Shi'ite, in 1980 it was ruled by the Sunni minority, headed by Saddam Hussein.

Iraq invaded Iran in September 1980, citing a long-simmering border dispute. But the real reason was Saddam's fear that Iran's Islamic revolution would inspire Iraqi Shi'ites, who were concentrated in the southern portion of the country bordering Iran, to rise up against him.

The bloody conflict lasted eight years, until August 1988. An estimated half-million combatants died, along with a similar number of civilians. Hussein used chemical weapons against the Iranians and in his own country against Kurds sympathetic to Iran. The war ended with the border between the two countries unchanged.

Iran lost much of its oil and gas production in the war. To make matters worse, in 1980 the U.S. government organized economic sanctions against the country to retaliate for the previous year's hostage takings, and in 1995, suspecting Iran of developing nuclear weapons, it expanded the sanctions. The UN Security Council imposed a series of harsher sanctions, beginning in 2006, after Iran refused to suspend its uranium enrichment program. The European Union layered on its own trade restrictions.

Although there are many leaks in the sanctions regime, there's no question that they hurt the country. Oil output still hasn't recovered to prewar levels of 6 to 7 million barrels per day. Access to outside capital is hindered, which slows the building of pipelines and other productive infrastructure. And Western investment has become a when-hell-freezes-over prospect.

Though Iran may be isolated from the United States and Western Europe, Tehran still has allies. Venezuela has advanced $4 billion for joint projects, including a bank. India has pledged to continue buying Iranian oil because Tehran has been an accommodating vendor for New Delhi, which struggles to pay. Greece opposed the European Union sanctions because Iran was one of very few suppliers willing to sell oil to the bankrupt Greeks on credit. South Korea and Japan are pleading with the United States for exemptions because of their reliance on Iranian oil. Economic ties between Russia and Iran have gotten stronger every year since Putin became president in 1999.

Iran is even making nice with Iraq's national government, now tenuously controlled by the Shi'ite majority. Its largest gas deal to date is going to its new BFF. Iraq needs natural gas, and lots of it, to power refineries, pipelines, and other infrastructure for exploiting its oil. The deal would feed Iraqi refineries over 700 million cubic feet of Iranian gas per day, which is a lot, about $4 billion worth a year under the terms of the deal. And there's talk of doubling the flow.

Finally, there's China. Iran's energy resources are a matter of national security for China, as Iran already supplies 15 percent of China's oil and natural gas. That makes Iran more important to China than Saudi Arabia is to the United States. China needs to protect its two-way trade with Iran, which is expected to hit $50 billion in 2015, so don't expect China to join U.S. and EU sanctions. China doesn't object to the West's effort to keep Iran from selling oil. In fact, China likes it, since it makes Iranian oil and gas that much cheaper to buy.

Iraq: The Quagmire

Iraq occupies a territory known in antiquity as Mesopotamia, the Cradle of Civilization, where humans first lived as permanently settled farming communities. But its recent history has not been all that civilized. And much of it has centered not on crops, but on oil—of which Iraq has a lot.

The country of Iraq is a recent invention. The area had been part of the Ottoman Empire for most of the years from the sixteenth century until the end of World War I.

With the acquiescence of U.S. President Woodrow Wilson, England and France chopped the Ottoman Empire into pieces they labeled Turkey, Syria, Lebanon, Palestine, the Gulf States, and Mesopotamia. The chopping was done with little consideration for the ethnic and religious differences within each piece or how a given group might overlap multiple countries. Notably, the Kurds were (mostly) split among northern Iraq, western Iran, and southern Turkey, and have been trying to coalesce into a country of their own ever since. They remain the largest ethnic group in the world without their own state.

Mesopotamia was administered by the British until they reformed it into the Kingdom of Iraq in 1921. In 1932, the kingdom was given full independence. With its religious and ethnic divisions, the kingdom has had a rocky history, including two Kurdish/Iraqi wars that killed many but settled nothing. In 1958, the monarchy was overthrown by a disgruntled military faction that promptly proclaimed the Republic of Iraq. It was not the kind of republic envisioned by James Madison. Instead, it was an authoritarian regime untethered from the traditional laws and practices that might restrain a monarchy. Most of the time, the office of president was held by whoever controlled the military.

One of them in turn was Saddam Hussein.

Saddam was a leader of the Sunni-dominated Ba'ath Party (fascism with sand dunes) and had played a key role in the 1968 coup that brought the party to power. In 1976, he became vice president and, in that office, stood next to an ailing head of state. Saddam developed a security force loyal to himself through which he could control relations between the government and the military. In the early 1970s, he orchestrated the nationalization of oil and other industries. Through the 1970s, he cemented his authority over the apparatuses of government as oil money helped Iraq's economy grow rapidly. Most of his appointees to positions of power were fellow Sunnis.

In 1979, he assumed the presidency, although he had been the real head of Iraq's government for several years. He ruled until being driven out, a quarter-century later, by the American-led invasion in 2003.

Iraq's Oil History

From 1925 to 1961, all production of oil in Iraq was controlled by the Turkish Petroleum Company (TPC), an organization that before World War I had acquired the rights to all the oil in the Ottoman Empire. TPC had been formed in 1912 by Calouste Gulbenkian, an Armenian entrepreneur who was already a prominent and successful player in the oil industry and who was nicknamed Mr. Five Percent for his practice of reserving 5 percent of everything for himself.

After World War I and the breakup of the Ottoman Empire, the company was renamed the Iraqi Petroleum Company (IPC). Gulbenkian sold half of it to British interests who were active in neighboring Iran and who were willing to fund the exploration and development of Iraqi oil deposits.

In 1927, IPC brought in a game-changing well in the Kirkuk field, in the Kurdish area of northern Iraq. By then, U.S. interests had their foot in the door and IPC was reorganized, with 23.75 percent going to each of the predecessors of today's BP, Royal Dutch Shell, and Total S.A., and to an American consortium of the antecedents of Exxon Mobil and Chevron. The balance went to Mr. Five Percent. Each of the parties agreed not to compete with one another in the Middle East (the Red Line Agreement).

The noncompete agreement led to a strain. The Americans and the British, on the one hand, had other sources of oil production and intended to develop the Iraqi fields at a measured pace. France, on the other hand, had its interest in Iraq and little else. With Iraq on "Slow," France wanted to develop other sources, but the noncompete agreement barred it from doing so on its own in the Mideast.

At the end of World War II, Iraq was decades behind Iran in developing its oil industry. It didn't have even one refinery. Iraqis wanted to exploit their resources, but, as in Iran, nationalist sentiment was growing and with it resentment of foreign control of oil production.

Iraq's military rulers understood the tension between the desire for independence from foreigners and the need for outside expertise. They feared that nationalization would bring Iraq a ruinous buyers' strike of the kind that shut down Iran's economy in 1952 and drove Mosaddegh from power and into prison.

It wasn't until the USSR arrived, with the Soviet-Iraqi agreement of 1969, that the government stood up to IPC and to British and U.S. interests.

The Soviets offered Iraq capital and technical help to build an oil refinery and pipelines to move crude oil and oil products. And that was only the opener. The Russians also offered assistance for hydroelectric plants, mining projects, and nuclear energy.

Moscow wanted more than access to Iraqi oil; involving itself in the country was a Cold War ploy. In easing Iraq's dependence on Western oil revenue and helping the country become more self-sufficient, the USSR would undermine U.S. influence and gain a foothold for itself in the Middle East. The Russians appealed directly to the Shi'ite majority, who were the most fervent nationalists and wanted to get rid of IPC altogether.

Westerners, especially the British and the Americans, had abused their positions over the years. As in Iran, they failed to deliver on promises of grand improvements, such as schools and hospitals. Disgruntled locals, mainly Shi'a, felt the foreigners were simply stealing from them. And there was a second but related target of resentment; whatever oil money stayed in Iraq all seemed to wind up in the pockets of the hated Sunni ruling class.

It was a political stew to Moscow's liking. Envisioning Soviet-friendly Shi'a ultimately taking control of their country, the Kremlin encouraged an assault on IPC.

In 1972, Saddam seized IPC's assets and handed them to the Iraq National Oil Company (INOC, an entity created in 1966 and still in existence). But from the Russians' point of view, the move backfired. Nationalization was seen as a great victory among the Shi'ites. However, Saddam and the Ba'ath Party still ran the military and the government, so the spoils of the nationalization helped keep them in power. The Shi'a got something to celebrate but nothing to spend. The Russians got nothing at all.

With nationalization, an oil industry that had been humming along went into a tailspin. The technical expertise that outsiders had been providing was lost, which was crippling for a not-so-modern country. Foreign investment dried up. In fact, INOC's own rules barred the company from granting concessions to or partnering with foreign corporations. Even service contracts required restrictions that few foreigners would want to live with.

Even more damaging to the oil industry was Saddam's appetite for war. He got involved in three of them, starting with the disastrous conflict with Iran.

The United States supported Saddam in his war against Iran, but after the UN-brokered ceasefire was signed, relations quickly deteriorated.

The First Gulf War came just two years after the end of the war with Iran. It was precipitated by Iraq's invasion of Kuwait.

Saddam beat up Iraq's rich little neighbor for three reasons.

The first was territorial. The Iraq defined by British cartographers in 1922 was virtually landlocked. Kuwait had Persian Gulf frontage that Saddam coveted. He claimed that the country's history as the Ottoman Empire's province of Basra made it rightfully Iraqi territory.

The second was debt. The Iran/Iraq War had left Iraq deeply indebted, primarily to Saudi Arabia and Kuwait. Iraq had been pressing both nations to forgive the debt, but they refused. Thus the invasion was like a hostile corporate takeover of a creditor.

The third was oil economics. Kuwait's oil fields were a tempting prize by themselves. In addition, Kuwait had been hurting Iraq by cheating on its Organization of Petroleum Exporting Countries (OPEC) quotas. The cartel's policy at the time was to limit production to keep the price near $18 per barrel; overproduction by Kuwait (and by the United Arab Emirates [UAE]) had pushed the price as low as $10. That cost Iraq

$7 billion per year in lost revenue, equal to its 1989 balance of payments deficit. Keeping Kuwait's oil in the ground was almost as attractive as stealing it.

The Iraqi government also claimed it was the victim of economic warfare, including slant drilling from Kuwait into Iraq's Rumaila oil field. In the summer of 1990, it threatened military action.

The trigger may have been clumsy communication by the United States. In a late-July meeting, U.S. ambassador April Glaspie told Saddam, "I know you need funds. We understand that, and our opinion is that you should have the opportunity to rebuild your country. But we have no opinion on the Arab-Arab conflicts, like your border disagreement with Kuwait. . . ."

Saddam took this to mean that if he moved against Kuwait, the United States would not intervene. Thus emboldened (and perhaps thinking he might catch a little help from the Russians), on August 2 Saddam ordered the invasion.

Carefully watching events from the sidelines was Saudi Arabia. The country is majority Sunni but includes a sometimes militant Shi'a minority in the oil-rich eastern part of the country.

Saudi-Iraqi relations, motivated by a shared fear of Shi'ite Iran, had been cordial during Iraq's war with Iran. Soon after the war, in 1989, the two governments signed a pact of noninterference and nonaggression. But while they shared interests, they did not share trust. The Saudis were driven to cooperate with Saddam by worries that a Shi'ite revolution in Iraq, should one occur, might spill over into Saudi Arabia. Yet they feared Saddam might see his thinly populated neighbor as so weak that, after he had captured Kuwait, he would try to swallow it as well.

Four days after Saddam's army entered Kuwait and a day after President George H. W. Bush proclaimed that the invasion "would not stand," Secretary of Defense Dick Cheney met with Saudi Arabia's King Fahd.

Each had an agenda. King Fahd feared that Saddam would push into his own country. The Americans, wanting to push Saddam out of Kuwait, needed a staging area, and Saudi Arabia was the most convenient choice: convenience for the United States, protection for the Saudis. But they had to hurry. The Iraqis were less than 300 miles from capturing the airfields and ports that American forces would need.

The mutual benefit was clear, but it was a touchy business nevertheless. The United States was asking permission to send hundreds of thousands of infidel troops into Islam's most holy land. This was not something to be taken for granted, even given Saudi Arabia's precarious position.

King Fahd needed only a couple of hours of persuasion, if in fact he needed to be persuaded at all. Permission was granted.

Attempts to talk Saddam out of Kuwait achieved nothing. President Bush recruited three dozen countries to join in the action, although the United States was providing three-quarters of the troops. (The Saudis, with some contribution from Kuwait and other Arab states, would wind up footing about 60 percent of the Gulf War's out-of-pocket costs.) The UN Security Council authorized "all means necessary" to eject Iraq from Kuwait. In mid-January, Congress gave the president the green light to invade.

Aerial bombardment of Iraq began on January 17. On February 24, U.S. troops entered Kuwait. A hundred hours later, it was over. In April, a Security Council resolution defined the terms of a ceasefire. Iraq agreed to recognize Kuwait's sovereignty, dispose of all nuclear, biological, and chemical weapons, cease production of such weapons, and allow weapons inspections to ensure compliance.

In the immediate aftermath of the Gulf War, Shi'a in the south of Iraq took their own fight to Saddam, encouraged by what they believed was a pledge of support from the United States. In the north, the Kurds, who had also been told they'd get American help, saw the moment as a golden opportunity to break away, and they too rose up. But the United States, expecting a coup from within Saddam's inner circle, did nothing to support either rebellion.

The coup didn't happen, nor did American military assistance to the north or south. Saddam crushed both uprisings.

The Gulf War didn't end in kiss and make up. Following the ceasefire, U.S. and British aircraft enforced a no-fly zone over Iraq. The Iraqis struggled to frustrate the weapons inspections. Hostilities resumed briefly in 1998, after which Iraq refused to admit weapons inspectors at all (until inspections restarted in 2002). In addition, Iraqi forces regularly exchanged fire with U.S. and British aircraft in the no-fly zone the two allies had imposed.

Shirking the conditions of the ceasefire kept Saddam at odds with the United States and culminated in the outbreak of another conflict, now generally just called the Iraq War, 12 years later.

There is no shortage of theories as to why the Bush administration in March 2003 decided to go to war against Saddam a second time: for violations of the ceasefire agreement; because Saddam was developing nuclear weapons; in retaliation for the assassination attempt on the younger Bush's father; because Israel wanted it; to promote the spread of democracy; to finish the job begun during the First Gulf War; for humanitarian reasons (i.e., to bring regime change to a people oppressed by a truly savage ruler); and of course—most commonly held by opponents of the invasion who toted No Blood for Oil signs—that the United States was merely making a grab for Iraq's petroleum at the behest of Big Oil.

There may be a little bit of truth in most or all of these theories. However, a hidden and probably very important cause is seldom mentioned.

It wasn't the oil per se, although bringing it under control was a nice side benefit. It was maintaining control of the currency in which all oil was being traded.

Until November 2000, no OPEC country had dared to violate the U.S. dollar pricing rule for oil. And while the U.S. dollar was still the world's reserve currency, that position was being compromised by a shrinkage in the United States' share of the world economy and by a deepening resentment over U.S. pushiness in global economic and political matters. While international trade without the dollar wasn't entirely practical, for many people around the world it was becoming an agreeable prospect.

It was the United States itself, ironically, that cracked the door open. To blunt criticism that the U.S.-led embargo of Iraqi oil was injuring innocent Iraqis, the Clinton administration agreed to the Oil for Food program, under which Iraq would be allowed to sell oil for cash that would be available exclusively to buy food, medicine, and other basic needs.

In late 2000, France, Germany, and a few other EU members joined with Saddam in defying the petrodollar process: They bought the oil, and Iraq bought the food, for euros, not dollars. Over the next six months, several other countries hinted at interest in non-U.S.-dollar oil trading, including Russia, Indonesia, and Venezuela. At about the same time, Iran was exploring its own exit from the petrodollar system.

In March 2003, American forces invaded Iraq. Barely two months later, the new Iraqi government announced that oil would once again be sold for dollars only.

Kurdistan—The Would-Be Country

Kurdistan is a country you won't find on the map. It has 25 million inhabitants, and they are the largest ethnic group in the world without a sovereign homeland.

The post–World War I partitioning of the Middle East scattered the Kurds among several countries. The British promised them their own home eventually, but so far it hasn't happened. Today they are the majority people in a wide swath stretching from southeastern Turkey through northern Iraq and northwestern Iran. Sizable minorities also are present in districts of Armenia, Georgia, Syria, and Azerbaijan.

They resist being digested by the countries that include them, so they are persecuted. In Iran, it is illegal to use a Kurdish name. Turkey continues to deny that Kurds are a distinct ethnicity, although many ethnic Turks think of them as gypsies. The official story (this is not a joke) is that Kurds are Turks who got lost in the mountains and forgot they were Turkish. In Iraq, Kurds have come close to carving out a sovereign state in the northern, oil-rich part of the country. Perhaps because of the strength that demonstrates, it is in Iraq that they have encountered the worst treatment.

Fearing that Kurds might side with the Iranians in the Iran/Iraq War, Saddam Hussein undertook a campaign of wholesale murder against them, including attacks with chemical weapons. More than 50,000 Kurds (or, by some estimates, 200,000) were slaughtered, and 2,000 villages were destroyed. Saddam also tried to "Arabize" the city of Kirkuk by driving out Kurds and resettling Arabs from central and southern Iraq.

Later, in the Second Gulf War in 2003, the Kurds joined the United States in attacking Saddam's government in Baghdad, a fact that no Iraqi national government is ever going to forget. Since the war, Kurds in northern Iraq have lived under an uneasy truce between their own Kurdistan Regional Government (KRG) and the government in Baghdad.

To Saddam, Iraq's Kurds were an enemy of the regime. To the Iraqi government that followed him, they are a minority that continues to spit at Baghdad's authority.

The Kurdistan Regional Government (KRG) is as close as the Kurds have gotten to self-rule. Since 1971, it has been an odd, semiautonomous authority controlling a region of northern Iraq while holding the Iraqi government at arm's length. It commands its own armed forces but still relies on the government in Baghdad for its budget. It's a reliance from which Kurds want to escape.

That escape is starting to happen. Kurdistan is one of the most successful and stable parts of Iraq—to Westerners, the not-so-crazy part. Though 94 percent of Kurdistanis are classified as Sunni, religious sentiment among them comes with tolerance. The sectarian strife that torments the rest of Iraq is absent.

Kurdistan produces oil that Baghdad claims as its own. The KRG disagrees. In practice, such arguments are won by the party that can deliver the oil to the buyer, and the KRG has recently arranged to do just that.

Foreign oil companies stood back from Iraq during the decade of American invasion and occupation. More recently, as U.S. involvement diminished, Baghdad became keen to revitalize its old oil fields. To that end, the central government signed a raft of multibillion-dollar deals with foreign operators.

The government's goal was a bit ambitious: a production rate of 8 million barrels per day by 2017. (In 2010 it was 2.4 million bpd.) At first, foreign oil companies fell over each other to stake their claims in Iraq. It should have been a bonanza for everyone involved. But the bonanza didn't happen.

In dealing with foreign oil companies, the Iraqi government missed the critical distinction between vast and infinite, as small children easily do. It asked foreign oil companies to provide the know-how and the billions of dollars of capital needed to develop the country's vast deposits in exchange for nickels. Rich as those resources are, there are minimum terms that any energy company would require, and Iraqi officials were too inept to calculate what those minimums might be.

When the world's biggest energy company, Exxon, turns its back on 115 billion barrels of proven oil reserves, that's a strong sign that the owner of the reserves doesn't know when to say yes to the best offer it is likely to get. Vast resources or not, if the contract is too stingy, Exxon is not going to bother. Many other companies have also concluded that working in Iraq is just not worth the risk and the effort. Iraq's recent oil auctions have drawn few bidders.

Baghdad now offers only service contracts, under which operators are paid a flat fee per barrel produced. For the operator, this works out to less than a 1 percent share of profits, with the Iraqi government taking the other 99 percent.

The low payments on offer from the Iraqi government would essentially turn Big Oil companies into hired hands. Baghdad wants even more than having its cake and eating it, too. It wants expert foreign bakers to buy the ingredients, bake the cake, frost the cake, and then slice and serve it—and say "Thank you" for minimum wages and no tips.

Nevertheless, some of Iraq's fields are so large that even a 1 percent take is marginally attractive for an outsider, as is the case for BP in the Rumaila field. Mostly, though, the profits are too slender to attract many takers, especially given the challenges of operating in a war-torn country. Some oil companies initially went along with Baghdad's terms in the hope that an appreciative government would offer them better production-sharing opportunities down the road. That hope has been disappointed, and now the biggest of Big Oil companies are turning away.

Their attention has moved to the north, where the KRG holds sway. Whatever has been paralyzing officials in Baghdad—whether it's arrogance, ignorance, wishful thinking, or an inability to evaluate a proposal—it is working to the advantage of the Kurds.

Kurdistan is offering developers a 20 percent share of the oil they produce. Despite the political risk, the hostility from Baghdad, and the fact that the area hosts less than a third of Iraqi oil, a 20 percent share makes Kurdistan a whole lot more attractive than the rest of Iraq. Kurdistan's infrastructure and security advantages are additional big pluses. There is less violence in the region than in the rest of the country, and it has functional airports, highways, and trains, as well as electricity that doesn't go down like the sun every day.

After carefully calculating the goodwill and opportunities they could lose in southern Iraq and the profit they could gain by dealing with Kurdistan, the oil giants are throwing their hats on Kurdistan's table. And almost as an afterthought, in doing so they are supporting Kurdistan's long-sought ambition to control its own resources in the fashion of a sovereign state.

Exxon Mobil, Chevron, and France's Total—three of the world's biggest oil companies—have reached accords with Kurdistan, adding to the three dozen production-sharing agreements the KRG has signed with smaller companies. To Iraq's central government, the deals are illegal and an insult to Baghdad's authority.

So far, retaliation has been economic rather than military. Baghdad has said it "will disqualify and terminate the contract of any company signing a deal with the Kurdistan region without the approval of the [Iraqi] oil ministry."

Acting on that policy, in 2012 Baghdad barred Exxon and Chevron from bidding on contracts anywhere in Iraq. It cut Exxon's participation in the West Qurna-1 field (with 8 billion barrels of reserves). And it has threatened to cancel Total's stake in the now-producing Halfaya field in southern Iraq unless Total stays out of Kurdistan.

Spokespeople from Exxon, Chevron, and Total have been publicly silent about Kurdistan. However, an official from one of the three companies, speaking off the record, put it this way:

> We understand completely that if we enter into a contract in the north, we're probably going to be blackballed in the south. So the question is: Have we exhausted all our options for getting a deal in the south on terms that we find acceptable? The answer for companies heading for the door is *yes*.[1]

Turkey is also thumbing its nose at Baghdad's authority over its northern region. In the spring of 2013, Turkey's state-run oil firm, Türkiye Petrolleri AO, struck a deal with Exxon for projects in Kurdistan. The agreement gives Iraqi Kurds a route for sending crude oil directly to world markets via a Turkish pipeline.

---

[1]Steve Levine, "Houston We Have a Country," Foreign Policy, July 31, 2012, www.foreignpolicy.com/articles/2012/07/31/houston_we_have_a_country.

Kurdistan's petroleum industry operates under all the geological, engineering, and economic risks and uncertainties of drilling for oil anywhere. In addition, it faces the political and military uncertainties of dealing with a breakaway district that may or may not succeed in asserting aspects of sovereignty in the face of Baghdad's objections. What is clear right now is that several of the world's biggest oil companies are betting on Kurdish oil, even though doing so deals them out of the rest of Iraq's immense oil potential.

The ramifications of all this are highly political. Iraq's prime minister took his complaints over the Exxon and Chevron deals straight to the White House. So far, while Obama "discourages oil dealings with the KRG," his administration admits that American companies have to make decisions based on economic considerations.

Kurdistan has left Baghdad in a bad spot. The Iraqi central government can continue offering low-paying service contracts for help in developing its oil resources and can blackball companies that deal with the KRG. But the blackball threat forces Big Oil to choose sides, and every foreign oil firm that cuts a deal with Kurdistan adds to the region's autonomy.

Assuming the current Baghdad government retains its hold on power, it has two other options.

The simple solution is to offer production-sharing terms that make business sense. Doing that would undercut the incentive for foreign energy companies to deal with Kurdistan. The Exxons and Chevrons of the world want to do business with Baghdad, provided the deal is reasonable.

Alternatively, Iraq could negotiate a handover of resource rights to Kurdistan and retain a share of what the Kurds collect, an arrangement that would cement the region's autonomy. That's not impossible, but given Baghdad's low aptitude for business calculation, it's a long shot.

From Big Oil's point of view, it hardly matters, as all three options bode well. If Iraq continues with the status quo, Big Oil can turn to Kurdistan. If Baghdad offers better terms, Big Oil will jump at exploiting Iraq's mammoth oil fields. And if Iraq and Kurdistan were to resolve their differences, Big Oil would have access to both regions.

Oil money tips the balance everywhere and regularly leads to political power. And that may well be the case here. By wooing Big Oil with reasonable terms, the KRG has enlisted Exxon, Chevron, Total, and a long list of other oil firms as de facto allies in its fight for full autonomy.

Neither truth nor freedom nor justice has a seat at the table in Iraq. Big Oil's goal is profit, and its deals with the KRG testify that the KRG has sovereign control over Kurdistan's resources. Future Kurdistani schoolchildren may be taught that Exxon was their country's Lafayette.

Afghanistan: The Bear Trap

The map places Afghanistan in Central Asia, not in the Middle East. I include it here because it figures prominently in the standoff between Russia and the West.

In April 1978, a military coup d'état brought the People's Democratic Party (PDPA) to power in Afghanistan, the so-called Saur Revolution. The new regime's agenda was socialist and secular; a first step was to rename the country the Democratic Republic of Afghanistan. It then signed a "Treaty of Friendship, Cooperation, and Good Neighborliness" with the USSR, and the PDPA so cozied up to the Soviets that the American ambassador in Kabul cabled home that "the Russian bear has moved south of the Hindu Kush."

This extension of Russian influence was what the British had resisted since the beginning of the Great Game, and the United States was concerned as well. It considered the Saur Revolution an extension of the Soviet empire. To many in Washington, it was something to be undone.

The first year of socialist rule went predictably poorly for a country as chronically fractious as Afghanistan. PDPA factions fought among themselves and against a menagerie of insurgents. The Afghan army shed battalions of deserters, many of whom left to join their chosen rebel groups. There were many to choose from.

Kabul invoked the Treaty and appealed to Moscow for help in holding power. The Soviets sent so-called advisors, much as the United States had in Vietnam. Then in December, the first soldiers of the Red Army crossed the border, and eventually 100,000 more followed. It was a big commitment, but not nearly enough to conquer one of the unruliest places on the planet.

The Soviets hoped to strengthen the Afghan army, sustain a competent, friendly government, and in time induct the populace into the ranks of socialism. But their alliance with the Afghan military was a disaster. Soviet practice was to use Afghan soldiers as cannon fodder while keeping Soviet soldiers safe inside armored vehicles. That destroyed the morale of the men the Russians supposedly had come to support. More Afghan soldiers deserted to the rebels, who reequipped them with a sense of purpose.

It was a costly, nine-year war of attrition, with a number of countries—most notably the United States and Saudi Arabia—supplying the anti-Soviet guerrillas, or mujahideen, with money and weapons. Even though all the mujahideen groups had a common enemy, their actions were uncoordinated. Most were affiliated with the seven expatriate organizations that directed their fighters from Pakistan. And virtually every regional warlord also maintained his own army, waging its own little war.

Aldous Huxley observed: "That men do not learn very much from the lessons of history is the most important of all the lessons that history has to teach." In the case of Afghanistan, there was plenty for Russians to learn from the American misadventure in Southeast Asia. But they entered Afghanistan seeming to know none of it.

Slowly, the Soviets were ground down. They couldn't win; they couldn't even fight effectively against guerrilla tactics. Their relations with China and Saudi Arabia suffered. And the whole unhappy experience was becoming a drain on their treasury. At home, opposition to the war grew. The introduction of American Stinger missiles in 1986 cost Russia its dominance of the skies, and after that it was just a matter of time. In 1989, the USSR pulled out. It was an ignominious defeat that cost the country not only in lives and money but also in domestic morale. The debacle contributed to the breakup of the Soviet Union, which led to the chaos in Russia that fostered Vladimir Putin's career.

Putin had watched the whole mess unfold from his perch in St. Petersburg, and its lessons were not lost on him. He took to heart that it's best to avoid wars, but that if fight you must, then do it in full force, as he would do in October 1999 with his scorched-earth suppression of the Chechens.

The outcome in Afghanistan pointed to his own, evolving grand strategy: Take control of energy. If you do, you will win the all-important economic war and will have little need to fight a possibly disastrous one with bullets.

The U.S. government had also made a mistake. It might reasonably have expected that supporting the mujahideen would gain some goodwill for the United States in the Muslim world. It didn't happen. Not only did the United States not make any new friends, but it also armed Osama bin Laden's rebel group, the foundation of al-Qaeda.

It doesn't seem to have occurred to Washington that once the Russians were gone, the mujahideen might refocus their xenophobia on the West.

Arming the mujahideen with modern weapons was as close as the United States ever got to directly attacking Soviet forces. Why did it bear the cost and the risk of intervening in a landlocked country, ruled largely by medieval warlords, ferocious in opposing outsiders, empty of oil and natural gas, and known for millennia as the "graveyard of empires"?

First, Washington policy makers provided money and weapons to the mujahideen in the hope of delivering a calamity to their Cold War opponent.

Second, though short on energy resources, Afghanistan is rich in minerals. It has iron, copper, zinc, cobalt, gold, and critical industrial metals like lithium and rare earths, and it has them in amounts large enough to make the country one of the most important mining centers in the world: the "Saudi Arabia of lithium," as one Pentagon analyst put it.

(In 2010, the United States Geological Survey claimed that American geologists had "newly discovered" vast amounts of untapped mineral deposits in Afghanistan worth nearly $3 trillion. It was an odd announcement. As far back as 1985, the Afghan Geological Survey Department had delineated the massive amounts of mineral wealth and had proposed extraction plans in cooperation with the USSR.)

Third, the country lies in the path of proposed Silk Road pipelines that would carry oil and gas from the Caspian Sea and Central Asian regions to the Arabian Sea without passing through Russian territory. The same general route could of course also be used to move Afghan mineral production by rail to Pakistan's deepwater port of Gwadar, on the Arabian Sea.

In March 1995, the governments of Turkmenistan and Pakistan joined a memorandum of understanding for a Trans-Afghanistan pipeline. Seven months later, Turkmenistan's president signed an agreement giving CentGas, a consortium led by Unocal and the Saudi Arabian Delta Oil Company, exclusive rights to develop his country's segment of the Trans-Afghanistan pipeline.

In 1997, a Taliban delegation spent several days in Texas, where Unocal officials promised that CentGas would teach Afghan locals the technical skills for pipeline construction. That resulted, in January 1998, in the Taliban selecting CentGas over Argentinian competitor Bridas Corporation and signing an agreement for the proposed project. But, in Afghanistan, things are never as simple as they seem.

The USSR's evacuation had left control of the Afghan government up for grabs, and the Taliban had come out on top and were in firm control of Kabul. But the Taliban still faced an insurgency from a ragtag, marginally effective bunch known as the Northern Alliance. For its part, the United States viewed the Taliban, who were fundamentalist Sunnis, as a nice counterbalance to their Iranian Shi'ite neighbors. Plus the Taliban were apparently on board with the important Trans-Afghanistan pipeline.

It looked as though things were going well. President Clinton took the Taliban to be at least mildly pro-Western, so he supported their claim to authority. Soon the State Department and Pakistan's intelligence service, the ISI, were funneling weapons and money to the Taliban to help them defeat the Northern Alliance.

Then, in August 1998, everything suddenly changed. The American embassies in Nairobi (Kenya) and Dar es Salaam (Tanzania) were bombed at the direction of Osama bin Laden. When the Taliban's leader, Mullah Mohammad Omar, announced that bin Laden had the Taliban's full support, all pipeline negotiations halted.

It should have come as no great surprise. The Taliban were known to have close ties to al-Qaeda, which had already been implicated in the 1993 bombing of the World Trade Center in New York City.

In any event, American relations with the Taliban went dead cold. As the prospects for a U.S.-controlled pipeline receded, there was always the chance that the project might be revived, but with another country, possibly Russia, at the helm (Gazprom had been an original member of the CentGas consortium but had withdrawn). So the United States had a reason to keep the military option available.

Then along came the events of September 11, 2001, which delivered a publicly acceptable purpose for acting in Afghanistan. Al-Qaeda, and specifically Osama bin Laden, was blamed for the attack, and the Taliban were tagged as accomplices. The United States invaded Afghanistan, ostensibly to destroy the former and punish the latter.

However, military operations in Afghanistan, including invasion, may have been in an advanced planning stage before 9/11. Niaz Naik, former Pakistani foreign secretary, told the BBC he was informed by senior American officials in mid-July 2001 that military action against Afghanistan was expected to go ahead by the middle of October at the latest (before the snows came).

Naik said the first objective was to kill or capture both bin Laden and the Taliban leader, Mullah Omar. But the larger purpose, according to Naik, was to replace the Taliban regime with a transitional government of moderate Afghans, possibly under the leadership of the former Afghan king Zahir Shah.

Then there's NSPD-9, a National Security Presidential Directive that reached President George W. Bush's desk, awaiting his signature, on September 4. NSPD-9 called on the Secretary of Defense to plan for military options "against Taliban targets in Afghanistan, including leadership, command-control, air and air defense, ground forces, and logistics," and "against al-Qaeda and associated terrorist facilities in Afghanistan, including leadership, command-control-communications, training, and logistics facilities."

Bush waited until October 25 to sign it, with minor changes and a preamble that reflected the events of 9/11.

And then the United States went to war: not just to drive some terrorists out of their caves and bomb them into extinction, and not just to punish the Taliban for harboring and supporting the terrorists, but to join with the Northern Alliance in an all-out assault on Kabul; to topple the Taliban and install a friendly government, no matter how corrupt; to destroy al-Qaeda's safe haven; to occupy the country while the new "democracy" sorted itself out; and to wage a guerrilla war against opposition forces that would drag on and on. And were there energy-related reasons as well?

Or to put it another way, whatever happened to that pipeline?

In December 2002, the leaders of Afghanistan, Pakistan, and India signed yet another agreement to build a 900-mile-long Silk Road pipeline. In 2005, the Asian Development Bank submitted a feasibility study prepared by British company Penspen to the governments of Afghanistan, Pakistan, and India. The then-U.S. ambassador to Turkmenistan, Ann Jacobsen, commented, "We are seriously looking at the project, and it is quite possible that American companies will join it." A further intergovernmental agreement to buy natural gas from Turkmenistan was signed in December 2010 by a group of nations that now includes India, which would host the terminus of the pipeline (known as TAPI).

Construction, however, has stalled. TAPI's overall feasibility remains questionable, since the southern part of the Afghan section runs through Taliban-controlled territory. That's been a major deterrent for commercial partners needed to build, finance, and operate the pipe. Few want in on a project that costs $8 billion yet is at the mercy of insurgents with a flair for sabotage.

And so the pipeline has languished for over a decade, but it is not dead. Turkmenistan's president wants to open new markets for his country, which holds the world's fourth-largest gas reserves. He has predicted that the agreements still needed for the project will be completed by the end of 2014. After that, construction will begin in 2015, he says confidently.

Time will tell.

Syria: Why Do We Care?

With 72 percent, Sunni Muslims are a majority in Syria. But the country is ruled by the Alawites, a Shi'a offshoot that makes up only 11 percent of the population. Most of the rest are other varieties of Shi'a (7 percent) and Christian (10 percent). The Sunni majority includes 2.5 million Kurds, who by law are denied citizenship, barred from public schools, and hindered from working. The entire happy lot add up to 22 million people.

President Bashar al-Assad's family has been running things for five decades, ever since the Syrian Ba'ath Party (more fascism with sand dunes) came to power in a coup in 1963. The other minority groups generally support Alawite rule as preferable to rule by the Sunni majority. That majority, however, has long chafed under the arrangement, with sympathy from Sunni regimes—especially Saudi Arabia—that would like to see an end to Alawite control. Iran and Iraq, being Shi'a, favor continued rule by the Alawites, as does Iran's ally, Russia.

It's an entirely nondemocratic dynamic. For years, the Sunni majority tolerated rule by the Alawites because the Alawites seemed too few in number to impose the worst of tyranny. From their side, the Alawites were committed, all-in, to holding on to power because ceding it to the Sunni majority would invite extermination. When you are a small minority bent on maintaining control over vastly greater numbers, only one strategy is available: measured brutality *until* you are challenged, and unrestrained brutality *when* you are challenged.

Today the country's president is following in the footsteps of his father, Hafez al-Assad, whose 30-year rule was marked by an event described by former British Foreign Secretary Malcolm Rifkind as the "single deadliest act by any Arab government against its own people in the modern Middle East." In 1982, Hafez sent his army to crush an opposition movement led by Sunni Muslims in Hama. His troops leveled much of the city with artillery fire and killed at least 10,000 and perhaps as many as 80,000 people.

For almost 20 years after the Hama massacre, dissidence in Syria was muted. Hafez died in 2000, and the presidency passed to his son. The younger Assad promised reform but has delivered little of it; he continues his father's zero-tolerance policy for opposition.

While Syria is nominally a republic, it has been in an officially declared state of emergency for the past half-century. The government is free to arrest and hold anyone. Torture is a standard police method. Anyone who is inconvenient for the regime risks joining the thousands who have simply disappeared.

The Syrian army is staffed with Alawites. Unlike in the armies of Tunisia and Egypt—whose soldiers couldn't be counted on to follow orders to kill protesters during the Arab Spring—the ranks of the Syrian army know that their fates are tied to Assad. If he goes, they go, and probably not in a nice way. Thus the military is unswervingly loyal to the president and will inflict whatever horror on the Sunni majority he orders.

The country's tensions bubbled below the surface for two decades. Then, in 2011, they boiled over.

Early that year, judging that civil war was about to explode in Syria and unsure that Assad could hang on, Vladimir Putin tried to bring both sides to the bargaining table, along with Russia and the United States. He attached two stipulations to Russian participation: Russia would be treated as an equal by the United States, and decisions about the future of the country and the composition of any transitional government would be made by Syrians alone, regardless of whether those decisions fit the American agenda.

Because of Assad's closeness with Iran and also to mollify the Saudis, Washington spurned the offer. Instead, it chose to encourage revolt and began funding selected anti–Assad insurgents. But the longer the war dragged on and the more terrible the list of atrocities grew, the greater the pressure became for the United States to wade in deeper. In 2013 President Obama, amid indications that Assad had killed thousands with chemical weapons, seemed about to order missile strikes against the Syrian government.

Putin neither wanted to confront the United States in the matter nor stand idly by while the United States bombed an ally of Russia. At the last minute, he proposed a deal under which Assad would divest himself of all chemical weapons and the United States would pledge not to take direct military action. The deal was struck, and Obama backed off.

It was a masterful bit of diplomacy. Putin averted a confrontation with the United States and in the same stroke positioned himself as friend and peacemaker to the Arab world.

So why do we care about this little country at all? Why back one side against the other? Why does the West green–light Turkey's involvement in cross–border clashes with Assad's troops?

The United States cares about Syria because the country is involved directly or indirectly in nearly every conflict in the Middle East. Syria is a clearinghouse for Mideast strife—Sunni versus Shi'a, Arabs versus Israelis, Persians versus Israelis, and Persians versus Arabs. Even Christians get to participate, as allies of the Alawites. Every Mideast player has a proxy or a natural ally or a natural enemy in Syria, so what happens there influences the security of every country, including Israel, Saudi Arabia, and its fellow Persian Gulf oil producers.

First and foremost, Syria is the third arm of the Iran-Hezbollah-Syria alliance, a consortium of Shi'a regimes that are congenitally hostile to Saudi Arabia and other Sunni-led powers and, for separate reasons, are hostile to Israel and the West in general.

The alliance is busy. It supports Hamas in Gaza with money and weapons and Hezbollah in Lebanon with the same. Both organizations border on Israel, for which each has a seething hatred. Hezbollah has dispatched fighters to Syria to oppose anti-Assad rebels. Iran has committed combat troops for the same purpose.

Russia has its own reasons for caring about Syria.

One of them is Tartus. Russia is committed to supporting the Alawite regime because it allows the Russian navy to use the Tartus naval base, which is the only military port available to Russia outside of the former Soviet Union. Russia also sells $150 million worth of arms to Syria every year, and it provides military and technical advisers to help repair and maintain those weapons and to train Syrian soldiers to use them.

In January 2014, Putin stepped up cooperation with Assad by sending armored vehicles, surveillance equipment, radars, electronic-warfare systems, spare parts for helicopters, drones, and guided bombs. Russia maintains that those sales are just part of a long-standing commercial contract.

The Russians also may be manning Syria's air defense systems. The capability of the systems would make any direct Western campaign—such as enforcement of a no-fly zone or the launch of punitive air strikes against Assad—slow and costly. And the presence of Russian personnel would make such a campaign very risky. Russian casualties would have unpredictable geopolitical consequences.

And of course there are energy connections for Russia.

First, the little stuff. In December 2013, a Russian oil and gas company, Soyuzneftegaz, signed a $90 million deal with Syria's oil ministry for exploration and production in an 845-square-mile block of Mediterranean waters off the Syrian coast.

Far more important is Syria's position as a key continental crossroads, between the energy riches of Eurasia and the Middle East and the energy-hungry markets of Europe. If Assad loses control, the new regime could allow cheap Qatari gas to flow via Syria to the Mediterranean, which would undermine Gazprom's dominance of the European gas market.

Even more important to Russia is Syria's involvement in the affairs of the Mideast. Putin plays chess. He knows that by moving the right piece in Syria, he can influence the game in any energy-producing country in the region.

Further, for Russia, Islam is a source of civil conflict and terrorism. Moscow is predisposed to be anti-Islamist, and it keeps a wary eye on growing Islamist sentiment in Turkey. The prospect of an Islamist alliance between Turkey and a post-Assad Syria, so close to Russia's borders, is worrisome. As far as Putin is concerned, protecting Assad's control of Syria protects Russian national security.

The Russians don't want Assad to lose the civil war, but they are in no hurry to see it end. The longer it goes on, the longer any pipeline through Syria gets postponed, and hence the bigger Putin's head start will be in building yet another pipeline to deepen Europe's reliance on Russian natural gas. And the longer the civil war continues, the more arms Russia can sell to Assad. This is another example of how Russia benefits from every problem in the Middle East.

Russia is nearing completion of South Stream, a pipeline to move gas from Russia to Italy (via the Black Sea, Romania, and Greece). Like the Nord Stream pipeline, it will bypass Ukraine and all of its problems. The main competitor to South Stream gas would be gas delivered by the proposed Trans-Anatolian Pipeline (TANAP), which would run across Turkey to connect Europe to Azerbaijan's massive Shah Deniz gas field.

With the civil war raging and shells straying across the border into Turkey, TANAP won't see much progress—and Putin will move closer to beating out Azerbaijan in supplying gas to Southern Europe.

For its part, the United States wants Assad to go just as much as Putin wants him to stay. Weakening the Shi'a axis has long been an American goal, primarily because the alliance supports Iran's ability to threaten Saudi Arabia.

Undermining the Shi'a axis has meant participating covertly in the civil war. The CIA is operating in southern Turkey to help its allies, chiefly Saudi Arabia, determine which anti-Assad forces should be the designated good guys who receive arms and other materiel. The supplies are paid for by Turkey, Saudi Arabia, and Qatar, which allows Washington to deny providing guns to the rebels.

This operation requires fluffing the pillows of more strange bedfellows—such as Syria's Muslim Brotherhood. But the United States has to try to avoid supplying weapons to outfits that are even more hostile to it, like al-Qaeda, the jihadist al-Nusra Front, and the Islamic State of Iraq and the Levant (ISIL), which wants to run the whole region as an Islamist caliphate. All of these have been sending battle-hardened veterans of the Iraq War into the fray.

It has been important for Washington and the media to portray Russia as the villain in the Syrian mess and Putin as one ruthless dictator siding with another. But the situation is rather more complicated.

Both major powers find themselves on thin ice in Syria. The United States runs the risk of succeeding. If Assad's enemies take power, they could turn out to be far more trouble than Assad. For his part, Putin struggles to wear his Arab-friendly face even as he props up a Shi'ite dictator hated by most of his subjects as well as by the rest of the Sunni Muslim world.

Bahrain's Importance

Bahrain is a tiny island state with outsized importance.

Its religious demographics are almost a mirror image of Syria's. In Bahrain, a 70 percent Shi'a majority is ruled by a Sunni monarchy, an arrangement that stretches all the way back to 1783. As in Syria, the majority is restless.

Though only a small-time oil producer (50,000 barrels per day), Bahrain profits from its location. Lying between Saudi Arabia and Iran, geography gives it a commanding military and commercial position on the Strait of Hormuz, through which 20 percent of the world's oil passes. Its deepwater port is ideally situated to service cargo ships transiting the central and upper Persian Gulf, and it is the terminus for Saudi Arabia's only international oil pipeline.

Perhaps most important, the world's largest offshore oil loading facility, Saudi Arabia's Ras Tanura complex, is a neighbor, just 65 miles away. Seventy-five percent of Saudi oil exports leave from this port and must pass by Bahrain.

Saudi Arabia (and, by extension, its American ally) emphatically does not want Shi'a Bahrain—less than 15 miles off the Saudi coast—to come under the influence of Shi'a Iran. Thus the House of Saud has a powerful interest in ensuring that Bahrain's ruling Sunnis, minority though they may be, remain in power.

That may not be easy. There has been tension in Bahrain since the Arab Spring. In early 2011, when street protests threatened to turn into rebellion against King Hamad bin Isa Al Khalifa, the Saudis neither hesitated nor sought American support. They sent 1,500 troops to help quiet the situation. The United Arab Emirates contributed another 500.

The protests were put down the way soldiers do things. Since then, there has been a reign of censorship, jailing, torture, disappearances, house-to-house raids, and death. Some Shi'ite mosques have been destroyed.

While the United States and Saudi Arabia prop up the monarchy, Russia refuses to take sides. You can be sure that in the event of regime change, Putin will be ready to become the Shi'ites' new best friend forever. But for now, he is cozying up to the Sunni rulers. In April 2014, Bahraini Crown Prince Salman Al Khalifa paid his first visit to the Kremlin, sent by the king to develop and enhance relations with Russia. Following the meeting, a memorandum of understanding was signed between the Russian Direct Investment Fund and the Bahraini sovereign fund Mumtalakat, and arrangements were made for a Bahraini airline to operate direct flights to Moscow.

For the moment, the Bahraini monarchy is firmly in control. But the unrest—including mass marches, violent clashes with police, and Molotov cocktails—continues to this day. It isn't going away. Regime change could come suddenly.

Israel

Israel is the United States' closest ally in the Middle East. It's the region's number one recipient of U.S. foreign aid, and no U.S. presidential campaign would omit a strong commitment to the country.

Oddly, U.S. presidential visits to the country are infrequent. Among recent White House occupants, Clinton was the most frequent visitor, four times. The younger Bush went twice. Reagan and the elder Bush never did. Obama didn't go until his second term.

Putin has been there twice and has referred to Israel as a "Russian-speaking country." It's not as outlandish a notion as you might think; about half of Israelis are, or are descended from, Jewish immigrants from Russia and Eastern Europe.

Despite Russia's support for Iran, Hamas, and Syria's Assad, Israel calculates that getting along with Russia can be a net positive. There are several points of affinity.

A politically active bloc of Russian speakers make up 20 percent of Israel's population, and 10,000 Russian Jews immigrate to Israel every year. There are growing economic ties between the countries: Bilateral trade already amounts to $3 billion annually, and a proposed free-trade agreement would expand that. Russia is a big source of tourist income for Israel, second after the United States as a source of tourists, numbering over 600,000 per year. Foreign Minister Avigdor Lieberman is USSR-born and maintains a close relationship with Moscow. Perhaps most important, the two nations share a chronic threat from Islam and are unsentimental about dealing with terrorism.

Israel was deferential to Russia's sensitivities during Moscow's 2008 war with Georgia, halting its arms trade with that country. That was a big piece of deference. Georgia's defense minister at the time, Davit Kezerashvili, had cultivated Israel as a supplier; he was born in Tbilisi to Jewish parents who moved with their son to Russia and then to Israel in 1992. Before the cutoff, Israel had delivered drones and rocket launchers to Georgia, among other items.

More recently, when Moscow swallowed Crimea, the Israelis shrugged. In March 2014, the Netanyahu government declined to vote on a UN General Assembly resolution on the situation in Crimea.

For years, Israel's Achilles' heel has been energy—or, more accurately, the lack thereof. Prime Minister Benjamin Netanyahu has joked that Moses led his people through the desert for 40 years to the only place in the Middle East without oil. Until 2000, decades of drilling and digging yielded no significant hydrocarbons, leaving Israel to spend

5 percent of its gross domestic product (GDP) buying fuel from its neighbors—with which relations were uneasy at best.

All that is changing. Trillions of cubic feet of natural gas have been discovered in Israeli waters, and 250 billion barrels of shale oil have been outlined on land. Whether Israel will become a significant oil producer is still very uncertain, as the economics of those shale oil deposits are far from proven, but the nation is already gearing up for a future funded by natural gas exports.

Even more significant than the country's new source of income will be newfound political might. Israel is already receiving visits from new friends and potential business partners, some of them countries that not long ago avoided or even shunned Israel. Russia has placed itself at the front of the pack with a 20-year deal between a subsidiary of Gazprom and Levant LNG Marketing Corporation for the exclusive purchase of liquefied natural gas from Israel's Tamar offshore gas field.

Anyone wanting access to Israel's natural gas will have to navigate a treacherous international obstacle course. Syria, Lebanon, Turkey, Greece, and Cyprus are all contesting maritime borders to lay some claim to Israel's vast offshore gas fields. Even Hamas may try.

Israel's natural gas story started in 2000, when a consortium led by an American firm, Noble Energy, drilled into the Mari-B field 56 miles off the Israeli coast. Nine months and a few holes later, the group had located 1 trillion cubic feet of recoverable natural gas, and in 2004 the Mari-B field was in production. Israelis embraced their new domestic energy resource: Consumption of natural gas rose as quickly as the country could produce it.

In 2006, Noble snapped up the chance to drill in the nearby Tamar block, whose exceptionally high underground pressures had frightened off other operators. They were right to take the risk. Two wells drilled in 2009 located 6 trillion cubic feet of recoverable gas. It was the largest deepwater natural gas discovery in the world that year, and it came just in time.

Israel's natural gas revolution had pushed consumption from almost zero to beyond Mari-B's ability to satisfy it. Israel was using natural gas to produce 20 percent of its electricity. Neighboring Egypt had lots of natural gas to sell, and in 2005 it opened the East Mediterranean Gas Company pipeline to connect El Arish, an Egyptian energy hub, with the Israeli port of Ashkelon. By 2008, Egypt was sending Israel over 200 million cubic feet of gas every day.

Today, however, Mari-B is running dry, and relations with Egypt are shaky. The 1979 peace treaty between Egypt and Israel was a treaty between governments, not between peoples. Much of the Egyptian public—including Islamists, Arab nationalists, and secular leftists—have long regarded the treaty with disgust. The deal that built and filled the gas pipeline was a product of the hated peace pact, and it has been denounced since the day it was signed as a device for Israel and Hosni Mubarak to cheat Egypt.

A series of bombings disabled the pipeline in 2011, and it hasn't been repaired. The days of Israel relying on Egypt for gas—and of Egypt collecting a nice revenue stream from Israel—are over.

The timing of offshore gas discoveries has been fortunate for Israel. Just as Egypt fell into turmoil and Mari-B began to dry up, a smaller offshore field called Noa came into production, and then the first wells at Tamar began producing.

Mari-B was a big discovery and Tamar was even bigger, but both were only a prelude. Shortly after delineating 9 trillion cubic feet at Tamar, Noble Energy spudded a drill into the nearby Leviathan field and hit a 500-foot home run. The Leviathan deserves its name; it is home to at least 17 trillion cubic feet of natural gas (estimates run as high as 25 Tcf).

Adding in several other, smaller deposits near Leviathan, Noble has now discovered 35 trillion cubic feet of gas and perhaps a lot more. That far exceeds what Israel can use, and the excess is available for export. (See Figure 10.2.)

Noble and partners plan to construct a liquefied natural gas (LNG) plant so that Tamar's output can be transported to Europe and Asia. They may build a floating facility, in part because coastal land in Israel is so precious. The Noble Group is watching Royal Dutch Shell's progress in building the world's first floating LNG plant for use off Australia.

For Europeans, Israeli LNG would be an alternative to gas from Russian pipelines. Putin knows he can't prevent Israeli gas from flowing, but he can try to influence where it flows and perhaps siphon off some of the profits along the way.

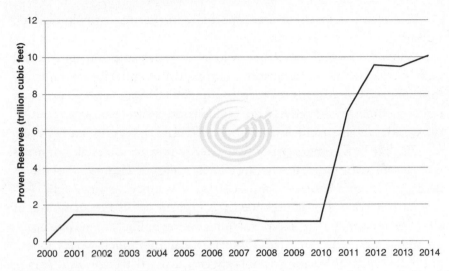

Figure 10.2   Israel's Natural Gas Reserves
SOURCE: Energy Information Administration. © Casey Research 2014.

One move was to improve Russia's standing in Cyprus. Even though the country is a member of the European Union, Russia stepped up with a $3.5 billion loan to help Cyprus recover from its banking disaster.

But the real prize would be a Russian/Israeli/Cypriot partnership. Apart from the potential of supplying Europe by pipeline, it would offer Russia, already the global leader in LNG supply, a major role in exporting Mediterranean gas to those parts of the highly lucrative and burgeoning Asian market—including China, India, and Japan—where piping the gas is not an option.

Even though it will be years before any LNG is shipped from Israel, Russia is so keen to get its hands on it that in 2012 Gazprom signed a letter of intent with the Noble Group to buy LNG from the Tamar project.

Then in early 2013, Gazprom cut a 20-year marketing deal for sales from the still hypothetical Tamar floating LNG plant. Gazprom is setting up an Israeli subsidiary (Gazprom Marketing) to handle the details, in partnership with Trading Switzerland and Levant LNG Marketing Corporation.

Gazprom Marketing is also reportedly in the mix to help develop Leviathan.

When the massive Leviathan field joins Tamar in production, Israel will be able to use every natural gas export avenue it can find. To that end, the country has been cultivating its relations with Cyprus and Greece, which could provide a pipeline route to Europe. It seems that gas wealth is aligning the interests of Israel, Russia, Cyprus, and Greece.

Even as Israel emerges as a new energy power, the Arab countries will remain rich, especially because their energy is cheaper to produce than the less conventional sources being developed in Israel and elsewhere. But what the Arab countries keep in money, they may lose in clout. With so many oil and gas streams coming online, we may be heading into a time when the world won't care all that much what happens in the Persian Gulf (as long as nobody gets frisky with nukes).

And that includes Russia. If it is someday forced to choose between its alliance with Iran and a booming economic partnership with Israel, Putin may choose the latter.

OPEC countries will be first to adjust to an energy-rich Israel, which will compete for sales to the European energy market.

Turkey will have a choice to make, too. When the Islamist AK party came to power in 2002, relations with Israel hit the skids. If Turkey remains hostile while Israel develops a cozy circle with Russia, Greece, and Cyprus, it will be isolated in the politics of the eastern Mediterranean.

Egypt will also struggle with Israel's rise. As much as many Egyptians decried gas sales to Israel, the Israelis did pay for what they received. Israel's natural gas production ends any hope of that income stream reviving.

Then there's the United States, whose importance to Israel will fade if the Jewish state becomes an energy giant with a dance card full of partners. In the long run, the United States could lose the most if its best Middle Eastern friend turns toward Russia.

Of all the players in the area, it is Russia that is most likely to benefit from Israel's emergence as a gas exporter.

Israel sees a need to protect its newfound energy riches. The Israeli Defense Forces in late 2012 approved a navy request for four new warships, at a cost of about $750 million. The navy is concerned that the gas rigs being built in Israeli waters will be attractive targets for terrorists, especially if Israel were to find itself in another war.

In particular, Hezbollah has the capability to attack offshore gas operations with land-based missiles. Other terrorist groups may be able to do the same. Syria also has antiship missiles that could reach the gas fields.

With such threats looming, it's no surprise that Israel, the most pragmatic of all nations, would welcome the Russian navy as a protector—especially if the United States comes to be seen as an untrustworthy ally.

Russia would have much to gain by offering its protection. It could enlist the cooperation of Israeli intelligence in stemming the tide of radical Islam, and it could gain a say in the exploitation of another giant source of natural gas. That might be attractive enough for Putin to accept the resulting damage to Russia's alliances with Syria and Iran. Abandoning those two countries would shift the balance of power in the region toward the Sunnis and would affect every Sunni/Shi'a conflict.

Bottom line: In an area whose politics revolve around energy resources, Israel has long been at a major disadvantage, scrambling to secure needed supplies of oil and gas. But no longer. Israel's newfound natural gas wealth will bring a sea change not only for the Jewish state but for the entire Middle East and everyone involved in its affairs. Israel is gaining clout, Russia might be changing sides, Iran is feeling vulnerable, Egypt is losing a major customer, and regional and global allegiances are shifting.

Rattling around the Shaky House of Saud

After World War I, it was clear to all that in warfare oil was as helpful as gunpowder. Having a reliable supply didn't guarantee victory, but not having one guaranteed defeat.

King Abdul Aziz Al Saud, of Saudi Arabia, understood the lesson.

For most of its history, the region now known as Saudi Arabia was the thinly populated home of a patchwork of scattered tribes. The Saudis were minor players. But their base, the Najd region in central Arabia, happened to be where Wahhabism, a reactionary fundamentalist sect of Sunni Islam, arose in the middle of the eighteenth century.

Founded by Muhammad ibn Abd al-Wahhab, Wahhabism was a revivalist movement that adhered strictly to fundamentalist interpretations of the Quran. Abd al-Wahhab preached against the moral decline of the peoples of the Arabian Peninsula and called them to unite under their true religion to gain political strength. He attracted the financial support and local political clout of the House of Muhammad ibn Saud in expanding his influence and in suppressing Shi'ites.

Over the following 150 years, Saudi territory waxed and waned. However, during the first third of the twentieth century, through wars of conquest, Abdul Aziz, then the head of the House of Saud, assembled the Kingdom of Saudi Arabia, proclaimed as such in 1932. The Sauds have been the royal family ever since.

The new kingdom started poor. It may have been blessed by Allah, but the Almighty had not endowed its inhabitants with much knowledge of what was lying beneath their feet. All they knew they had was Mecca. The city is the holiest place in the Islamic world, and every true believer is called to make at least one pilgrimage to it in his or her lifetime.

Pilgrims to Mecca supplied most of the kingdom's income. But the global depression of the 1930s cut the king's revenue by 60 percent. The king needed to find another source of money or risk losing his kingdom.

Abdul Aziz looked to his neighbors and saw the oil wealth in Iran and Iraq. He thought there might be something like it at home. But even if there were, he'd need help getting the oil out of the ground, so he decided to open his land to foreign oil companies.

Exploration in Saudi Arabia began in 1933, when Standard Oil of California (Socal, now Chevron) obtained the first concession. At the time, the Red Line Agreement brokered by Mr. Five Percent was still in effect, so no member of the Turkish Petroleum Company (TPC) was free to negotiate its own deal with the kingdom. But Socal wasn't part of the consortium that made up TPC. It alone bid for the assets and concessions.

Socal walked off with the prize. Oil there was, and in greater abundance than anywhere else on Earth. Winning in Saudi Arabia eventually pushed Socal to the top of the industry.

The first commercial production came online in 1938, at Dhahran. Socal formed a subsidiary, the Arabian American Oil Company

(Aramco) in 1944, for its operations in the country. As it turned out, the king had been wise to go outside the existing syndicate. By the time Aramco was founded, the split with the Saudis was 50–50—far better than what Iran got from APOC.

The 50–50 split brought the kingdom a gigantic windfall when, in 1948, Aramco tapped into Ghawar. This area, 174 miles long by 19 miles wide, in east central Saudi Arabia toward Qatar and the Persian Gulf, is by far the largest conventional oil field in the world. It produces over 60 percent of Saudi oil and more than 6 percent of the globe's.

The kingdom keeps per-field production numbers close to its vest, but it is estimated that Ghawar yields 5 million barrels of oil and 2 billion cubic feet of gas per day. Its reserves are immense even if, as is widely believed, they are overstated by Saudi oil officials. Assume they are only half of what the government says. That still translates into 40 years of production at current rates.

Compared with Iraq or Iran, Saudi Arabia is sparsely populated. That meant the gusher of money went into fewer pockets, and the king needed to spend less of it to maintain control. While the population quickly grew, so did production. Saudi Arabia could develop its resources and its country together, harmoniously. Citizens grew rich and had no reason to challenge the Sauds' authority. Nor was there much religious strife, as the kingdom was more than 80 percent Sunni.

The Aramco arrangement continued for almost 30 years, until the 1973 oil crisis prompted the Sauds to begin taking control of the country's petroleum industry. The Sauds moved slowly, engineering a 25 percent takeover in 1973, then 60 percent in 1974, and finally assuming complete ownership in 1980. The company changed its name to Saudi Aramco in 1988, and today it reigns as the largest producer of crude oil in the world. With its massive reserves and complete integration of production, refining, and shipping, Saudi Aramco will be waving a scepter for years to come. And the head of the House of Saud will remain one of the richest and most powerful men alive.

Even so, the Saudis always understood that they were too small to go it alone, so they sought both political and commercial allies.

In 1945 they joined Egypt, Iraq, Lebanon, Syria, and Yemen in the Arab League, an organization dedicated to the "independence and sovereignty ... of the Arab countries." The League has since expanded to 21 members (not counting Syria, which in 2011 was suspended because of Assad's bad manners).

Later, in 1981, Saudi Arabia joined with Bahrain, Kuwait, Oman, Qatar, and the United Arab Emirates to form the Cooperation Council for the Arab States of the Gulf. Its purposes include supporting a military organization, the Peninsula Shield Force, to defend against attack on any member state, including attacks by a member's own citizens, such as the 2011 uprising in Bahrain.

In 1960, Saudi Arabia joined with Iran, Iraq, Kuwait, and Venezuela to form the Organization of Petroleum Exporting Countries. Nine other countries would join later. OPEC was conceived as a permanent organization with cartel power to control prices by controlling output.

For its first decade, OPEC had little apparent effect, but in the 1970s it turned the energy world upside down by ending the era of cheap oil. Prices rose sharply on two separate occasions, the Arab embargo in 1973 and the Iranian Revolution in 1979.

The 1973 oil embargo was the Arab world's pushback to the United States and other countries that had resupplied Israel during the October 1973 Yom Kippur War, support that had proven disastrous for Egypt and Syria. While an act of hostility, the embargo gave rise to a convergence of interests that has been of the utmost importance ever since.

The embargo quadrupled the price of oil and reminded the titans of the industrial West of the sharp sword that a handful of small, backward nations held over them. This was particularly true for the United States, which was the country most dependent on imported oil. For the United States, expensive oil was tolerable, but unreliable supply wasn't.

U.S. dependence on foreign oil had grown from 22 percent in 1970 to 36 percent in 1973, and at the time the trend looked irreversible. Unfortunately, much of the world's oil supply was coming from countries that were hostile to the United States, such as Russia, or that were politically unstable, like much of the Middle East (or both). Washington judged that the single most potent guarantor of the reliability of its oil supply would be a Saudi Arabia that was allied with the United States and at peace both internally and with its neighbors.

The puzzle was how to broach an oil deal with a country that had you on its black list. First, obviously, the parties to the Yom Kippur War had to be reconciled. Though a ceasefire had been arranged in October, tensions and mistrust still ran high.

President Richard Nixon and Secretary of State Henry Kissinger saw peace talks between Israel and Egypt and negotiations with Arab OPEC members over the embargo as distinct matters. But they also understood the linkage between them in the minds of Arab leaders. Thus the United States began parallel negotiations with Egypt, Syria, and Israel to accomplish an Israeli pullout from the Sinai and the Golan Heights, and with Saudi Arabia and other oil producers to end the embargo. The First Egyptian-Israeli Disengagement Agreement followed, in January 1974. Though a full peace treaty failed to materialize, the prospect of a real negotiated end to hostilities was enough to convince the relevant OPEC countries to lift the oil embargo two months later.

At the same time, Kissinger was talking separately with the Saudis. They knew they were exposed to their militarily stronger neighbors who coveted Saudi Arabia's vast wealth. And the Soviets might add to the threat, either directly or by sponsoring an invading state.

Sectarian hostility enhanced the danger. Iran was 90 percent Shi'a; Iraq, though for the time being ruled by Sunnis, was 65 percent Shi'a; and next-door Bahrain, small but rich, was 70 percent Shi'a. The Saudis could imagine a war in which Iran or Iraq or the two together with Bahrain would make a grab for their country and do so under the banner of restoring true Islam to the holy places of Arabia.

Saudi Arabia needed a patron. And no major power was likely to stand up, unless . . .

Protection was what Kissinger came selling. As outlined in Chapter 3, the United States offered to support the House of Saud forevermore and defend the kingdom against external aggressors. (Yes, it would continue to support Israel, too; that was just something the Saudis would have to tolerate.) In return, the Saudis would be the bellwether leading oil traders to the exclusive use of U.S. currency—and would agree to invest any unneeded profits in U.S. Treasury bonds, notes, and bills.

The deal was struck, and soon thereafter, Kuwait signed up for much the same.

Washington was confident that as Saudi Arabia had the biggest voice in OPEC, the other members would follow its lead. In 1975, they all did.

Thus 1974 turned out to be a banner year for the United States. War ended, Israel was preserved, oil again flowed from the Middle East, a solid relationship with Saudi Arabia was forged, and, most important of all, the petrodollar was born.

Where was the Soviet Union in all this? On the other side, of course. The USSR wanted to be seen as a friend to OPEC. It never competed with the cartel for markets, and it helped out with energy technology and infrastructure. During the Yom Kippur War, it aided Egypt and Syria. The Soviets wanted to enhance Western dependence on OPEC and to create the right environment for future cooperation with cartel members. Putin would follow a similar policy by embracing pariahs like post-shah Islamic Iran.

The American/Saudi alliance has underwritten stability in the Arabian Peninsula for a good long while. But it may have reached its "Use by" date.

In its twilight years, the Soviet Union suffered from a succession of weak leaders who kept dying on the job. Brezhnev, Andropov, and Chernenko all succumbed within a span of three years. When President Reagan was informed of Chernenko's passing, he reportedly said, "How am I supposed to get anyplace with the Russians if they keep dying on me?"

This may be just what a U.S. president will soon be saying about the rulers of Saudi Arabia.

The similarities are striking. The USSR in its latter stages was a socially repressed and ethnically divided society living in a resource-rich but economically poor country, led by an ensemble of autocratic old men who kept dying without clear plans for succession. All of this was set smack in the middle of a global battle for power.

Today's Saudi Arabia isn't poor, but it is headed for economic trouble. Rapid increases in social spending and in domestic fuel consumption are chewing up the kingdom's all-important oil revenues, which have not exactly been equitably distributed. The money has made average citizens comfortable, yes, but it has left them looking up at a ruling class thickly populated by millionaires and billionaires.

While the House of Saud might present itself as a stable, strong, and cohesive royal family, in truth the king and his successors are growing old and incapable in a throne room crowded with contenders. Meanwhile, the Islamists—the only other organized social group in the country—are waiting outside the door.

The present King of Saudi Arabia, Abdullah Aziz bin Saud, turned 90 years old in August 2014. Under Saudi Arabia's rules of succession, upon the king's death the throne passes not from father to son but from brother to brother. And brothers, ipso facto, tend to be of similar age. Predictably, none of King Abdullah's brothers is exactly young and vigorous and ready to tackle the problems of a medieval country trying to hold things together in a digital world.

Crown Prince Salman bin Abdulaziz Al Saud, the putative next in line to the throne, is already 78 and was drawn to the top only by the death of his two elder brothers. The average age of the surviving brothers, including the king, is now over 80 years.

This is not to say it's a done deal that Salman will succeed to the throne (if in fact he even survives the king). The Saud family is rich in princes, 7,000 of them, the fruit of multiple wives and unlimited family budgets. Among this royal battalion, there undoubtedly is someone with the right mix of youth, clearheadedness, and piety to lead Saudi Arabia through the troubles of succession and into the future. But how would he rise to the top?

Whenever a throne room is crowded with would-be successors, it's easy for a brawl to break out, which favors the most ruthless over the best qualified. The chance that Prince Right will emerge the winner is remote. More likely is a combative individual filled with resentment of the West and spoiling for war with Shi'ites.

The United States doesn't want this (and might not tolerate it). It would prefer to let a string of relatively docile old men each take his turn as king, which means one ruler after another in his seventies or eighties, men who are unlikely to rock the boat.

But they will also lack the energy or even the time to enact significant reforms. And reforms are needed. Here's a short list of the endemic problems that are battering the world's premier oil producer: high unemployment, a corrupt bureaucracy, a nothing-but-oil economy, a weak education system, and a generation of frustrated youth.

While the country creaks under the strain of those problems, the three pillars that have supported the royal family are weakening. The oil revenue long used to buy public contentment is falling behind the public's perception of what it deserves to be given. The Wahhabi Islamic establishment—which has been allied with the House of Saud from the beginning—has become quarrelsome and is losing public credibility. And the royal family itself is struggling to maintain its façade of infrangible solidity.

Whereas the regime once controlled the population by controlling access to information, that age is now almost over. The Internet has connected young Saudis with the rest of the world. What they see is prompting questions about their society, and they are beginning to make their own decisions.

Even the religious establishment is losing its strength. Increasingly, young Saudis are turning to the Quran for guidance rather than following the decrees of any religious leader. It's like a Protestant Reformation in the desert.

This is not exactly the kind of boil manageable by octogenarians taking turns.

Thus, unsurprisingly, when the Arab Spring broke out in Tunisia and Egypt, the spirit of protest leaked into Saudi Arabia. Few of the protesters were demanding democracy. Nor were they trying to oust the royal family. No, the young Saudis who took to the streets had more practical demands.

At the top of the list was jobs. Despite the preponderance of elders at the top of government and an average life expectancy of 75 years, high birth rates have kept the country as a whole astoundingly young on average. Sixty percent of Saudi citizens are under age 20. But among young adults, the unemployment rate is nearly 40 percent. These young people want the opportunity to better their lot, but they can't find work and so default to living on government handouts.

Those handouts have been shrinking. Saudi Arabia's population has grown 380 percent in the past 40 years, far faster than oil production. So there are fewer dollars per head every year.

The short-term fix has been redistribution, the only thing those old guys in the House of Saud really know how to do. So in the wake of the Arab Spring, King Abdullah drowned protestors in money, a $130 billion spending package for new housing, bigger payrolls, and fatter unemployment payouts. It was quite a windfall. Saudi Arabia's entire annual budget is just $180 billion, so the king almost doubled spending to appease the protestors.

The tactic cannot work forever. Even in Saudi Arabia, there is only so much oil money. The Saudi royals already need an oil price of at least $80 per barrel to support all their social programs, and with domestic oil consumption rocketing upward, that baseline price will keep climbing.

And the unrest continues.

After King Abdullah offered his billions of dollars in social spending, many protestors went home—except in the country's oil-rich eastern provinces, where the protests never stopped.

Since the Arab Spring, Shi'ite Saudis in the eastern Qatif region have been demonstrating regularly, demanding the release of all political prisoners, freedom of expression, and an end to ethnic and religious discrimination. When Saudi security forces turned on the demonstrators in November 2011, killing five, the protests took on a distinctly anti-Saud tone. A popular banner read: "For 100 years we have lived in fear, injustice, and intimidation."

In response to long discrimination against Shi'ites, the Eastern Province Movement has been calling for the establishment of a constitutional monarchy. While this is a reasonable enough demand by Western standards, in Saudi Arabia it constitutes treason.

And that's from the older, more cautious elements of the population. Among the young, many advocate the overthrow of the Sauds.

In June 2012, King Abdullah ordered the country's security forces to a state of high alert due to a "turbulent situation" in the eastern region. Demonstrations are illegal in Saudi Arabia, so anti-riot units deployed armored vehicles in downtown Qatif. The government accused Iranian Shi'ites of stirring up dissent. In late 2012, the government required all mobile phone users to register their subscriber identification module (SIM) cards, which means text messaging about demonstrations is no longer anonymous.

Confrontations are growing more violent. Dozens have been killed over the past four years. In February 2014, Saudi security forces attacked anti-regime protestors in the town of Awamiyah in the Qatif region of the Eastern Province and used live fire.

A Saudi court sentenced seven people to prison for up to 20 years for taking part in the Qatif protests and for tossing petrol bombs at security forces.

Thousands took to the streets to mourn those killed in Qatif, and the funeral procession quickly turned into yet another demonstration. Activists say there are more than 30,000 political prisoners in Saudi Arabia and demand their release.

The Eastern Shi'a are well positioned to sabotage the area's oil fields, if they so choose. But they are not the only threat to the monarchy. Al-Qaeda in the Arabian Peninsula (AQAP), the product of a January 2009 merger of Yemeni and Saudi al-Qaeda branches, is committed to toppling the king. Operatives work throughout the country and do so with support from tribal leaders. Bringing down the House of Saud would be a pivotal victory for al-Qaeda and would destabilize the entire region.

All told, external threats, internal divisions, and domestic struggles leave the Saudi royal family's hold on power tenuous. And that makes its recent differences with the United States all the more troubling.

It's no secret that the Saudis are unhappy with President Obama's foreign policy. Because they supply the United States with oil and park their money in U.S. Treasuries, they believe the United States should fight their battles for them. And it isn't doing that.

Prince Bandar bin Sultan—director of the Saudi Intelligence Agency from mid-2012 to early 2014 and the Saudi ambassador to Washington for 22 years before that—has shown European diplomats a long list of grievances. The United States, in the Saudi view, has failed to support the Sunni rebels fighting Syrian President Bashar al-Assad; has done too little to help the Sunni Palestinians deal with Israel; is growing too close to Shi'ite Tehran; and failed to support the Saudis when they crushed the 2011 anti-government revolt in Bahrain.

The relatively young, 65-year-old Bandar is among the most hawkish of Saudi princes. He once offered to pay all of Washington's costs for intervening in Syria and has threatened Putin with terror attacks if Russia doesn't abandon Assad. He now maintains that the kingdom will make a "major shift" in relations with the United States. It's not known whether he reflects the views of King Abdullah, with whom he has fallen out in the past, or whether he might have personal designs on the throne.

Another former director of the Saudi Intelligence Agency and member of the royal family, Prince Turki al-Faisal, in late 2013 accused Obama of "dithering" on Syria and Israeli-Palestinian peace. Calling the president's Syria policy "lamentable," Prince Turki went on to say: "The current charade of international control over Bashar's chemical arsenal would be funny if it were not so blatantly perfidious, and designed not only to give Mr. Obama an opportunity to back down [from military strikes], but also to help Assad to butcher his people."[2]

These are remarkably harsh words from someone so highly placed.

It may seem unlikely that Saudi Arabia would distance itself from its longtime patron; it's still beholden to the United States for military support. In addition, the bulk of its $700 billion worth of foreign reserves remains in dollars. But there are limits to the disrespect the Saudis will tolerate. Primarily because of U.S. inaction on Syria, "All options are on the table now, and for sure there will be some impact," a member of the royal family said.

So what would happen if, for whatever reason, the shaky House of Saud actually did crumble?

Apart from the monarchy, religion is Saudi Arabia's only source of social structure. There are no political parties, no unions, and no social organizations aside from a few charities run by members of the royal family. Were the Sauds to fall, the only players ready to step into the vacuum would be the Islamists.

The shift to the Muslim Brotherhood was unnerving to much of Egypt, but that was nothing compared to what would happen in Saudi Arabia. Islamist leadership on the peninsula would not be the tepid variety that came to Egypt. Saudi Islamists, as noted, are Wahhabi Muslims, practitioners of the strictest and most reactionary strain of the religion; they are Osama bin Laden's coreligionists.

The Sauds are nominally Wahhabi, and they enforce its stringent code on their people. But for eight decades they've been living in the lap of luxury. Despite the support they give Syrian rebels and their intervention in Bahrain, they have, by the standards of their more radical brethren, gone soft.

[2]Amena Bakr and Warren Strobel, "Saudi Arabia warns of shift away from U.S. over Syria, Iran," Reuters, October 22, 2013, www.reuters.com/article/2013/10/22/us-saudi-usa-idUSBRE99L0K120131022.

Were the Sauds to fall and the radical Islamists to inherit the government, peace with the neighboring Shi'a Islamic Republic of Iran would be unlikely. There is a shooting war everywhere the two sects meet. Both branches of the faith believe the other has strayed so far from the path that its followers are infidels. Odds of open warfare between Saudi Arabia and Iran would go sky-high the moment Islamists prevailed in Riyadh. And that would have unpredictable but obviously dire consequences for the region and would threaten the entire world with a calamitous loss of oil supplies.

Even worse—at least from the American point of view—a Wahhabi Islamist Saudi Arabia might attack the devils of the West by shutting off the oil taps completely. It would be the 1973 oil crisis all over again, but in an even more oil-dependent world. The price of oil shot up 300 percent in 1973; you can imagine what it would do today. Even if there were merely an equivalent hike, we'd be looking at over $300 a barrel.

The end of the era of friendly U.S.-Saudi relations would be bad enough in itself. The kingdom has been a partner of the United States for a long time. It has helped stabilize the Middle East and has kept the other OPEC countries in line.

But the real calamity would be the demise of the petrodollar.

If Saudi Arabia turns away from the West—whether because of internal conflicts or because of a rupture with the United States—who is it likely to turn *to*? One certain suitor is Putin's Russia, which would come with an offer to set up a ruble/rial trade system. China would probably show up with a proposal to use the yuan. And who knows who else?

Like it or not, the petrodollar is moving into its twilight. For more than 40 years, Saudi Arabia has been its de facto sponsor. When that sponsorship ends, the end of the petrodollar will quickly follow.

Let's look at the consequences in greater detail.

Chapter 11

Twilight of the Petrodollar

In Chapter 3, I explained how the petrodollar system began and how it now reinforces the dollar's status as the world's reserve currency. Then we looked at Vladimir Putin's grand strategy for waging the Colder War and unseating the dollar.

Now we come to the present and to the signs that the dollar's position is vulnerable.

What we're watching is a remake of an old movie: *The Rise and Fall of the British Pound*. So, for some useful perspective, let's hit the replay button and watch that epic production again.

Before World War I, the British pound sterling was the world's premier currency—not quite like the dollar today, but close.

It was the success of British entrepreneurs that gave the pound the inside track. The system of manufacturing they developed was vastly more efficient than the small craft shops it was replacing, which gave British products a big competitive advantage in export markets. Other countries sold raw materials to Britain, and value-adding Britain turned them into manufactured products, notably textiles and metal goods.

Britain became "the workshop of the world," turning out relatively low-cost products by the boatload. The world wanted them, but to buy British products, you needed British pounds, so everyone wanted them, too.

Britain also maintained a strong military, particularly its navy, and it accumulated so many colonial possessions that, as they used to say, "the sun never sets on the British Empire." The colonies, some a source of great riches, helped reinforce the pound's dominance. If you wanted to buy from a British colony, you needed pounds. And if you wanted to sell to a British colony, you could expect to be paid in pounds, probably through a bank in London, which was becoming the world's undisputed financial center.

It was a sweet deal while it lasted. But one by one, other countries entered the age of industry, and they brought competition to markets that the British had virtually owned. And as administration of the colonies passed from the early financial adventurers who had made them profitable into the hands of government functionaries, many became costly to maintain. They were a burden and a drag on the economy rather than a boost.

Then came World War I. It ended with Britain mired in debt, which did terrible damage to the pound's brand name. The United States, in contrast, came out of the war with huge holdings of gold from exporting food and other goods to countries at war. The war also served as a bloody, four-year advertisement for the United States as a safe place to store wealth. In the eyes of the world, the dollar began to emerge as a reserve currency, first as simply a serviceable alternative to the pound, and then, at least for some, as a superior one.

Britain's physical damage and added debt from World War II finished off the pound as an international currency. The empire disintegrated, and Britain reverted to being a small but prosperous country with some prominence in world affairs, but nothing like dominance.

The United States picked up the position that Britain had lost. World War II added to the U.S. Treasury's already impressive gold holdings (more exports to a war-torn world) and served as a follow-on ad campaign for the United States as the safest place in the world to store wealth. The dollar had become unambiguously the world's reserve currency— almost everyone's first choice for international trade and for diversifying out of the risks of holding the local currency.

As noted earlier, in 1973 a deal between the United States and Saudi Arabia cemented the dollar in place as the most practical currency for buying and selling crude oil. This allowed the United States to import the world's oil essentially for free, since its central bank, the Federal Reserve, could create from thin air all the money needed to buy all the oil its citizens wanted. It allowed the United States to do much else as well.

The currency monopoly on the oil trade put the dollar laps ahead of any possible competitor for status as the world's reserve currency. Everyone needed oil, so everyone needed dollars. If you had anything to sell in an export market, you were happy to be paid in dollars, because you knew you were going to need them for oil. If there was something you wanted to buy from another country, you knew that the seller would gladly accept dollars because the seller could use them to buy oil—or almost anything else. If you were participating in the world economy, it was dollars in, dollars out. Your own local currency was useful only locally.

From Russia to China, from Brazil to South Korea, every country fell under the dollar's hegemony.

Demand for U.S. dollars grew, pushing up the greenback's value. The strong dollar allowed Americans to buy imported goods on the cheap, which is to say that the petrodollar system was subsidizing U.S. consumers at the expense of consumers in the rest of the world. Of course, there was a downside to that: cheap imports hammered the U.S. manufacturing sector. In 1970, manufacturing was 23 percent of the total economy. Today it's just 12 percent.

By putting the dollar so far ahead of any possible competing currency, the petrodollar system allowed the United States to exploit (critics might say abuse) the dollar's status as the world's reserve currency. It could run a perpetual balance of payments deficit; that is, it could spend more dollars in other countries than outsiders were spending in the United States—and not just by small amounts, but by billions each day.

The dollar's position as first among the currencies of the world gave the same status to debt instruments (IOUs) denominated in dollars. Among the countries that were accumulating the dollars Americans were spending—like Saudi Arabia, China, and Japan— the first choice for storing the money was in U.S. Treasury bills and bonds. That provided a new, deep pool of lenders to accommodate U.S. government deficits, which, rather predictably, skyrocketed. There's nothing a politician enjoys more than spending money that no one has to pay in taxes.

Today the U.S. government borrows from practically the entire world without preparing for the day it will have to repay the money—because it can always print it.

If you suspect there is something unsustainable about this arrangement, you're right. It can't go on forever, but the petrodollar system has allowed it to go on for so long that it seems normal and natural. It isn't. Here's where living on the petrodollar for 40 years has taken the United States:

- Government debt now exceeds 100 percent of what the country produces every year—its gross domestic product (GDP). That puts the U.S. economy in what historically has been the danger zone for ruinous trouble of one kind or another—economic stagnation, default, or runaway inflation.
- Most manufacturing industries are languishing.
- The economy has been left with little capacity for recovering from shocks. Despite the unprecedented money printing and deficit spending evoked by the recent recession, recovery has been pitifully slow. Unemployment has been declining, but the pace has been a tease.
- To keep the economy from slipping back into recession, the Federal Reserve has depressed interest rates to levels that mock savers.
- Investment markets can't go anywhere without creating a bubble that eventually bursts, as happened with dot-com stocks and real estate, and is happening now with bonds.

Is this the picture of a healthy superpower? Or is it the picture of a vulnerable giant close to exhausting its advantage?

The world is moving toward sloughing off the U.S. dollar. As it proceeds in that direction, the U.S. currency will lose its position as the global reserve asset. Holders of trillions in dollar-denominated assets will become sellers, and the value of the dollar will plummet.

This is another way of saying the dreaded word *inflation*. If we're lucky, inflation will merely be nasty. If luck deserts us, we get massive inflation; double-digit interest rates; crippling increases in the cost of food, clothing, and gasoline; and bad, bad news for the stock market.

The 2008–2009 recession, in retrospect, will look like a bump in the road.

The consequences for Americans, who have been living well on a dollar that the world wants and needs, are that dire. The eventual outcome for the world—which currency winds up as top dog, or whether any currency does—is unknowable.

What *is* utterly predictable is that the U.S. government will use any means available to try to counter threats to dollar hegemony. In an earlier chapter, I advanced the notion that the 2003 invasion of Iraq was driven by, as much as anything else, the threat to the petrodollar that came from Saddam Hussein redirecting the Oil for Food program from dollars to euros.

Something similar could be said of the uprising in Libya. Muammar Qaddafi's regime was fragile, but the timing of its end is instructive. Qaddafi began encouraging Arab and African nations to abandon both the dollar and the euro and instead use a new currency, the gold dinar. Not long after, Qaddafi was history, pushed out by rebels with assistance from the United States and NATO.

It's also telling that the conflict gave Washington legal cover for freezing $30 billion of troublesome Libyan assets. The money had been earmarked as Libya's contribution to three key components of an African economic federation: the African Investment Bank in Libya; the African Monetary Fund, to be based in Cameroon; and the African Central Bank in Nigeria, which was about to start printing the new, dollar-displacing African currency.

Darts at the Dollar

Russia and China are encouraging the abandonment of the dollar by developing international trade facilities that operate without touching U.S. currency.

In late 2010, Putin and Chinese Premier Wen Jiabao announced an agreement to settle certain trades in rubles and renminbi (another name for yuan). At the time, Wen Jiabao stated, "China will firmly follow the path of peaceful development and support the renaissance of Russia as a great power." This was the first agreement between the two nations that directly challenged the U.S. dollar's status as the dominant global currency.

In early 2012, China and Japan, which are the world's second- and third-largest economies and far from the world's best friends, followed suit. Their arrangement will allow firms to convert directly between yen and yuan instead of using U.S. dollars as an intermediary. That was the first time China allowed swapping yuan for any currency other than the dollar.

To put the deal into practice, the Japanese government said the Bank of Japan would buy 65 billion yuan ($10 billion worth) of Chinese government debt for its own reserves. That's only a tiny part of Japan's nearly $1.3 trillion of foreign-exchange reserves—mostly dollars—but it's a start.

Markets for swapping the two currencies will operate in Tokyo and Shanghai.

In September 2013, the Chinese government announced that the country's banking system was ready for anyone in the world who wished to buy or sell crude oil using the yuan rather than the dollar.

Other anti-dollar-currency events for China that year:

- A currency swap facility between the People's Bank of China (the central bank) and Banco Central do Brasil (Brazil's central bank) for $30 billion worth of Brazilian reals and Chinese yuan. Each central bank will be able to settle trade between the two countries without using dollars. China is Brazil's largest trading partner.
- A similar arrangement with Australia for $31 billion worth of yuan and Aussie dollars, again to facilitate trade without touching U.S. dollars.
- A similar arrangement with the United Arab Emirates (UAE) for $6 billion worth of Chinese yuan and UAE dirhams.
- A similar arrangement with Turkey for $1.6 billion of yuan and Turkish lira.

In June 2013, Wen Jiabao visited Chile to propose a currency swap arrangement, Chilean pesos versus Chinese yuan.

At the end of the year, South Korea and China announced they would allow their banks to draw on an existing 64 trillion won

($59 billion) swap arrangement between the two countries' central banks to settle import/export transactions.

To support all these arrangements, in March 2014 China opened two centers to process yuan-denominated trades, one in London and one in Frankfurt.

And in July 2014, China joined in yet another currency swap, with the Swiss National Bank, for 150 billion yuan versus 21 billion Swiss francs (worth about $23 billion). The deal allows the Swiss central bank to invest in the Chinese bond market.

Other countries are following the lead given by Russia and China.

Also in July 2014, the BRICS countries (Brazil, Russia, India, China, and South Africa) took a huge step toward autonomy at an economic summit in Fortaleza, Brazil. First, they agreed to the creation of a New Development Bank (NDB), based in Shanghai, which will help fund development needs of the BRICS countries and other emerging markets. It has an authorized capitalization of $100 billion.

Second, they also agreed to fund a Contingent Reserve Arrangement, or currency reserve pool, initially capitalized at $100 billion. It is designed to help protect the BRICS countries against short-term liquidity pressures and international financial shocks.

What currencies will be involved are not yet known, but these five countries are clearly moving to disengage from the Bank for International Settlements (BIS) and the International Monetary Fund (IMF)—both of which are subject to the dollar's current dominion.

The Dollar Shoots Itself

Unwittingly, the United States is aiding the dedollarization of the world, most notably through the economic sanctions it organized to discourage Iran from developing nuclear weapons. The sanctioning countries agreed, among other things, not to import oil from Iran. Although a November 2013 agreement brokered by Putin suspends some elements of the sanctions, that primary one remains active.

The U.S. government prefers sanctions over a military attack for a simple reason: Iran would not be the kind of pushover Iraq was. U.S. naval vessels attacking Iran from the Gulf would be met with a swarm of small suicide craft. And Iran could easily attack the oil tankers (big, slow targets) passing between Saudi Arabia and Bahrain and the Strait of Hormuz, which would choke off 20 percent of the world's oil supply.

And then there's Putin. Russia is not likely to sit on its hands while the United States bombs one of its allies. So, Johnny, don't get your gun.

When the sanctions were laid, U.S. allies, including much of Europe and parts of Asia, fell into step quickly, excluding or reducing imports of Iranian oil. Iran's oil exports initially fell by half, but Iran didn't roll over.

Oil is highly fungible, which means one barrel of crude may be interchangeable with another. Once it leaves its home country, it's difficult to determine where a barrel of oil originated, if its handlers desire to make it so. And it's not just barrels that are hard to track. Even though oil is carried on ships so large they are dubbed supertankers, it is surprisingly difficult to keep tabs on every tanker or its cargo.

Under international law, a cargo ship is required to carry a satellite tracking device, but the ship's master has discretion to turn it off for safety reasons if permission is given from the ship's home country. Iranian captains have been exercising that discretion, and now most of the country's 39 tankers are sailing "off radar." Only seven of Iran's very large crude carriers (VLCCs) are still operating their onboard transponders, while only two of the country's nine smaller Suezmax[1] tankers are trackable.

So millions of barrels of Iranian oil held in storage in Iranian tankers have been "disappearing." Officially, there is just a shrugging of shoulders. No one admits to knowing where the oil goes.

Iran's National Iranian Tanker Company (NITC) has begun taking delivery of 12 new supertankers built in China, which will add to its capacity for whisper shipping its oil.

Iran has proven that sanctions can be evaded, but all the tricks and maneuvers come at a cost.

Added freight costs for each voyage come to nearly $5 million, or $2.50 to $4.00 per barrel, depending on the size of the ship. Iran is also shelling out millions of additional dollars to insure each shipment, because most of the insurance industry operates from sanction-compliant

---

[1] "Suezmax" refers to a ship not too large to pass through the Suez Canal.

countries. Iran must deal with the few insurers that are located elsewhere, primarily in China and Russia.

And since business is business, buyers are demanding easy credit terms from the National Iranian Oil Company (NIOC). The buyer may get as long as six months to pay for each 2-million-barrel cargo, a grace period that costs Tehran another $5 to $8 per barrel.

All told, the added freight costs, insurance, and generous credit terms can wipe out 10 percent to 12 percent of the value of each supertanker load. It has been a serious burden, but it hasn't been a crushing one.

The sanctions' prohibition on accepting shipments of Iranian oil has a counterpart—a blockade on payments to Iran. In particular, the sanctions forced the Society for Worldwide Interbank Financial Telecommunication (SWIFT)[2] to refuse wire transfers to or from Iranian banks. That closed the conventional avenue for settling transactions between anyone outside Iran and anyone inside Iran, which would have been painfully effective if every country actually supported the sanctions. But that hasn't been the case.

A good number of countries have gotten past needing to kowtow to the United States. Some explicitly objected to U.S. sanctions on Iran and refused to cooperate. Others are more politic, choosing instead to trade with Iran through avenues that sidestep the sanctions, such as routing goods and money through third countries. (China has made a business out of helping.) Others simply ignore the sanctions but without saying so.

For still others, circumstances trump any impulse to cooperate with the United States. They depend on Iran for so much of their oil that complying with sanctions would be too painful to consider. India is a major user of Iranian oil, China is another, and South Korea is a third. They are not going to trade their own economic health for a pat on the back from the United States.

Trading with Iran without openly mocking the sanctions has become an art, largely developed by the Iranians themselves. When you ban people from SWIFT, they don't pound sand; they devise alternatives.

---

[2]This Belgian company handles all international bank wire transfers.

Iran is selling oil to India for gold and rupees. There also is a deal with China that swaps oil for a Walmart's worth of Chinese products. And South Korea, as well as China, is quietly paying for oil with its own currency.

One trick required the cooperation of Turkey, whose state-owned Halkbank ran oil payments through a so-called golden loophole. Between March 2012 and July 2013, the Turks shipped $13 billion of gold to Tehran directly or through the UAE. In return, the Turks received Iranian natural gas and oil. But because sanctions barred paying for the petroleum in dollars or euros, the Turks paid in Turkish lira, which the Iranians used to buy the gold that was already sitting in Tehran. Thus Iran got more gold and Turkey could say it was sending cash to private citizens, thus not violating sanctions.

President Obama closed the golden loophole in January 2013, classifying any such transactions after that date as a violation of sanctions.

Barter may be the next work-around. Iran and Russia are negotiating an oil-for-goods swap worth $1.5 billion per month to boost Iranian oil exports. Russia would accept up to one-half million barrels per day in exchange for Russian goods. Since Russia doesn't need the oil, it would resell it on the world market for rubles.

The U.S. government has demanded that Russia back away from its proposal and has threatened tighter enforcement of the prohibition on Iranian oil. What that might entail is open to conjecture. Would the United States seize vessels carrying Iranian oil purchased by Russia? That would surely push strained U.S.-Russian relations past the breaking point, with potentially horrific consequences.

All in all, non-dollar-denominated trade with a long list of friendly nations has been keeping Iran's finances afloat. Sanctions predicated on Iran's need to use the U.S. dollar in fact leave loopholes wide enough for VLCCs to sail right through.

And that's the irony. The sanctions are teaching Iran and its oil customers how to live without dollars. Other countries are watching and learning.

It's a classic self-inflicted foot wound: *Sanctions intended as an exercise of U.S. supremacy are in fact showing the world how to neutralize the primary tool of U.S. economic control.* Those unhappy with U.S. overinvolvement in world affairs are inspired to discover ways to escape dependence on the dollar.

The United States intended to demonstrate to the world that it still carried the biggest stick. Instead, it has shown that getting whacked with the stick needn't hurt that much.

U.S. sanctions against Russia for its involvement in Ukraine are having the same perverse effect on the dollar as sanctions against Iran.

In March 2014, furious over the blocking of a remittance from the Russian embassy in Kazakhstan to Sogaz Insurance Group via JPMorgan in New York, Putin ordered the Russian central bank to proceed immediately with Project Double Eagle.

Double Eagle will build a new "national payment settlement system" that will be a Russian alternative to SWIFT. It would enable trade partners to price oil in gold, which Russia has been stockpiling. That will allow users to move away from the dollar (and the euro), and conduct their business in something physical and more substantial than fiat money. The BRICS countries are cheering it on.

Russia's Ministry of Foreign Affairs calls SWIFT the "glue" that binds the global monetary system to the dollar, which it is. The ministry boasts (and it just might be right) that the Russian alternative will "destroy [SWIFT] in a fortnight." It also claims that the other BRICS countries are ready to join the new exchange as soon as it comes online.

As an angry Valentina Matviyenko, the speaker of Russia's upper house of parliament, colorfully put it, "Some hotheaded decision makers have already forgotten that the global economic crisis of 2008—which is still taking its toll on the world—started with a collapse of certain credit institutions in the United States, Great Britain, and other countries. This is why we believe that any hostile financial actions [toward Russia] are a double-edged sword and even the slightest error will send the boomerang back to the aborigines."

The Tide of Commerce

Rapid economic growth outside the United States over the past two decades is also undermining the dollar's importance.

In 2009, China pushed past the United States to become Africa's biggest trading partner. In 2012, Chinese-African trade exceeded $200 billion.

Inconveniently for the dollar, much of the trade is energy related. China gets one-third of its oil from Africa and is very engaged in the African petroleum industry. Examples:

- In 2006, China purchased a 45 percent stake in a Nigerian offshore oil and gas field for $2.3 billion.
- In 2010, it made a $23 billion agreement to build three oil refineries and a fuel complex in Nigeria.
- In 2013, Sinopec Group agreed to buy Marathon Oil's 10 percent stake in an Angolan offshore oil and gas field for $1.52 billion.
- In 2013, the China National Petroleum Corporation (CNPC) acquired a $4.2 billion stake in a Mozambique offshore natural gas field.

With those deals comes growth in the use of Chinese currency in Africa. In January 2014, Nigeria's central bank said it would sell U.S. dollars to increase its yuan holdings from 2 percent of total foreign-exchange reserves to 7 percent. A day later, Zimbabwe's central bank announced that it would add the yuan to its roster of official currencies.

Russia and India are close to a major energy alliance. In March 2014, Rosneft CEO Igor Sechin visited India to discuss cooperation between Rosneft and India's state-run Oil and Natural Gas Corporation (ONGC). Rosneft announced it had agreed to ship gas to ONGC from Rosneft's yet-to-be built LNG plant in Sakhalin, on Russia's Pacific coast. It's a virtual lock that dollars will not be involved.

An additional factor is the rise of consumerism in the large developing nations, like China, India, and Brazil. As at-home demand for goods rises, it tends to have a stabilizing effect on the indigenous currency, and nations that see increasing exports to these countries are more apt to switch their business out of the dollar.

Then there's gold, the historical choice for stability in times of financial turmoil. In 2009, as the U.S. Federal Reserve was churning out new dollars at an unprecedented pace, the world's central banks turned into net gold buyers (after years of selling off their reserves). The year 2013

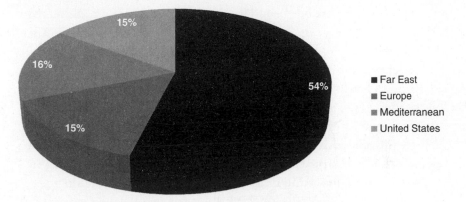

Figure 11.1   Saudi Crude Oil Exports by Destination, 2012
SOURCE: Energy Information Administration. © Casey Research 2014.

saw record buying of gold in China and Russia, as well as much of the developing world, led by Iraq and Brazil.

Germany's Bundesbank has put on the noisiest demonstration of interest in gold (which is to say, interest in securing an alternative to the dollar). In 2013, it sought to repatriate 300 metric tons of gold it had stored in the vault of the New York Fed. A Bundesbank spokesperson said the relocation was "in case of a currency crisis."[3]

Back to Riyadh

The dollar's hold on its reserve status now depends on the petrodollar system, which in turn depends on Saudi Arabia. And the Kingdom of Saudi Arabia is increasingly looking eastward.

As noted, Iranian oil is important for China—9 percent of China's imports. But oil from Saudi Arabia is even more important; the Saudis send 19 percent of all the oil China imports. (See Figure 11.1.)

Trade between Saudi Arabia and China has increased almost 58-fold in the past two decades, from $1.28 billion in 1990 to $74 billion

[3] Interestingly, the United States said it would take until 2020 to deliver that much gold. So far, it is not close to even that turtle-like pace. Just five tons were returned in year 1 (less than 2 percent), leading some skeptics to question whether the United States actually has as much gold as it claims.

in 2012. Saudi Arabia has been China's top partner in the Middle East for 11 consecutive years. The two countries just keep growing closer. In 2012, they agreed to build the world's largest refinery on Saudi soil, a joint venture worth $8.5 billion.

In 2009, Saudi exports to China exceeded those to the United States for the first time, and the country now exports three times more to five Asian countries (China, Japan, South Korea, India, and Singapore) than to Europe and North America combined. All this—along with the United States' shale revolution and its decreasing need for imported oil—points to China as the growth market for Saudi petroleum.

Saudi Arabia is not the only Muslim power to have deepened its economic ties with China over the past decade. Egypt, Indonesia, Iran, Iraq, Kazakhstan, Malaysia, Mauritania, Nigeria, Pakistan, Sudan, and Turkey have done so as well. But Saudi Arabia has gone the furthest.

The Chinese and Saudis are still using dollars in their trade, but for how long is an open question. Saudi Arabia is not likely to pull the plug anytime soon. American guarantees to support the monarchy in case of insurrection and defend it against invasion still carry a lot of weight. With Shi'ite Iran and newly minted (though besieged) Shi'ite Iraq on Saudi Arabia's doorstep, that protection remains critical.

But Saudi/American relations are cool at best. There's a lot of irritation in the relationship for the kingdom. For instance, the United States has beaten the "democracy" drum in the Middle East since 9/11, which has not been pleasing to the distinctly undemocratic ears of the Saudi monarchy.

Saudi officials view U.S. post–Cold War hegemony in the Middle East as destabilizing in its overall effect. Saudi Arabia sees itself as suffering for reckless and poorly executed American foreign policy. The United States toppled Saddam Hussein against Riyadh's advice, and now Iraq threatens to come apart. Plus, the U.S. government continues to fail to pressure Israel to make the concessions to the Palestinians required under the Saudi Initiative of 2002.

The Saudis saw the U.S. decision to remove Saddam as wrong-headed from the beginning, knowing that any democratically elected national Iraqi government would be Shi'ite majority and open to cooperation with Iran. Thus when the Bahrain protests erupted in 2011, the Saudis did not wait for a permission slip from the White House before sending troops to assist in a harsh crackdown to defend Bahrain's Sunni monarchy.

Saudi Arabia views American officials, and particularly the Obama administration, as clueless about Middle Eastern realities. The unfolding of the Arab Spring has led many in Riyadh to question Washington's loyalty to the kingdom and its allies. When protests erupted across Egypt in 2011, the Saudis were disappointed at the passivity of the Obama administration as a strategic partner of 30 years (the Mubarak regime) disintegrated. Washington's subsequent decision to reduce military aid to General Sisi has further irked the Saudis, who fear Sisi's enemy, the Muslim Brotherhood.

Many Saudis also accuse the United States of betraying the anti-Assad rebels in Syria, and Riyadh was angered when the Obama administration decided not to strike Assad's forces after their alleged use of chemical weapons.

And there is Iran itself. Barack Obama has made conciliatory gestures toward Iran virtually from the beginning of his presidency. While sanctions remain the stick, Riyadh sees negotiations with Iran as an overly generous carrot. From Saudi Arabia's point of view, the whole process signals a possible shift in the regional balance of power that would leave the kingdom exposed.

The Saudis do not, therefore, see U.S. negotiations with Iran as a positive. They see them as a slap to Riyadh's face, and yet another reason to question Washington's commitment to the kingdom.

Putin, who was the first Russian leader ever to visit Saudi Arabia, in 2007, sees it all unfolding. He recognizes that Saudi participation in the proposed Double Eagle payments system or something like it would make dethroning the U.S. dollar much easier.

Saudi Arabia has kept holding its hand out to Russia, specifically by offering a $15 billion arms contract to the Russians if they will soften their support of Assad. Russia won't rush a decision that big, but with the United States pulling back on involvement in the Middle East, it's only a matter of time before Saudi Arabia and Russia begin working together more closely, most likely starting with a weapons deal. But it won't happen quickly, as Saudi Arabia is a supporter of the Islamic State of Iraq and the Levant (ISIL) and most of Assad's other enemies, while Russia is Assad's ally.

Before it happens, China will already have a close relationship with Saudi Arabia, as it is rapidly advancing in that direction. And because China and Russia are now working so closely, the Chinese-Saudi relationship will help to draw Russia closer to Saudi Arabia.

Much will depend on Saudi Arabia switching away from the petrodollar, but in the meantime, it will be in Saudi Arabia's interest to play with both sides, the United States and the Sino-Russian axis. Rather than standing with the United States or jumping ship, Saudi Arabia will take a middle path, which will be enough to give Putin the opening he wants.

It is still a matter for conjecture, but at some point the Saudis may decide two things:

- First, that by not dealing more forcefully with Iran and Syria, the United States has reneged on its promise to keep the monarchy safe, so Saudi Arabia has no reason to continue honoring its part of the 1973 petrodollar agreement.
- Second, that using U.S. dollars in every transaction is foolish, an unnecessary bit of overhead, especially in dealing with the Chinese.

If these ideas take root and Russia presents itself as a reliable protector, the Saudis will ditch the buck, and Putin's work will be done.

Chapter 12

Post-Petrodollar America

This is the climax of the story I promised at the beginning of *The Colder War*. It describes the financial tsunami headed for the West in general and for the United States in particular, and how the maneuverings of Russia's diminutive earthquake generator, Vladimir Putin, will disrupt your life.

What you've read is what some in Washington already understand but are not willing to acknowledge publicly. Putin and his allies are embarked on a mission to sabotage the petrodollar. You now know this, and you know its importance. It is certain to happen—not *if*, but *when*. So the critical question is: How will it all unfold?

When the petrodollar era ends, will it go with a bang or a whimper?

History has little guidance to offer. The decline of the British pound, as noted in the preceding chapter, took 30 years and two world wars; the unwinding of the empire took even longer. Is something similar in store for the United States? Perhaps, but three factors argue persuasively that the undoing of the dollar will be comparatively abrupt and disturbing.

First, in its heyday, Britain ruled a vastly different world. Many of the great population centers economically were all but living in the Dark Ages and posed no threat to British hegemony. Today there are multiple centers of financial power—including Russia, China, and Brazil—with the technical ability to build dollarless systems and with sufficient size to attract wide international participation.

Second, ubiquitous computing capacity will make it easier to leave the dollar. In pen-and-ledger days, maintaining accounts in multiple currencies just wasn't practical for any but the largest businesses. Today, thanks to modern data handling, any business that wants to can have a multicurrency bank account and run a multicurrency accounting system. So the need for a reserve currency that serves as a financial common language for international business is no longer pressing. It will be far easier to wave good-bye to the dollar than it would have been to leave the pound.

Third, the volume of the assets that will be shunned will be unprecedented. The British, because they were constrained by the pound's redeemability for gold, never came close to the extravagance with which the United States has abused its position as the issuer of the world's reserve currency.

The United States slipped away from gold discipline in 1971, when President Nixon "closed the gold window." Since then, exporting dollars and dollar-denominated IOUs has been a major growth industry. That was never the case with the pound, so the volume of dollar assets that foreigners will be shifting away from will be much bigger and will move like a landslide.

Softening Up

The U.S. economy's relative position in the world has declined over the past several decades as one country after another has modernized and played economic catch-up. The United States is no longer the behemoth astride a ruined world that it was after World War II. Most cars built in 1946 were built in the United States. In 2013, it accounted for only 12 percent of world auto production.

On the other hand, the United States is still by far the world's strongest military power and will continue to be for some years to come. It can rain death on any selected patch of earth, and the threat of doing so can intimidate any troublesome country not equipped with nuclear weapons. It's clearly preferable to have that power than to be on the other side of the transaction, but it comes with drawbacks, both of which are damaging to the dollar.

First, there's the cost. In 2013, the United States spent $643 billion on its military—over one-third of the world's total military spending and just shy of 20 percent of total U.S. federal spending.

The United States no longer can afford it. Of every dollar Washington has been spending, 46 cents is borrowed money. Even if Russia and China weren't cheering for the dollar to drop dead, and even if Putin took up knitting, the river of IOUs running out of the United States and into foreign investment portfolios would eventually drown the dollar. So the U.S. military's megabudget, which accounts for nearly half the U.S. government's deficit, works to soften up the dollar for its attackers.

Second, no country likes being pushed around. Possessing overwhelming power has its advantages, but only a near-saintly degree of self-restraint can save that power from attracting resentment. For the United States, such self-restraint hasn't been part of the program, and now, reasonably or not, the world is full of resentment. As the need for U.S. currency declines, the resentful will find dumping the dollar entirely agreeable, a satisfying exercise in passive aggression.

The Process

The exit from the dollar will run on two tracks, both of which lead to trouble for the United States. One track is for the dollars themselves. The other is for Treasury bills and other IOUs denominated in dollars. Whether it happens rapidly or slowly, here is how the process works.

Foreigners hold over $600 billion in hand-to-hand U.S. currency (e.g., $100 bills) and over $1 trillion in checking deposits at U.S. banks—about 65 percent and 30 percent, respectively, of the two items. When they decide they no longer need most of it because other currencies are serving well for international trade, they'll unload the excess by selling dollars for those other currencies.

The immediate effect will be a drop in the foreign-exchange value of the dollar; a dollar won't buy as many Russian rubles, Chinese yuan, Brazilian reals, or units of any other currency as it once did, which will translate into higher prices for goods imported into the United States. All that stuff from China that you can buy at Walmart won't be so cheap anymore, nor will cars from Germany or South Korea, or coffee from South America, or cocoa from Africa, or shirts from a dozen poor countries that today crave dollars. In other words, an early result of the world distancing itself from U.S. currency will be price inflation in the United States.

A separate vector feeding price inflation will come into play. The dollars that foreigners are unloading will find their way to the wallets of individuals and businesses in the United States—the dollars will have nowhere else to go. That extra cash will reinforce the inflationary process already under way.

Foreigners hold over $5 trillion in U.S. Treasury securities and bank certificates of deposit (CDs), about 47 percent of the total outstanding. As the dollar's hold on reserve currency status slips away, the primary motive for owning those assets will slip away with it. The U.S. Treasury and commercial banks in the United States will be forced to offer higher yields to persuade foreigners to roll over their investments as they mature, which will push up interest rates throughout U.S. credit markets. Prices of existing dollar-denominated bonds will fall.

Then the two tracks—the effects of dumping dollars themselves and the effects of diminished demand for dollar-denominated IOUs—will meet. Higher rates of price inflation will operate as a second-stage booster for interest rates, as savers and lenders insist on being compensated for the purchasing power that is draining out of their dollars.

The process won't just be financial news. It will change the way Americans live, and it will change the U.S. government's notion of what is possible and what is not.

For most Americans, it will mean a period of stagnant or declining living standards. Imported goods will become more expensive, as will borrowing to buy a house or for anything else. It will be a hard lesson that tomorrow is not inevitably better than today.

For the U.S. government, it will mean learning to live as just one more borrower in the international capital markets. Letting debt grow faster than the economy will no longer be an option. The politicians will be forced to decide what not to spend money on.

On the Fast Tracks

For most Americans, it's not going to be good times. Whether the unwinding of the dollar's hegemony turns into a depression and a truly painful experience for millions of people depends on how rapid and abrupt the process is.

What happens if the petrodollar system breaks down relatively rapidly, over the course of a year or two, instead of slowly fading away? This is the worst-case scenario for the Colder War—not a withdrawal but a flight from the dollar. You wouldn't want it to happen, but you shouldn't assume it won't.

The past six years of ultralow interest rates have pushed bond prices higher and higher. A flight from the dollar would send interest rates at least up to the highs of the 1970s and early 1980s (when the rate on the 30-year Treasury bond peaked near 15 percent) and slash the trading prices of existing bonds by 35 percent to 55 percent. Homeowners with adjustable-rate mortgages would get crushed. Results for the stock market would be even more violent.

The Federal Reserve could forestall the process temporarily by creating even more trillions of fiat dollars out of thin air to buy up the bonds being dumped by foreigners. But the bond dumpers would quickly trade the newly minted bucks for more immediately useful currencies, which would further depress the exchange value of the dollar, which means imported goods would become even more expensive for Americans and price inflation would get even worse. And as the newly created but unwanted dollars returned to the United States, they would become yet another force driving inflation.

Rapidly rising interest rates would have nasty consequences throughout the U.S. economy.

U.S. banks would be in trouble. The fall in the value of their bond holdings and the gap between yields on old loans and the higher rates they would need to pay to retain deposits would push many institutions toward insolvency. The Federal Deposit Insurance Corporation (FDIC)'s puny insurance fund wouldn't be enough to buy even a Band-Aid for the problem. You could count on the Federal Reserve to deal with the problem by printing still more money—which would pay for still more inflation, which would exceed the rates suffered in the 1970s. A 20 percent annual inflation rate would be within reach.

And something even worse could happen to the financial system. The daisy chain of derivative investments that runs in and out of the world's biggest banks, insurance companies, brokerages, and hedge funds could come apart, with truly apocalyptic consequences, as explained nearby in "The Bomb in Your Basement."

The U.S. government's option of last resort would be to default on debt held by foreigners, which would produce the most interesting day ever in the history of global financial markets. Panic, chaos, pandemonium—no word would be adequate to describe it. But a default with lipstick and makeup, such as surprising foreign investors with a high rate of withholding tax on their interest earnings, is a possibility. Other countries have weaseled out of debt they couldn't pay and then climbed out of the deep pile of wreckage that resulted, although it has never been done on the scale that a U.S. default would represent.

It is more likely that the U.S. government will raid individual retirement accounts (IRAs) and 401(k)s by requiring them to hold a minimum percentage in Treasuries—for the account owner's supposed protection, of course.

Rising interest rates would cripple the economy. Not only do they harm the housing industry, but they discourage people from borrowing money. Business start-ups would become rare, as would any expansion of existing businesses. Frightened consumers would slow their spending. Unemployment would reach depression levels.

At best, it would be stagflation, a state of high unemployment, snail-paced or negative economic growth, and rapid price inflation. The combination of higher prices for necessities and lower wages would demote much of the middle class to working poor status and impoverish those creeping along on fixed incomes.

The U.S. government would be forced to slash expenditures—drastically. It wouldn't be able to continue borrowing 46 percent of what it spends, at least not for long, since at high interest rates the interest on the debt would quickly become ruinous. Cutting spending would mean a much smaller military and a big decline in the services and handouts that a wide swath of the population now takes for granted.

Americans living on government largesse would be hit hard, and they'd be joined by millions of newly unemployed. When the ranks of the disgruntled begin to swell, things could get very noisy very fast, and the noise could turn into street violence. Members of the Occupy movement would be remembered for their nice manners. Episodes of martial law are a possibility.

International trade wouldn't cease, but it would switch to alternative currencies. The ruble and the yuan are the top candidates. I'm sure that in his dreams Vladimir Putin envisions the ruble as the world's new reserve currency, but there's no guarantee that any one currency would replace the dollar.

Another possibility is that gold would recover its historical role in international trade. Russia, China, India, and others have been buying gold over the past decade and would be ready for such a development. In fact, this may be where Putin is trying to go, since Russia is now the world's number-three gold producer and its output is growing rapidly. A gold ruble has already been proposed for use within Russia.

The Bomb in Your Basement

A simple derivative is a financial contract that derives its value from the performance of another, underlying asset—such as a particular stock, a bond issue, a defined basket of stocks or bonds, an interest rate, or other financial index. Other derivatives are more complex; their value depends on whether the underlying asset outperforms or underperforms a given standard. Some of them are inverts; their value rises when the value of the underlying asset declines.

Imagine a laboratory where a mad scientist dismembers animals of different species and reassembles the parts into novel

(Continued)

structures. That's how strange the world of derivatives gets. And it gets even stranger. The asset underlying a derivative may itself be a derivative whose underlying asset is or includes still other derivatives. The chains can be very long and complex, a tangle of claims and obligations by the many banks and other institutions involved.

The financial mathematics customarily used for valuing derivatives and assessing their risk levels assume that the behavior of the ultimate underlying assets and financial indexes will never stray too far from normal. Generally that assumption works nicely. But if a truly abnormal event occurs, something that might not happen more than once in a century, something like the world rejecting yesterday's international reserve currency, the only answer you'll get from the math for estimating value and risk will be "Duh."

That result would be worse than a wave of catastrophic losses by banks and insurance companies. It would be catastrophic losses with lights out, since the complexity of many derivatives would prevent the participants from quickly assessing who lost what. All the participants (including, most likely, the bank where you keep your money) would look bankrupt, as many of them would in fact be.

Depending on who's doing the measuring, the notional value of all derivatives currently outstanding is $600 trillion. In a dollar meltdown, that would make for a lot of confusion. During the 2008–2009 financial crisis, the markets got a taste of how bad it can get. If there is a rapid flight from the dollar, they'll get a banquet's worth.

In 2008 and 2009, trust evaporated. Banks refused to lend to other banks because no one knew what the other guy's collateral might be worth. The financial system seized up, and we came within a whisker of finding out what could happen in the event of a dollar meltdown.

Banks would fail, brokerages would fail, credit would dry up, debtors would default en masse, and individual investors would see their accounts swept away, their life savings lost. A global depression would ensue.

There is no financial event in history to compare this with.

Last Exit

None of this is yet inevitable. In fact, the recipe for the United States to avoid it is not at all complex.

- Stop runaway government spending. If the growth in government debt is held below the growth rate of the economy, the dollar's ability to withstand attack will strengthen mightily.
- Stop accepting everyone's invitation to participate in everyone's conflict. That will allow a country protected by two oceans to spend less on its military and still be secure.
- Stop everything—especially tax rules and handouts—that encourages people not to work, not to produce, and not to save.
- Stop allowing superstition-based regulation to interfere with the development of domestic energy resources.

That solution is still available. And it is simple, but brutally so. Judge for yourself the likelihood that it will be applied.

What You Can Do

While they are waiting for the problem to be defused by thoughtful, farsighted official action, what can Americans do to protect themselves from the risk of the dollar getting whacked?

- **Step 1.** The single most helpful step, and it is a simple one, is to trade some of your dollars for mankind's natural reserve currency, which is gold. It could be gold coins such as the gold Eagles produced by the U.S. Mint, Canadian Maple Leafs, or South African Krugerrands. Even better, get some of all three, and don't store the gold in a local bank, but rather in a very safe location that would leave the coins accessible when you need them. Owning physical silver is also prudent.

- **Step 2.** Open an account with a non-U.S. bank, to make it easy to hold some of your cash in the form of foreign currencies, preferably in a jurisdiction you want to spend some time in.

Having assured yourself of multiple sources of liquidity, you can prudently turn to profiting from the disorder that is likely to come when the dollar is dethroned. That event will be accompanied by the Putinization of global resources, a historic economic shift that will be disastrous for the unprepared but that will make some people rich.

Where to begin?

There is no better profit opportunity than speculating in publicly listed junior resource companies. Stocks of small oil, gas, uranium, and other resource companies are highly volatile. Careless buying can be ruinous to your financial health. But when one of these little stocks does well, it doesn't go up 10 or 20 percent; it goes up 10 or 20 *times*—or even more.

Profits from junior resource companies have changed my life, and Mr. Putin's long-term plan can give you the opportunity for a similar experience.

The most important element for winning big with junior resource companies is to bet on the right people. You don't need to be a geologist or engineer, or have an MBA.

You do need to focus on investing in the right management teams, the people whose knowledge and experience tell you they can stack the deck in favor of success. They know how to navigate through the obstacles that destroy so many little companies. Without shrewd decision makers, environmental and regulatory problems can poison the development of the best deposits, and failing to raise needed capital at each step in the process of turning an interesting patch of ground into a producing mine or oil field can bring the most promising project to a halt.

There is an old saying in the junior resource sector: "Average management will screw up the best rocks in the best jurisdictions, and the best management teams will find the best rocks in the best jurisdictions."

Bringing Modern Technology to Old Fields

One of today's biggest opportunities is bringing modern technology to past-producing oil and gas fields and mining deposits. For example, in the United States, hydraulic fracturing combined with horizontal drilling has unlocked gas and oil deposits that were known but were previously uneconomic—such as the now very profitable Barnett and Bakken shale formations.

While Putin is busy with his resource projects in Asia, smart and savvy management teams will be revisiting dormant oil and natural gas fields in Europe, which were producing oil and gas before the first petroleum well was drilled in the United States. They'll be bringing modern technologies, such as horizontal drilling, to collect the hydrocarbons that are still waiting and that European consumers will be desperate to buy.

Throughout the book, we've seen how Vladimir Putin is positioning Russia to control the global resources chessboard. Fortunes will be made by investors who correctly position themselves in companies that effectively add one more square to that chessboard, a square where Western Europe can find alternatives to energy from Russia.

Expect more conflict between Russia and the West. And expect the conflict to make access to energy and other resources even more valuable than it is today. Understanding that fact is the key to profiting from Putin's vision.

I hope you'll use it.

Afterword

E ven as I'm preparing to button up the manuscript for *The Colder War* and send it off to the publisher, events keep adding to the story, and I'm about to summarize the most recent. New events are sure to occur, so go to www.caseyresearch.com/colderwar for the most recent updates.

On July 17, 2014, Flight MH17 from Amsterdam to Kuala Lumpur was shot out of the sky just east of Donetsk in Ukraine and about 50 kilometers from the border with Russia. As a result, 298 people died, apparently because pro-Russian separatists had acquired a Russian SA-11 (Buk) missile and mistook an airliner for a Ukrainian military plane. Russia denies any responsibility and blames Ukraine. Ukraine denies any responsibility and blames Russia.

The European Union and the United States have responded with more sanctions against Russia. But the new measures, like their predecessors, cut with a double-edged blade. The ruble's foreign-exchange value dropped by almost 10 percent—bad news for Russian consumers and for Russian companies that have borrowed in foreign currencies, but a bonanza for Russian exporters of natural gas, oil, and uranium, and anything else produced domestically.

The Islamic State of Iraq and Syria (ISIS) has been extending its ungentle control over much of Iraq. President Obama's removal of U.S. soldiers from the country left a power vacuum that ISIS is filling with the use of weapons and other military supplies left over from earlier U.S. involvement. The United States has just begun to respond, alarmed by ISIS's threat to Kurdistan and its oil fields, and to the last U.S. military base in Iraq.

Israel and Hamas have been battling each other in the Gaza Strip. The notable difference from the Gaza strife of 2008 is today's hostility toward Israel in European media and also in global social media like Facebook and even in the United States. Perhaps the world has forgotten, or would rather not consider, that Hamas's goal includes removing Jews, all of them, not just from Palestine but from the whole region.

While all of this adds to the story, it doesn't alter the story line. Every brick the United States throws at a Russian window bounces back. Every U.S. sanction against Russia offers a profit opportunity for a company or country that switches out of the dollar. Every U.S. criticism of Russia demonstrates its inability to do anything but criticize. Every futile U.S. effort to control events in the Middle East demonstrates that a promise of U.S. protection is a thin reason for a government to feel safe—especially if it is the government of Saudi Arabia.

The story isn't finished, but I thank you for reading the part I've set out. For readers of *The Colder War*, go to www.caseyresearch.com /colderwar for updates and to subscribe to my free weekly e-letter. I hope you'll visit. You've already paid for the book, so the updates are free.

References

Vladimir Putin

Fennell, Thomas. Translation of Vladimir Putin's thesis "Mineral and Raw Materials Resources and the Development Strategy for the Russian Economy." *The Atlantic*, August 20, 2008. www.theatlantic.com/daily-dish/archive/2008/08/putins-thesis-raw-text/212739/.

Goldman, Marshall L. *Petrostate: Putin, Power, and the New Russia*. New York: Oxford University Press, 2008. http://books.google.com/books?id=9VreAGr8sk4C&printsec=frontcover&dq=petrostate&hl=en&sa=X&ei=HeDoU4bnG4-TyATIpYDoDA&ved=0CB4Q6AEwAA#v=onepage&q=petrostate&f=false.

Lynch, Allen. *Vladimir Putin and Russian Statecraft*. Washington, DC: Potomac Books, 2011. http://books.google.ca/books?id=OHnY1Qm9OYQC&printsec=frontcover&dq=vladimir+putin+and+russian+statecraft&hl=en&sa=X&ei=ft_oU-b2Eov-yQTO94DgDQ&ved=0CCYQ6AEwAA#v=onepage&q=vladimir%20putin%20and%20russian%20statecraft&f=false.

Putin, Vladimir. "A New Integration Project for Eurasia: The Future in the Making." *Izvestia*, October 3, 2011. www.russianmission.eu/en/news/article-prime-minister-vladimir-putin-new-integration-project-eurasia-future-making-izvestia-3-.

Putin, Vladimir. "Russia and the Changing World." *Moscow News*, February 27, 2014. www.mn.ru/politics/20120227/312306749.html.

Putin, Vladimir. "Russia in Focus—The Challenges We Must Face." *Izvestia*, January 16, 2012. http://rt.com/politics/official-word/putin-russia-focus-challenges-845/.

Russia

Bogetic, Zeljko, et al. "The World Bank in Russia—Russian Economic Report No. 18." World Bank, March 2009. http://siteresources.worldbank.org/INTRUSSIANFEDERATION/Resources/rer18eng.pdf.

Donaldson, Robert H. "Boris Yeltsin's Foreign Policy Legacy." Presentation to the 41st Annual Meeting of the International Studies Association, Los Angeles, California, March 18, 2000. www.personal.utulsa.edu/~robert-donaldson/yeltsin.htm.

Graham, James. "The Collapse of the Soviet Union." *History Orb*. www.historyorb.com/russia/intro.php.

"Prominent Russians: Peter the Great." *Russiapedia; Russia Today*. http://russiapedia.rt.com/prominent-russians/the-romanov-dynasty/peter-i/.

"SCO to Admit New Members." *Russian Radio*, August 1, 2014. http://indian.ruvr.ru/2014_08_01/SCO–admit-new-members/.

Yakovlev, Andrei. "State-Business Relations and Improvement of Corporate Governance in Russia." BOFIT Discussion Paper, 2008. www.suomenpankki.fi/bofit_en/tutkimus/tutkimusjulkaisut/dp/Documents/dp2608.pdf.

Khodorkovsky and Putin

Gessen, Masha. "The Wrath of Putin." *Vanity Fair*, April 2012. www.vanityfair.com/politics/2012/04/vladimir-putin-mikhail-khodorkovsky-russia.

The Great Game

Fromkin, David. "The Great Game in Asia." *Foreign Affairs*, Spring 1980. www.foreignaffairs.com/articles/33619/david-fromkin/the-great-game-in-asia.

Chechnya

Anderson, Scott. "Putin: The Dark Rise to Power." *GQ Magazine*, September 6, 2009; reprinted by KavkazCenter. www.kavkazcenter.com/eng/content/2009/09/06/10979.shtml.

Oliker, Olga. "Russia's Chechen Wars 1994–2000." Monograph Reports, RAND Corporation, 2001. www.rand.org/pubs/monograph_reports/MR1289.html.

Steele, Jonathan. "It's Over, and Putin Won." *The Guardian*, September 29, 2008. www.theguardian.com/commentisfree/2008/sep/30/russia.chechnya.

Ukraine

Cohen, Stephen F. "Distorting Russia." *The Nation*, March 3, 2014. www.thenation.com/article/178344/distorting-russia.

Emmerson, Charles. "Ukraine and Russia's History Wars." *History Today*, March 4, 2014. www.historytoday.com/blog/2014/03/ukraine-and-russia%E2%80%99s-history-wars.

Gaouette, Nicole. "Putin's Motives Rooted in History Remain a Mystery Abroad." *Bloomberg*, March 18, 2014. www.bloomberg.com/news/2014-03-17/putin-s-motives-rooted-in-history-remain-a-mystery-abroad.html.

Goodman, Amy, and Juan Gonzalez. "We Are Not Beginning a New Cold War, We Are Well into It: Stephen Cohen on Russia-Ukraine Crisis." *Democracy Now!*, April 18, 2014; reprinted by *Truth Out*. http://truth-out.org/news/item/23171-we-are-not-beginning-a-new-cold-war-we-are-well-into-it-stephen-cohen-on-russia-ukraine-crisis.

Putin, Vladimir. "Vladimir Putin Talks to Reporters about Ukraine." *World News Daily*, Information Clearing House, March 8, 2014. www.informationclearinghouse.info/article37889.htm.

Color Revolutions and the Role of NGOs

Wilson, Jeanne L. "Colour Revolutions: The View from Moscow and Beijing." Wheaton College, Norton, Massachusetts. https://www.ucl.ac.uk/ceelbas/workshops/Jeanne_Wilson_paper.pdf.

The Middle East

Fildis, Ayse Tekdal. "The Troubles in Syria: Spawned by French Divide and Rule." *Middle East Policy Council*, Winter 2011. www.mepc.org/journal/middle-east-policy-archives/troubles-syria-spawned-french-divide-and-rule.

"The History of Saudi Arabia." Royal Embassy of Saudi Arabia, Washington, DC. www.saudiembassy.net/about/country-information/history.aspx.

"Iran History." *Pars Times—Greater Iran and Beyond*. www.parstimes.com/history/.

Scheinmann, Gabriel. "The Map That Ruined the Middle East." *The Tower*, July 2013. www.thetower.org/article/the-map-that-ruined-the-middle-east/.

StevenAU. "Wahhabi Islam: General Overview." *Free Republic*, July 17, 2004. www.freerepublic.com/focus/f-news/1173310/posts.

Valdes, Juan Jose, Lauren E. James, and Eve Conant. "Iraq: 1,200 Years of Turbulent History in Five Maps." *National Geographic*, July 2, 2014. http://news.nationalgeographic.com/news/2014/07/140702-iraq-history-maps/.

Various articles on Afghan history. Afghanistan Online. www.afghan-web.com/history/.

"What Is the Difference between Sunni and Shiite Muslims—And What Does It Matter?" History News Network, October 5, 2005. http://hnn.us/article/934.

Energy

"Excerpt GEAB 72 (February 2013)—2013–2015: The End of the Petrodollar's Rule over the World." *GlobalEurope Anticipation Bulletin*, February 15, 2013. www.leap2020.eu/Excerpt-GEAB-72-February-2013-2013-2015-The-end-of-the-petrodollar-s-rule-over-the-world_a14922.html.

Kaplan, Robert D. "The Geopolitics of Energy." *Forbes*, April 4, 2014. www.forbes.com/sites/stratfor/2014/04/04/the-geopolitics-of-energy/.

Mitrova, Tatiana. "The Geopolitics of Russian Natural Gas." Harvard University's Belfer Center and Rice University's Baker Institute Center for Energy Studies, February 2014. http://belfercenter.ksg.harvard.edu/files/CES-pub-GeoGasRussia-022114.pdf.

"Oil History Timeline." *Oil 150*. www.oil150.com/about-oil/timeline/.

Saul, Jonathan, and Parisa Hafezi. "Exclusive: Iran, Russia Negotiating Big Oil-for-Goods Deal." Reuters, January 10, 2014. www.reuters.com/article/2014/01/10/us-iran-russia-oil-idUSBREA090DK20140110.

Terentieva, Alexandra. "Russia Goes Uranium Mining around the World." *Global Geopolitics and Political Economy*, March 31, 2010. http://globalgeo politics.net/wordpress/2010/03/31/russia-goes-uranium-mining-around-the -world/.

Money

Cohen, Benjamin. "Bretton Woods System." Prepared for the Routledge Encyclopedia of International Political Economy. www.polsci.ucsb.edu/ faculty/cohen/inpress/bretton.html.

"The History of Money." Federal Reserve Bank of Minneapolis. https:// www.minneapolisfed.org/community_education/teacher/history.cfm.

McLeay, Michael, Amar Radia, and Ryland Thomas. "Money Creation in the Modern Economy." *Bank of England, Quarterly Bulletin 2014 Q1*. www.bankofengland.co.uk/publications/Documents/quarterlybulletin/2014/ qb14q1prereleasemoneycreation.pdf.

Oweiss, Ibrahim M. "Economics of Petrodollars." Address before the Conference on the World Monetary Crisis, Arden House, Harriman Campus, Columbia University, New York, March 1–3, 1974. http://faculty.georgetown.edu/ imo3/petrod/petro2.htm.

Robinson, Jerry. "The Rise of the Petrodollar System: 'Dollars for Oil.'" *Financial Sense*, February 23, 2012. www.financialsense.com/contributors/jerry -robinson/the-rise-of-the-petrodollar-system-dollars-for-oil.

Threats to Dollar Hegemony

"China and Russia Abandon the Dollar in New Bilateral Trade Agreement." *Daily Mail UK*, November 25, 2010. www.dailymail.co.uk/news/article -1332882/China-Russia-abandon-dollar-new-bilateral-trade-agreement.html.

MacLucas, Neil, and Richard Silk. "Swiss, Chinese Central Banks Enter Currency Swap Agreement." *Dow Jones Business News*, July 21, 2014. www.nasdaq.com/article/swiss chinese central banks enter currency swap -agreement-20140721-00068.

Robinson, Jerry. "Preparing for the Collapse of the Petrodollar System." *Jerry Robinson's FTM Daily*. http://ftmdaily.com/preparing-for-the-collapse-of -the-petrodollar-system/.

"Russia Prepares to Attack the Petrodollar." *Voice of Russia*, April 4, 2014. http://voiceofrussia.com/2014_04_04/Russia-prepares-to-attack-the -petrodollar-2335/.

Soldatkin, Vladimir, and Florence Tan. "UPDATE1—Russian Oil Firm Says Asian Buyers Willing to Use Euros." Reuters, April 10, 2014.   www.reuters.com/article/2014/04/10/russia-gazpromneft-euros -idUSL6N0N22EH20140410.

Zhu, Grace. "BRICS Create $100 Billion Emergency Reserve Fund." *Dow Jones Business News*, July 15, 2014. www.nasdaq.com/article/brics-create-100 -billion-emergency-reserve-fund-20140715-01338.

About the Author

Marin Katusa is one of the most well-connected deal makers and successful portfolio managers in the energy and resource exploration sectors. If there's a deal being done, chances are Marin is in the room, is familiar with everyone, and knows exactly how to play it.

The one place you're not likely to find Marin is behind a desk. He gets into the field and scrutinizes mines and energy projects firsthand (he has racked up hundreds of site tours). Marin has rubbed elbows with energy ministers, generals, oligarchs, and billionaires all over the world. He has strapped on a flak jacket to survey lucrative projects in Russia, Iraq, Ukraine, Kuwait, Mongolia, Kosovo, Colombia, and many other dangerous yet resource-rich jurisdictions that require the protection of heavily armed private security forces.

After starting out as a mathematics professor, Marin left academics to apply his models to portfolio management. His funds have been among the top-performing in the resources sector over the past five years in Canada.

Over that time, he has outperformed the comparable index, the TSX-V, by an astounding 600 percent after all costs and fees.

He is one of the most sought-after speakers and financial minds in the sector. He's a regular contributor to the Business News Network (BNN) and is interviewed around the world, appearing on CNBC, RT (formerly Russia Today), and CBC, as well as in *Bloomberg* and *Forbes*.

Marin is a founding director of Copper Mountain, one of only a few companies that ever went from private to public and built an operating mine in four years. Today, Copper Mountain is Canada's third-largest copper mine.

Since 2007, he has been serving as the chief energy investment strategist for Casey Research. Every year since, his newsletters, *Casey Energy Confidential* and the *Casey Energy Report*, have outperformed their benchmarks, including multiple 10-bagger recommendations.

He also handpicked the Casey NexTen, a top 10 list of the most successful young resource entrepreneurs of our time who have built true value for shareholders over the past decade. Marin is a large shareholder via his funds in each of the companies run by these superstars.

Marin is one of the most active financiers for early-stage, junior resource companies in Canada. He was the lead financier in the first two financings for Cuadrilla Resources, now one of the largest and most successful unconventional natural gas players in the United Kingdom.

He also structured the financing and the sale of Turkana and the world-class 10BB oil block in Kenya to Africa Oil, a Lundin-held company with a market capitalization of over CDN$2 billion.

Over the years, Marin has been involved in raising over CDN$1 billion in capital for early-stage and producing resource companies.

Marin is always on the lookout for the next big investment opportunity outside of well-traveled paths. You can read his monthly advisory services at www.caseyresearch.com/.

Index

Investing in *The Colder War*

The global strategic war over energy is here, and it is sending ripple effects through every sector of the economy. The *smart* money is positioning itself to take advantage.

Save 47% – Exclusive Offer for Book Owners

Exposing the West's shortsighted policies and the renewed threat from an old enemy now using our own weapons against us are the main reasons I wrote this book.

But first and foremost I'm an investor. Being in the room while worldwide resource deals were struck shaped my understanding of the political reality I describe in *The Colder War*. The same understanding has shaped my portfolio.

In my advisory, *The Colder War Letter*, I uncover the investment opportunities emerging from the global quagmire.

Get my latest insights and investment advice—at an exclusive discount for readers of my book.

Marin Katusa,
Senior Editor,
The Colder War Letter

Exclusive Discount for Book Fans: Save 47% on a Risk-Free Subscription to *The Colder War Letter*

I am completely convinced that the fortunate few with the foresight to invest in the opportunities the global energy battle is offering will end up with vast profits.

Normally a steal at $149, right now you can get *The Colder War Letter* for just $79...a 47% discount.

Your satisfaction is guaranteed: If you don't like *The Colder War Letter*, cancel within 90 days and receive a full refund.

**To order, visit http://www.colderwar.com/reader-offer
or call 888-51CASEY.**

Or return this form via mail to:

The Colder War Letter
c/o Casey Research
PO Box 1427
Stowe, VT 05672

Name: _____

Email: _____

Credit Card Number: _____

Expiration Date: __/__ Billing Zip/Postcode: _____

The Colder War Letter is delivered online. All orders renew automatically at $79/year, billed to the credit card provided. You'll never pay more as long as you remain a subscriber.